Evading Class in Contemporary British Literature

Previous Publications

Reconsidering Drugs: Mapping Victorian and Modern Drug Discourses (2000)

Evading Class in Contemporary British Literature

Lawrence Driscoll

palgrave
macmillan

EVADING CLASS IN CONTEMPORARY BRITISH LITERATURE

First published in 2009 by
PALGRAVE MACMILLAN®
in the United States—a division of St. Martin's Press LLC,
175 Fifth Avenue, New York, NY 10010.

Where this book is distributed in the UK, Europe and the rest of the world, this is by Palgrave Macmillan, a division of Macmillan Publishers Limited, registered in England, company number 785998, of Houndmills, Basingstoke, Hampshire RG21 6XS.

Palgrave Macmillan is the global academic imprint of the above companies and has companies and representatives throughout the world.

Palgrave® and Macmillan® are registered trademarks in the United States, the United Kingdom, Europe and other countries.

ISBN: 978–0–230–61527–4

Library of Congress Cataloging-in-Publication Data

Driscoll, Lawrence Victor.
Evading class in contemporary British literature / Lawrence Driscoll.
p. cm.
Includes bibliographical references.

1. English literature—20th century—History and criticism. 2. Social classes in literature. 3. English literature—21st century—History and criticism. 4. Working class in literature. 5. Postmodernism (Literature) 6. Social classes—England—History—20th century. 7. Social classes—England—History—21st century. I. Title.

PR888.S6D75 2009
820.9'3552—dc22 2008043014

A catalogue record of the book is available from the British Library.

Design by Newgen Imaging Systems (P) Ltd., Chennai, India.

First edition: July 2009

For Tomoko and Oscar

The ideas of the ruling class are in every epoch the ruling ideas... In so far, therefore, as they rule as a class and determine the extent and compass of an epoch, it is self-evident that they do this in their whole range, hence among other things they rule also as thinkers, as producers of ideas, and regulate the production and distribution of the ideas of their age....

—*Marx and Engels, The German Ideology (1846)*

Contents

Acknowledgments

No book is an island, and all texts have many tentacles that reach out toward those who helped to give it life. In particular, I feel that I must thank Diane Fidler and Rita Duhig for planting some vital seeds long long ago. These were then cultivated by Paul Giles, Shaun Richards, David Cairns, and Richard Ellis who provided the critical grounding that made this book possible. In addition, I must thank Santa Monica College for providing me with the professional environment in which to carry out my work while also bringing me into contact with some splendid students. I would like to thank Susan Sterr, David Zehr, and James Pacchioli for being such great colleagues, who along with Gordon Dossett and Jeremy Brigstocke are always able to steer me in the right direction. Jane Lillienfeld helped me some years ago, and I still wish to thank her for the support and encouragement she gave me. I would also like to thank the Librarians at the University of California, Los Angeles, who were tireless in helping me with my research. I would also like to thank Brigitte Shull at Palgrave for all of her hard work and for her faith in this book. The people I worked with in the English Department at Kingston-Upon-Thames University in London also deserve a special thank you as they went out of their way to look after me during my sabbatical in 2004. Thanks also to Hiroko and Toshio for giving me the only air-conditioned room in their house in which to write while I was in Japan. My mother also deserves a medal for tirelessly sending me various British magazines, newspapers, and endless copies of Private Eye and for being such a great sport in flying all around the world to visit us. I would also like to offer, once again, my thanks to Simon and Jo for their unconditional friendship and love, as well as for their guidance, and a beautiful Star of Jasmine. Ron Gottesman and Beth Shube, (as well as Alison and Blake) also deserve a special mention for always being there for us. Finally, thanks go to my wife Tomoko for her endless patience, love, and support during the production of this book.

Introduction: Questions of Class in the Contemporary British Novel

Class! Yes, it's still here. Terrific staying power and all against the historical odds. What is it with that old, old crap? The class system just doesn't know when to call it a day.

—*Martin Amis*[1]

the class war is over

—*Tony Blair, Labour Party Conference, 1999*[2]

The central aim of this book is to offer a critique postmodern theory's idealization of contemporary British literature and culture as a space of fluid, flexible decentered subjects, and to argue that beneath this celebration of hybridity and difference lie clear evasions and erasures of class. Using a variety of materialist theories, this book explores how the ideological and political pressure to erase class in the period from Margaret Thatcher to Tony Blair produces the return of class as a troubling subterranean and repressed element in contemporary literature, theory, and culture. Offering critical readings from a range of recently canonized middle-class authors such as Martin Amis, Zadie Smith, Ian McEwan, Peter Ackroyd, Jonathan Coe, as well as Kazuo Ishiguro, Pat Barker, Will Self, and Alan Hollinghurst, I hope to reveal that the contemporary British novel, assisted by "class blind" postideological literary theories, both articulates and silences questions of class, thereby enabling and sustaining the ideological notion of a "classless" contemporary British literature and culture.

In *After Theory*, Terry Eagleton called for a change of direction in the field of academic analysis: "The postmodern prejudice against norms, unities and consensuses is a politically catastrophic one."[3] However, we still find ourselves faced with an academic discourse overwhelming focused on identity politics and the belief that a "lack of stable identities . . . is the last word in radicalism."[4] This critical assault on the normative has meant that, while gender, sexuality, and race have been thoroughly examined, it has been at the expense of class, with the result, as Peter Hitchcock has pointed out, that class has clearly been "under theorized in terms of the literary, as if what is problematic for the social scientist is transparent or inconsequential for the literary critic."[5] Gary Day points out that this evasion of class has its roots in the contradictions of post-structuralism:

> On the one hand, it recognized that cultural products were embedded in a wider social context but, on the other, it seemed to imply that their meanings could be endlessly multiplied without any sense of constraint. It is this latter aspect which has been stressed most in the subsequent development of post-structuralism. The result was that while the cultural context of the work continued to be elaborated, its economic one was progressively ignored.[6]

Given that the humanities and literary criticism has generally insisted on treating class in this transparent way, it means, as Wendy Brown points out, that the current focus on "identity politics . . . preserves capitalism from critique [and] sustains the invisibility and articulateness of class—not incidentally but endemically . . . Could we have stumbled upon one reason why class is invariably named but rarely theorized or developed in the multiculturalist mantra, 'race, class, gender, sexuality.' "[7] So while Cultural Studies as an academic field began by inquiring into matters of class, those origins have been dissolved in favor of other more hip topics that are bracketed under identity politics and difference. As Stefan Collini points out: "In the frequently incanted quartet of race, class and gender and sexual orientation, there is no doubt that class has been the least fashionable . . . despite the fact that all the evidence suggests that class remains the single most powerful determinant of life chances."[8] Philip Tew has also recently warned us that "class blindness . . . haunts contemporary British fiction and academic exegesis."[9] Moreover, for Žižek, class is not simply one of four elements that can be added to a list, but it is the ground upon which all of the others are played out: "the social organization of production (the 'mode of production') is not just one among many levels of social organization, it is the site of 'contradiction,' of structural instability, of the central social antagonism...which, as such, spills over into all other levels."[10]

Turning our attention back to the roots of Cultural Studies, I will therefore set out to examine how this blindness to class concerns has distorted our readings of the contemporary British novel and limited our ability to read the current literary landscape other than through the rather limited lenses of the postmodern.[11] I would argue that the current postmodern emphasis on the margins, fragments, and difference/identity has left the academy and the general reading public void of what Eagleton terms "memories of collective, and effective, political action."[12] This "cultural turn" in postmodernism, while celebrated as somehow being a radical tool to deconstruct Western culture has in fact, as Judith Williamson states, "proven surprisingly compatible with the dominant neo-liberal and utilitarian politico-economic logics of the last two decades of the century...[and that] the ideology of difference is not in fact, different from the ideologies that imprison us all."[13]

This book therefore argues that from Thatcher to Blair a transformation has occurred in which an ideological shift has attempted to erase the category of class from public discourse, while in the academy, postmodern theories have bolstered this erasure through its focus on margins and the micropolitics of desire.[14] My argument is that working-class experience has been revised and rewritten during this period so as to eliminate it as an object of knowledge and power and that this rewriting of both middle- and working-class identity can be delineated and traced through the pages of the contemporary British novel as well as in recent cultural productions in British television and cinema.

I will therefore examine the question of class by critiquing British middle-class novelists from 1979 to the present to see how their texts have been comfortably assimilated into the canon through the conduit of postmodern theory. Some of the questions that I will be raising will include: What kinds of questions about class do these novels and theories permit or prohibit? What conclusions about class do they draw or avoid? In addition, I think we need to ask ourselves how these conclusions and omissions are linked to the political and ideological changes in Britain during this period. Similarly, in what ways has the current trend for postmodern readings of these texts served to obscure the working-class subject, while simultaneously desiring to interpellate the reader into a middle-class subject position in the hope of producing a supposedly "classless" norm? My aim has been to choose the contemporary canon to see clearly how a *middle-class* tradition is being shaped and preserved. The aim of this book is thus not to posit an alternative socialist-realist canon by celebrating the gritty realism of working-class writers, but instead, to investigate the ways in which the *representation* of class positions in British culture allows us to see how the middle-class institutions of Literature/Culture and academia have appropriated, channeled, and rebranded the troubling working-class subject, while at the same time reshaping both the middle- and working-class subject into one who is supposedly "free" from history, and the "limits" of the past. Each chapter explores the tension between the postmodern framing of the British contemporary literary canon and the advantages of shifting the debate into a cultural materialist arena in which questions of class could once again begin to play a vital role in our understanding of these texts.

Although it is true that there are exceptions to be found among the class backgrounds of the canonical authors of the British novel (e.g., working-class authors such as Caryl Phillips or Dennis Potter who both graduated from Oxford), generally the large bulk of "famous" authors today come down to us from a rather narrow educational/class segment of British society. The creation of this group of canonical authors, is, as Andrew Milner points out, dependent on the educational system: "[I]t is clear that the universities have been of fundamental importance to the establishment and maintenance of a relatively autonomous intelligentsia: its common class interests and internal bonds of affiliation…The emergence of a distinct intellectual class…remains crucially dependent on…higher education."[15] Therefore, I think it is vital to remind ourselves that when we read the canonized contemporary British novel we are dealing with a literary form produced not by "Britain" but by a small middle-class section of society and one which is encouraged by various media to see itself as the spokesperson for all classes. Tew remarks that most middle-class writers have a capacity "to pick obsessively over their own middle-class identities to the exclusion of almost everything else" and the result is that "[m]ost middle-class literature fails to extricate itself sufficiently from [its own] prejudices" such that there is plenty of "class bias subtly inflected in both fiction and criticism."[16] For Tew, this class bias is "an uncomfortable and mostly unacknowledged factor within the literary field that most academics refuse to address sufficiently."[17] While it is clear that "a particular class affiliation is a constant," he also feels that the postmodern distrust of grand narratives seems not to have affected these novelists' (and some critics) ability to generate an "intellectual hegemony based on a relative uniformity of self-reflection and self-representation."[18] It is this uniformity and self-reflection that this book aims to examine and critique.

This book is thus a Brechtian "making strange" in which I hope we can see the academy's postmodern theorizing and the British canon as collusion with, rather than a critique of, bourgeois ideology. I have no desire to be fashionably postmodern, but will be persistent in raising the troubling question of class. Quite simply, now that the dust has settled on the desire to read contemporary British literature as a series of hybrid subjects free falling into endless freedoms and pluralities, what stubbornly remains to be read and theorized, is class.

Focusing on the period 1979–2007, I will set out to establish that current postmodern readings of contemporary British literature have reached an epistemological cul-de-sac. Tracing post-structuralism's dominance in the academic and cultural scene I will address the strengths as well as the weaknesses of these approaches. Cultural materialist models of literary analysis will be introduced so as to resituate these texts as part of a historical moment of cultural and ideological production, and to see how, as John Kirk says, "hegemonic culture seeks to 'place', 'arrange' and displace the realities of class."[19] In several instances, I have also spent time looking at newspaper and book review commentaries on the various novels I have selected. The intention behind this is not to avoid the academic debates but to examine the symbiosis between academic debates and the popular media. In addition, I felt that it was important to look closely at how these novels are read, packaged, spoken of, and consumed by the reading public as it is in the realm of the popular where the cultural meanings of a text are often shaped and sustained.

In *The Modern British Novel 1878–2001*, Malcolm Bradbury tells us that the postwar British novel exists in a different world from that of Dickens: "A society of class, rank and deference, it had seen its hierarchies give way to new classlessness...."[20] The same argument that Britain is now a classless society is also echoed in Richard Bradford's popular university-level recommended reading book, *The Novel Now:* "Postwar British society underwent changes, mostly the same as those experienced by virtually all other Western democracies: class distinctions became gradually less prominent...."[21] In many ways Bradbury and Bradford are not alone, as the notion that Britain has become a classless society is heard across the political spectrum.

It has been suggested by Andrew Milner that "the most straightforward explanation for this growing lack of theoretical interest in class difference would be that class has ceased to be of central empirical significance to our culture."[22] Milner shows us that this erasure of class is not confined to Thatcher, John Major and Blair but shows up unquestioned in the work of such major postmodern theorists as Lyotard and Baudrillard:

> For Lyotard...class struggle has blurred to the point of losing all...radicality [while for] Baudrillard " 'the social does not exist anymore.' And with the social, so too go socialism, social class and the proletariat...[in the words of Baudrillard] 'the concept of class will have dissolved....' "[23]

These ideas are also echoed by post-Marxist theorists, like Laclau and Mouffe: "class struggle is just one species of identity politics, and one which is becoming less and less important...."[24] Generating a post-Marxist position, they argue that the "unity and homogeneity of class subjects [is a] set of precariously integrated positions which...cannot be referred to any necessary point of future unification."[25] Instead what they see is a postmodern field in which there is only a "contradictory plurality" which as Hall points out, means that "there is no reason why anything is or isn't potentially articulable with anything" and that having erased class we are left with "the notion of society as a totally open discursive field."[26] The same erasure of class can also be seen in popular arguments from some quarters of sociology. For example, the highly influential Zygmunt Bauman has concluded that "the entire conceptual repertoire of mainstream sociology, class included, seems devoted to the study and the service of 'unfreedom' and hence [is] irreparably 'modern' in character."[27] This is not just a theoretical view, and as Milner points out, "the argument finds some resonance even amongst the more empirically minded: Ray Pahl, for example, has described the concept of class as 'ceasing to do any useful work' [while] Holton and Turner regard it as tied to the 'tired comparison between conflict and consensus.' "[28] Another popular argument centers on the proposal by Ulrich Beck regarding "individualization" in which people have become " 'disembedded' from their old communal modes of life" by globalization and the information society to the point that class no longer matters.[29] This move away from class is also echoed in government policy. John H. Goldthorpe and Michelle Jackson point out that Blair has been eager to see the end of class and its replacement with a more fluid concept rooted in individualism:

> In particular, the aim has been to redefine policy objectives in this regard so that emphasis falls far more on *equality of opportunity* than on *equality of condition*. In a speech early in his second administration Tony Blair (*Guardian*, June 10, 2002) stressed the need to promote mobility as being *in itself* "the great force for social equality in dynamic market economies." Underlying this claim is the idea that high rates of mobility can serve to mitigate the socially divisive effects of the large inequalities in income and wealth that such economies generate by restricting their intergenerational continuity and, further, by providing them with some form of "meritocratic" legitimation. Yet more explicitly in this latter respect, Ruth Kelly, speaking as Secretary of State for Education (Institute for Public Policy Research, 26 July, 2005), represented social mobility as being the key to a "just society": that is, a society where "success" depends not on individuals' backgrounds but on "their ability and efforts."[30]

This postclass argument is also repeated in the work of Lord Anthony Giddens, former Director of the London School of Economics. As with other postclass theorists, Giddens's work also argues that there are no viable alternatives to the capitalist system and that people are free to define themselves by their self-chosen lifestyle. As Atkinson points out, Bauman, Giddens, and Beck all regularly appear "on the pages of those who are keen to cite detractors of class."[31]

However, there are major sociologists who have highlighted that class (in theory and in practice) is alive and well. For example, in July 2007 a major and long-awaited report was published by the Joseph Rowntree Foundation entitled "Poverty and Wealth across Britain from 1968 to 2005." Some of the key points of the report were as follows:

- Britain is moving back towards levels of inequality in wealth and poverty last seen more than 40 years ago.
- Over the last 15 years, more households have become poor...[and] the overall number of "breadline poor" households increased–households where people live below the standard poverty line. This number has consistently been above 17 per cent, peaking at 27 per cent in 2001.
- Already-wealthy areas have tended to become disproportionately wealthier. There is evidence of increasing polarization, where rich and poor now live further apart. In areas of some cities over half of all households are now breadline poor.

- The general pattern is of increases in social equality during the 1970s, followed by rising inequality in the 1980s and 1990s.
- Both poor and wealthy households have become more and more geographically segregated from the rest of society.[32]

So, rather than a classless British society that is then being simply "reflected" in the "fluid and hybrid" literature of a classless society, it would seem that the opposite is the case: Britain has become more divided by class and inequality, not less.[33] Such conclusions are reinforced by the influential sociologist John Westergaard, who, in examining class since 1980 openly states that perceptions of classlessness are purely ideological:

> The facts about class—in Britain and a number of other western countries—show that inequality has widened quite dramatically since about 1980. But, over just this same period, fashionable theories and influential ideologies have appeared to say almost the opposite. While rich and poor have in fact grown further apart, predominant ideology has set out to dismiss this; and both predominant ideology and leading social theory have come to argue that it does not matter much any longer. If we are to believe the commentators, the politicians and the academic theorists who have set this tone in the current debate, then class inequality has lost social force; it has lost moral force; it has lost political force.[34]

Moreover, he concludes that "fashionable class-denying theory and ideology . . . naively infers, from new complexities of political group formation, an erosion of economic-categorical class which is, quite plainly, contrary to the fact."[35]

The policies of the Welfare State remained untouched since 1945, but by the end of the 1970s after a series of global economic changes, Thatcherism emerges as a right-wing ideology that was "openly committed to challenging the socio-political settlement of the 1940s—to taking apart the 'class compromise' associated with postwar social reconstruction."[36] The changes that took place were designed to shift the country away from what Thatcher saw as the "socialist" policies of the postwar consensus, and toward a culture driven by the free market:

> The main means to this have included: legal curbs on trade union power; thinning out previous measures for protection of low-paid labour; deregulation in other forms, privatization of once-public enterprises;

> reductions in direct taxation to foster initiative; and a general reliance on market competition for growth and industrial discipline. On the other hand, and in parallel, radical-right policy has sought to hold back public expenditure—so in particular to trim down public welfare provision....[37]

Not surprisingly, as John Kirk points out, both Reaganism and Thatcherism were "a type of radical individualism conducive to a reinvigorated consumer capitalism...a position oddly commensurate with poststructuralist/postmodernist suspicions of class as a master narrative...."[38] The basic structure of these policy changes was continued under Major and Blair and the ideological response has been to assume that these policies have brought us to the threshold of a mythical "classless" society. This view has been reinforced by Simon Jenkins' recent work *Thatcher and Sons: A Revolution in Three Acts.* Jenkins argues that there are really four Thatcherite prime ministers: Thatcher, Major, Blair and Brown. Reviewing the book in the *Observer,* Ned Temko points out the (uncannily postmodern) parallels between Thatcher and Blair: both were " 'total politicians' who didn't read much, didn't much care for their own parties, had no experience of actually managing anything, seemed 'to be from nowhere and everywhere' and who 'had convictions on everything but ideas on little.' "[39] As Susan Watkins has pointed out, New Labour, far from challenging Thatcherism, has only intensified Thatcher's revolution: "From the start...New Labour was pledged to consolidate the Thatcherite paradigm rather than create a new model...Gross transfers to the rich from the poor have continued under New Labour...Other social indicators are equally bleak. Literacy levels have now fallen below those of the United States...."[40] Slavoj Žižek also asserts that Blair has been more of a Thatcherite than Thatcher herself: "[T]he Thatcher revolution was in itself chaotic, impulsive...it was only the 'Third Way' Blairite government that was able to *institutionalize* it, to stabilize it into new institutional forms...."[41] Historian Arthur Marwick also echoes Žižek and Watkins when he reminds us what has happened since the Thatcher revolution:

> In the mid nineties the situation in regard to class was, naturally enough, not greatly changed from the situation in the late eighties... inequalities in income and living conditions between well-off and badly off were intensifying still further...the basic class framework remained....[42]

In addition, Marwick makes it clear that Blair changed nothing:

> Quite obviously Blair's "meritocratic middle-class," as he envisaged it, extended to the proliferating fat cats who, in fact, could readily join, and reinforce, the ever-enduring upper-class. Class content, certainly from the time of Thatcher, was in flux; class attitudes much less so...What most securely underpinned the class system was the educational mess...what most palpably demonstrated it was inexcusable economic inequality, actually growing under the Blair governments, though it had been at its highest between 1985 and 1992.[43]

David Cannadine in *Class in Britain* reinforces this by suggesting that while class may have been sidelined and "disregarded by many historians and abandoned by almost all politicians" it is also true that "there has been no 'fall of class' at all. It is still with us, still around us, still within us...."[44]

Revisionist theories of class, alongside postmodern literary criticism, continue to argue that class is no longer a viable issue, but Westergaard points out that the key points of the revisionist argument do not stand up to empirical analysis. For example, revisionist theories tend to make their arguments along three major lines: (1) distribution of real incomes, (2) distribution of property, and (3) social mobility. Westergaard points out that in all three areas there have either been no substantial changes or there have been losses for the poorer sections of the population and gains for the richer sections of the nation. So, in terms of the distribution of real incomes Westergaard shows that "over the ten years from 1980 to 1990, earnings among the top-tenth of white-collar employees rose in real terms by about 40%...the blue-collar median wage rose by little more than 10% over the full ten years, while the poorest-paid tenth among blue collar men gained hardly anything in real terms...the class gaps have widened across the range."[45] Second, in terms of distribution of property, Westergaard points out that given Thatcher's plan to let people buy their council houses and through the selling of public companies, we would expect to see an expansion of private property ownership, but in fact the opposite has occurred so that "overall stakes in private property of all kinds has in fact become more concentrated, not less."[46] Lastly, in terms of social mobility, while the notion of "free opportunity for all" has been a major bulwark of the ideological justification for dismantling the postwar consensus, Westergaard makes it clear that "[c]omprehensive studies of social mobility across the population as a whole, [which] continued into the 1980s, have as yet shown no significant reduction of those relative inequalities of opportunity between classes...it is predominantly people in the downward reaches of the class structure who, far from gaining opportunities, have very tangibly lost them."[47]

Revisionist theories of class also suggest that class is no longer the central axis by which to examine contemporary culture since it has been overtaken by the more fashionable postmodern categories of identity politics such as age, gender, or race. Such theories are obviously welcomed by bourgeois culture because as Fredric Jameson points out: "Such theories have the obvious ideological mission of demonstrating, to their own relief, that the new social formation in question no longer obeys the laws of classical capitalism, namely, the primacy of industrial production and the omnipresence of class struggle."[48] Westergaard makes it clear that although it is currently fashionable to look at Britain in this way, the facts on the ground tell a different story. For example, arguments about the age division of contemporary British culture usually try to suggest that classical models of class are no longer appropriate because it is the older sections of the population that are poor and that the younger generations possess a greater degree of wealth. However, Westergaard points out that "old age by itself does not bring poverty: it does so only in circumstances which are set by class structure [and] class inequality after working life matches—even tends to exceed—class inequality during working life."[49] Another common revisionist argument is that class is irrelevant because "class" should be measured by how many earners there are in any given household, and not by the "class" of work that they do. Westergaard suggests that once again "the conclusion does not fit with the factual evidence" and that if there are multiple wage earners in a household, it will tend to be in middle-class households that only serves to "strengthen the impact of class rather than to weaken it...dual earning has boosted middle- and upper-class household incomes more, over time, than it has boosted working-class incomes."[50] So, far from dissolving, class has actually hardened and Westergaard states that "class has...been declared dead...at a time...when its economic configuration has become even sharper."[51]

The revisionist argument that gender divisions have superseded traditional class models also doesn't bear much scrutiny. As Westergaard points out "a major line of revisionist theory [postulates] that class division is much less salient now, because gender divisions cut across it."[52] Yet, the pattern of employment and promotion and pay, rather than undermining any traditional analysis of British class structures, only serves to reinforce them. As Westergaard makes clear:

> [A]t every level, women are usually worse off than their male counterparts. Level for level of work, their pay tends to be poorer; their pensions, if any, tend to be much lower; their opportunities for careers are much more restricted; their confinement to routine grade work, and their risks of demotion, are much greater... Yet none of this involves any sort of suspension of the force of class structure on economic life. The class structure of the labour market for women parallels that for men.[53]

The same revisionist argument is also made for race in which theoretical sociologists echo literary and critical theorists who say that race somehow "trumps" class. Once again, Westergaard's data reveals that although it is true that there are certainly "new—and nasty—lines of racial inequality...those lines have in no way supplanted the lines of class inequality...inequality by gender interacts with inequality by race: the one has not displaced the other."[54] If these arguments fail to convince us, then revisionists have finally postulated that "patterns of consumption" have supplanted the old traditional class lines, in which consumers are central and not producers/workers.[55] Sadly, these arguments also prove specious: "In general, 'consumer power' from private resources remains a highly unequal power, when overall private resources—that is to say, real incomes—remain highly unequal, and have grown more unequal over the years since about 1980."[56] So it would seem that despite an ideological desire to see class erased, displaced, obscured, or replaced by some more market-friendly apolitical category, the reality is that Britain remains a society strictly divided along class lines by an economic system that preserves and indeed exacerbates class distinctions.

In *A Class Act: The Myth of Britain's Classless Society,* Adonis and Pollard make it clear that all of Britain's cherished institutions from education, to the courts, the media, the military and housing, despite major "changes" since 1945, all continue to perpetuate a class society. Given that this book is concerned with academics, intellectuals, and authors, it is worthwhile noting that it is the institution of "Education, [which preserves] the meritocratic ideal and chronic inequality [which] underpin class divisions in modern Britain...and that class divisions, based on education, remain stark despite transformation in the educational experience of the population across the century."[57] So while politicians and postmodern commentators champion the emergence of a classless society, Adonis and Pollard suggest that over the period "brute economic forces [have made] for a more, not less, divided society" (10). In agreement with Westergaard, they point out that there are clear "income divisions underpinning the class hierarchy, which were stark to start with and widened further during the 1980s, [during] a decade when income inequality grew faster in the UK than in any developed country apart from New Zealand" (11). Their figures speak for themselves: "In 1979 the bottom tenth of the population received 4.1 per cent of the national income; by 1991 this was down to 2.5 per cent, while over the same period the share taken by the top tenth increased from 20 to 26 per cent" (11). In fact, rather than a classless society, they show that what we have seen since Thatcher has been the continued growth of an underclass that has split off from the working class alongside the rise of what Adonis and Pollard term a "Super Class." The underclass is not some new class, but quite simply a whole "Servant Class" (12) that has sprung into being to serve the needs of the now (more) rich and (more) powerful super class: "In the mid-1980s Mintel, the market researchers, estimated that £524 million a year was spent on cooks, cleaners, child minders and gardeners; by 1997 the figure was thought to be £4 billion" (101). They argue that overall, the "mobility [between classes] is no greater than, say, during the Industrial Revolution" (16). While we are constantly bombarded with narratives of people who have made it across the class divide, Adonis and Pollard remind us that "minorities are on the ladder; majorities stay put, even in periods of rapid occupational change, when opportunities to rise are abundant" (15). This frozen-class society is thus held in place by a whole host of what Althusser would term the Repressive State Apparatuses (the courts, the military, the police) and by an army of amorphous Ideological State Apparatuses (the media, arts, education, etc.). Adonis and Pollard thus show that across the board in Britain, from the House of Lords to the BBC, from the National Health Service to the Inns of Court, and from Eton to Inner London schools, England's institutions continue to preserve the class barriers that they may even in some cases think they are out to dismantle.

Of all these institutions, Adonis and Pollard point out that the British education system does more to perpetuate the class structure of Britain than anything else: "Half of the entrants to Oxford and Cambridge universities in 1995 came from private schools, although the independent sector accounted for only 7% of the total school population" (24). While 88 percent of private school pupils go on to higher education, only 27 percent go from the State Schools and in London "[o]ne in five of all seven year olds in state schools are earning zero on reading tests" (50). Since the 1970s, it is also clear that while access to private education has actually risen for the wealthy private sector, the state schools have deteriorated as they have succumbed to the quasi-Darwinian pressures of the market. The result is that the quality of working-class education is appallingly low: "Four out of five eleven year olds in Islington, for example, cannot pass even a basic reading test" (45). Adonis and Pollard point out that classless apologists say that it is "only" 7 percent of the population who are in private education as if this group is somehow "atypical, marginal, unusually selfish, or all three." But, as they remind us, "Only 7 per cent means 610,000 pupils and more than a million parents": "The pupils represent a large part of the academic cream of their generation; the parents constitute a majority of those with children among the higher professional and managerial class, and include virtually all of the Super Class...." (47). The upper echelons of the military also read like a "public school directory" while in the supposedly meritocratic civil service "Two thirds of the eighteen civil service permanent secretaries attended Oxbridge" (47, 59). The conservative party is "firmly in the grip of private schools," while eighteen out of John Major's twenty-three cabinet ministers were privately educated, and this, coming from John Major who openly boasted of how Britain was a "classless society." New Labour has fared no better. Tony Blair was educated at Fettes College (Scotland's Eton) before going to Oxford, and his Cabinet was also drawn from the ranks of Oxbridge. Oxford has provided nine of this century's prime ministers (including Blair), and Cambridge has provided three, out of a total of nineteen. Therefore a supposedly classless country of 57 million "is governed by 2 per cent of her graduate total" (59).

What concerns us here is that education and literature (such as The Inns of Court or the House of Commons) operate as institutions that are structured, maintained, and rewritten when needed, by middle-class interests and ideology.[58] In short, the purpose of these institutions, and thus the purpose of literature, is to secure and maintain a hegemonic position for the middle class, and, as John Kirk points out, it is through such institutions that a "national memory" is sustained.[59] Fentress and Wickham point out, however, that this national memory is not equally available to all since it "is always 'articulated or created by the bourgeoisie, or for the bourgeoisie, or for the bourgeoisie *first.*'"[60] Such institutions, like the institution of literature, are thus able to rewrite class identity as a "national" identity, enabling the bourgeoisie to legitimize its own "structures of political and economic dominance, by which the elite justifies itself as an elite."[61]

Postideological criticism leads us to believe that literature, especially our own contemporary literature, is automatically going to be "counter-cultural" or "radical" in some way, or that it is naturally "post-colonial" or "anti-bourgeois" and that we "liberal" and open-minded readers and critics should therefore automatically be on the side of literature because what "we" want is obviously the same as what literature wants. But to rewrite Freud's infamous question about women: What does literature want? What is it that the institution of literature desires?[62] A tentative answer is that what literature desires is that it be allowed to continue producing its hegemonic discourses unimpeded and it would like us to desire, accept, and consume those narratives as if they emerged from a nation of classless subjects.

A clear way to approach this question is to examine the material foundations that give rise to literature and theory in the first place. As Aijaz Ahmad reminds us:

> [I]t would be hard to think of a Marxism which would not foreground, in any discussion of theory, the issue of the institutional sites from which that theory emanates, the actual class practices and concrete social locations, in systems of power and powerlessness, of the agents who produce it, the circuits through which it circulates and the class fractions who endow it with whatever power it gains.[63]

In turn, if we wish to examine literature through a material lens Ahmad feels that we cannot continue without raising the "suppressed questions of institutional site and individual location."[64] In simple terms, as Terry Eagleton states, "Literature, in the meaning of the word we have inherited, *is* an ideology. It has the most intimate relations to questions of social power."[65] In short, Ahmad's suggestion is that we need to engage in a procedure that will involve looking closely at the material and institutional positions of our canonized British authors. Looking only at the "images" of contemporary British writers we get the impression, encouraged by various marketing and media sources, that we are looking at a broad spectrum of society that comes to us (again through the lens of identity politics and difference) primarily because of their race and gender: we see various images of

Ian McEwan, Jeanette Winterson, and Zadie Smith for example, alongside images of Martin Amis, Hanif Kureishi, and Hari Kunzru, and we feel as if this represents some kind of classless "cross section" of a pluralistic British society. Yet these images tell us nothing about class, and in fact our reliance on the image is itself symptomatic of the identity politics that contemporary theory is embroiled in.[66] It is as if we only need to "see" them to "know" what they are going to be writing about and in turn how we should respond to their work. Yet how is it that *these* writers have been selected and handed down to us as "our" canon? If we examine them through the lens of the "institutional sites" of their education (which, as the sociologists covered in this introduction would agree on, gives us an indication of their economic and social class), then the "concrete social locations" as Ahmad terms it, of contemporary British writers becomes much clearer:

Educated at Oxford University: Martin Amis, Julian Barnes, Alan Bennett, William Boyd, Melvyn Bragg, Christine Brooke-Rose, Amit Chaudhuri, Caryl Churchill, Margaret Forster, John Fowles, Maggie Gee, Alan Hollinghurst, John Lanchester, Penelope Lively, Timothy Mo, Iris Murdoch, Anthony Powell, Craig Raine, Michele Roberts, Will Self, Adam Thorpe, Alan Wall, A. N. Wilson, and Jeanette Winterson.

Educated at Cambridge University: Peter Ackroyd, J. G. Ballard, A. S. Byatt, Jonathan Coe, Margaret Drabble, Sebastian Faulks, Tibor Fischer, Nick Hornby, Ian Jack, Howard Jacobson, Nick Laird (Zadie Smith's husband), Adam Mars-Jones, Jane Rogers, Salman Rushdie, and Graham Swift.

Educated at the London School of Economics: Pat Barker and Hilary Mantel.

Educated at the University of East Anglia: Malcolm Bradbury, Kazuo Ishiguro, Ian McEwan, Glenn Patterson, and Rose Tremain.

Educated at the University of London: Jim Crace, Louis De Bernieres, Jenny Diski, Buchi Emecheta, Susan Hill, Hanif Kureishi, David Lodge, and Patrick McGrath.[67]

While many of these names are well-established figures in the canon, the so-called new generation of contemporary writers is also cultivated from the same institutions. The 2003 edition of *Granta's Best of Young British Novelists* (itself conceived and edited over the years by Cambridge graduate/writer Ian Jack) contains twenty young writers: this "new" group includes Monica Ali, Hari Kunzru, Philip Hensher, Toby Litt, Rachel Cusk, Ben Rice, and Adam Thirwell (all of whom are from Oxford). The selection also includes Susan Elderkin, Peter

Ho Davies, Robert McLiam Wilson, Nicola Barker, and Zadie Smith (all of whom are from Cambridge). In short, out of the twenty new writers, twelve (60 percent) are from Oxbridge. Three of the twenty had also gone through the University of East Anglia writing program (just like McEwan, Ishiguro, and Pat Barker) and were tutored either by Malcolm Bradbury and/or Rose Tremain. The canonical group of writers chosen here makes a total of sixty-six authors: fifty-four of them (i.e., more than 80 percent) are from Oxbridge.

What we can now see is that the "important" contemporary British novelists do not really represent a "range" or even a "cross section" of British contemporary experience, but constitute a group of novelists who emerge from a rather narrow middle-class/university experience. Philip Tew has touched on this problem in *The Contemporary British Novel*: "Various contemporary authors continue to concern themselves...with issues of a singular class perspective...The world of many such writers is a postindustrial remodeling of the bourgeois world of novelists such as Jane Austen. Often, the cast of characters and concerns assumes the cultural relevance of a narrow class experience...."[68]

The literary productions of this narrow social group is then marketed, read, filmed, written about, taught, and reviewed as if it was representative of a "universal" experience reflecting a majority perspective on the current state of British society and the issues that "Britain" and its "people" confronts. Once we begin to see our canon in this light, we are closer to understanding how these textual productions are actually operating as an institution that is sustained by an ideology, an ideology that is also reinforced by the institution of criticism. I would argue that when we consider our contemporary novelists in this way we are surely in the presence of an ideological "institution" that has the same problems, weaknesses, and desires as The House of Lords or Chancery, and as critics we do not have to be automatically subservient or deferential to what this institution is saying about British culture and society. In fact, I would posit that if we admit to the narrowness of our canon it behooves us to have a healthy skepticism toward this rather insular institution. In the same way that England's legal and economic institutions reproduce the conditions of production, as Althusser would say, so too, literature also plays its ideological part in ensuring that the culture reproduces itself along lines that are favorable, albeit consciously or unconsciously, to dominant class interests. It may sound as if I am suggesting that we need to be against literature, and critics may be tempted to defend literature as the last bastion against the deadening effects of the market and mass culture, but that is precisely the position that we need to take. As Raymond Williams has pointed out, "Literature" is never an ideologically neutral zone by any means, and cannot be so, despite how we may wish to see it. Moreover, what gets to be seen as literature, is not the result of chance, nor is it simply "the best of what is said," but, as Williams makes clear, it is the result of a class-based tradition of self-selection:

> It was a selection which culminated in, and in a circular way defined, the "literary values" which "criticism" was asserting...Selectivity and self-definition, which were the evident processes of "criticism" of this kind, were, however, projected as "literature" itself, as "literary values" and even finally as "essential Englishness": the absolute ratification of a limited and specializing consensual process. To oppose the terms of this ratification was to be "against literature."[69]

Following Williams then, I feel that if we are going to move toward a less hermetic form of literary criticism and if, in turn we truly desire to open the critical windows and usher in a fresh way of seeing how contemporary British literature operates, we must strive to be "against literature" however uncomfortable this may seem to an academic field that often goes to great lengths (aided by postmodern theory) to offer ideologically complicit readings of these authors. As Williams points out, Literary Criticism is specifically designed to be the ideological reinforcement behind literature: "Thus these forms of the concept of *literature* and *criticism* are, in the perspective of historical social development, forms of a class specialization and control of a general social practice, and of a class limitation of the questions which it might raise."[70] Only by dismantling these reinforcements can literature be exposed to a radical critique. As Žižek has pointed out, only then can criticism become truly critical: "The act proper is an intervention which does not merely operate within a given background, but disturbs its coordinates and thus renders it visible *as* a background."[71] A proper act of criticism must therefore aim at "rendering palpable" the texts' "political dimension."[72]

But this is by no means an easy task, as the recent shifts that have taken place in literary theory have made it harder for criticism to be *critical* of the institution of literature. As Eagleton makes clear, "Socialism has lost out to sado-masochism. Among students of culture, the body is an immensely fashionable topic, but it is usually the erotic body, not the famished one. There is a keen interest in coupling bodies, but not in labouring ones."[73] The result has been that while the margins have become central, the collective and the social have been erased:

> For some postmodern thought, consensus is tyrannical and solidarity nothing but soulless conformity. But whereas liberals oppose this conformity with the individual, postmodernists, some of whom doubt the very reality of the individual, counter it instead with margins and minorities. It is what stands askew to society as a whole—the marginal, mad, deviant, perverse, transgressive—which is most politically fertile. There can be little value in mainstream social life.[74]

Accordingly we are left with an empty pluralism: "...since the working-class stood for political solidarity, it is scarcely surprising that we should now have a form of radicalism which is deeply distrustful of all that. Postmodernism does not believe in individualism...but it does not believe in working-class community either. Instead, it puts its trust in pluralism."[75] The subject that such a theory produces is also a strange Gollum-like figure: "The creature who emerges from postmodern thought is centreless, hedonistic, self-inventing, ceaselessly adaptive."[76]

Mirroring the postmodern subject, literary criticism on the postwar British novel has also emerged as a strange creature. In *English Fiction since 1984: Narrating a Nation*, Brian Finney reveals the place that postmodern thought has come to when reading the British novel. Having just examined the narrow class base of the English novel above, Finney feels that it offers "a bewildering variety of narrative modes, voices and tones," and Britain is therefore a nation in which everything is "so thoroughly interconnected" that Cool Britannia now produces a hip and trendy body of literature that is no longer "cozily provincial" and has been somehow "freed from the middle-class monologue."[77] This new breed of writers that he examines (Ackroyd, Amis, McEwan, Barnes, Byatt, Rushdie, Carter, Kureishi, Ishiguro, Swift, and Winterson) is praised because they "no longer exclusively address an insular middle-class readership" (3). Sounding like Bob Hoskins addressing the boat of champagne-swilling gangsters, councilors, and bent cops in *The Long Good Friday*, we are told that England is now "part of the new global economy, and that London [is] a multicultural and international capital" (4). Alongside this is the celebration of the eradicated ego, the vanished Self: "The poststructuralist self or subject is not an autonomous, unified entity. It is a multiple construct...Levis Strauss...felt...that there is no 'I,' no 'me,'" or in the words of John Banville "there is no self." There is instead an "infinite succession of selves" bringing about a "fluid sense of multiple identity" (7). Finney feels that people thus become "mutants" and "hybridization" is the order of the day, while "an omniscient narrator is an anachronism" (7, 12). Since we are now in this fluid space, it is not surprising that the theoretical tools to critically assess these writers also comes from within the postmodern critical field. Finney's logic is that since these writers emerged in this theoretical milieu and are cognizant of it he feels that we should also look to those theories to help us read their work: "it seems appropriate to draw on this body of theoretical work when interpreting their fiction" (6). Finney is also part of this critical echo chamber when he tells us that he too has no fixed theoretical abode, but is similarly fluid and nomadic, and like Barthes' *bricoleur* does not "identify with any particular formulation of poststructuralist theory, but use[s] it eclectically, choosing where appropriate whatever theoretical approach best illuminates the fictional text concerned" (6).

However, when these poststructuralist tools are applied to the texts we find that this "fluid sense of multiple identity" just runs away, leaving us high and dry (7). What kind of conclusions does this criticism make? Finney's chapter on Jeanette Winterson ends by discussing "the enigmatic status of the ending...ungendered sexuality can only live in the privileged, imagined world of textuality" (189); the chapter on Graham Swift's *Last Orders* ends with the image of how "our" identity is parallel to Jack's scattered ashes as "part of the continuum between the living and the dead" (204). The chapter on Angela Carter ends with the notion of how there is a "never-ending process by which subjects narrate themselves and which only encounter closure with death" (176). With Ishiguro we are informed that as an author he remains, like James Joyce's formulation, "within or behind or beyond or above his handiwork, leaving the aesthetic image...to work on us principally in aesthetic and figurative ways" (154). The last word in the chapter on Kureishi is given to the Tory bandwagon-hopping character Eva who says that "Individualism flourishing isn't something that either socialism or conservatism caters for...." To which Finney points out that Karim's father affirms this remark by suggesting that all Britain needs is an increase in "the way of the spirit" (137). The chapter on Rushdie closes with a peppering of Homi Bhabha and discussions of migrant discourses from the old and the new, and that only in the "liminal borderland" can these two mingle (123). The discussion of McEwan's *Atonement* similarly echoes these conclusions: "The novel ends on a note of ambiguity" (100). Regarding Byatt's *Angels and Insects,* we learn "that we are made by the past and remake it in the present," while in *Time's Arrow* Amis "wages an ironic war of words on [those who have] employed grand narratives..." (66, 86). The chapter on Barnes leads to the conclusion that *The History of the World in 10 and ½ Chapters* "can be seen to belong to the same genre as Rushdie's novels, fiction written on and about the margins of life past and present that nevertheless comes to occupy its center" (51). The chapter on Ackroyd sustains the same line of argument: "the ending [of *Chatterton*] celebrates the triumph of art and the autonomy of the literary work over the contingencies of life and their historical representation" (32).

Reading the contemporary British novel in this way is not dialectical and it is not really "criticism" of the texts, but serves paradoxically to transform the novels into coherent narratives about fragmentation and margins. As with a wide range of postmodern literary criticism, there appears to be no truly troubling contradictions in the readings or in the texts themselves. Throughout Finney's entire text there is no suggestion that any of these authors might be wrong about anything: in all cases they are basically praised for cleverly showing us the true postmodern road that we should all take. In this sense we find ourselves immersed, not in a classless society, but in a classless body of criticism.[78]

Obviously, class is ubiquitous in the contemporary novel, and as Tew points out, far from supposedly vanishing like the working-class narrative, the middle-class narrative is strong and resilient: "It can be one of the most recursive, regressive and resistant of narratives," which determines "an aesthetic and intellectual hegemony based on a relative uniformity of self-reflection and self-representation," and as far as the common reader is concerned, when we pick up a contemporary novel, the characters that are "mostly assumed as being normative are middle-class presences."[79] For Žižek, this middle-class norm arises because the self-created identity of the "middle class" is built on a paradox, in that it is not so much a class in itself, but is simply defining itself by a negation, by what it is not:

> ...today, the only class which, in its "subjective" self perception, explicitly conceives of and presents itself as a class is the notorious "middle-class" which is precisely the "non-class": the allegedly hard-working

> middle strata of society which define themselves...by a double opposition to both "extremes" of the social space.... The "middle-class" grounds its identity in the exclusion of both extremes which, when they are directly counterpoised, give us "class antagonism" at its purest...[which] by expelling both poles of the antagonism into the position of antisocial "extremes" which corrode the healthy social body (multinational corporations and intruding immigrants), presents itself as the neutral common ground of Society.[80]

The result, as we see in Finney, and as Philip Tew accurately points out, is that "a particular class affiliation is a constant [which becomes] the bedrock of [contemporary British] writing."[81] Reading the contemporary British novel in this way means that it is always being treated in a vacuum, where we cannot engage in truly productive readings since the novels and the criticism revolves through a self-perpetuating and hermetically sealed circuit. For example, Philip Tew's comments quoted earlier about the middle class are themselves contained in his chapter on class, which means that while issues of class can be addressed and aired, by being one chapter among many it functions as a kind of bracketing, so that questions of class are to be brought up *here*, which then forestalls them being brought up elsewhere. Once the "class" chapter is over, he returns to talking about the contemporary novel as if it was once again politically and ideologically transparent. So for example, Martin Amis's *Money* is dealt with in his next chapter but only within the framework of the chapters' concerns: "Space and Styles—Urban Identities."[82] The same safety mechanism of bracketing class also arises in Chapter Two of Dominic Head's *Modern British Fiction 1950–2000*.

As Fredric Jameson points out, if we are to read the contemporary British novel dialectically we must break this hermeneutic circle and shed light on the voice that these texts (and criticisms) have silenced:

> [S]ince, by definition the cultural monuments and masterworks that have survived tend necessarily to perpetuate only a single voice in this class dialogue, the voice of a hegemonic class, they cannot be properly assigned their relational place in a dialogical system without the restoration or artificial reconstruction of the voice to which they were initially opposed, a voice for the most part which is stifled and reduced to silence...or reappropriated in their turn by the hegemonic culture.[83]

Positing a working-class canon to supplant the current one is beside the point. Jameson reminds us of the dangers of this when he states that an "affirmation of such non-hegemonic cultural voices remains ineffective if it is limited to the merely 'sociological' perspective of the pluralistic rediscovery of other isolated social groups."[84] Moreover, extending the list of authors to say, "Here, let's include these working-class authors as Literature," would only extend the institution of literature, and reaffirm its status as an institution rather than being an act proper that could transform the field of literature altogether.

What I aim to examine here is how the middle-class authors who are presented to us as "canonical" are working with questions of class, how they are representing it, and why these representations take the narrative forms that they do, to illuminate why these novels are perhaps singled out for praise and canonized. John Kirk has suggested that "class itself becomes the 'Third space' which disrupts and destabilizes any easy notions or bland celebration of difference... [and that] anxieties around class arise in the dialectic of simultaneous working-class absence and presence."[85] Paradoxically then, if we wish to build a critique of middle-class ideology (and what is holding it together) we are much better off looking at the canonical novels, where these class tensions are most forceful, rather than by simply erecting and celebrating a working-class counter-canon. Facing these novels and the anxieties that class invariably produces in them is vital, because, as Ian Buchanan points out: "cultural texts provoke such anxieties as these to *manage* them... What the text must manage is precisely the dangerous and disruptive desire for change its utopian elements betoken."[86] The result is that we want to be able to see the institution of literature at work as it draws off the utopian impulses that these middle-class novels invariably are working to contain. According to Buchanan, a text engages in two contradictory kinds of work: "it must solicit our interest by offering up the possibility of the quite real satisfaction of a genuinely changed society; it must then contain that desire by persuading it to be satisfied with the less than genuine symbolic change."[87] It is this contradictory strategy that I aim to explore in these texts, and so, by critically reading the current canon of middle-class novels it should provide us with a foothold from which to short-circuit the usual classless postmodern approaches to these texts. Ideally we should read our contemporary canon so as to become conscious of how these novels are "managing" the problem of class, and in turn how they build, repair, and redesign their own hegemonic positions. As Jameson points out "The literary or aesthetic act always entertains some active relationship with the Real, yet in order to do so, it cannot simply allow 'reality' to persevere inertly in its own being, outside the text and at a distance. It must rather draw the Real into its own texture...language manages to carry the Real within itself as its own intrinsic or immanent subtext."[88] By examining this group of canonical writers, I hope to shed light on how these texts are thus engaging with the real and in the words of Jameson, echoing Pierre Macherey, show how the novel has an ideological function: "the function of inventing imaginary or formal 'solutions' to unresolvable social contradictions."[89]

In the chapters that follow, I aim to read the contemporary British novel in a way that avoids slipping into either the classless pluralism of postmodern theory, or from simply finding these novels guilty of false consciousness. Instead, I have set out to open up the institution of literature to critical examination so as to shed light on what these texts gain (and lose) by dealing with class in the ways that they do. Each chapter deals with more than one author so that we can see how across the field of the middle-class novel, similar patterns, contradictions, anxieties, and solutions begin to emerge and shape themselves. Treating these authors as an institution also allows us to see them not in individual terms but as branches of a larger grouping in which overarching ideological positions can be mapped and made to reveal themselves.

Chapter One is concerned with examining the work of Pat Barker, Ian McEwan, and Kazuo Ishiguro. Separately, these novelists would appear to be working in different spheres, yet when read alongside each other we see how all three are articulating a desire to position their characters within narratives that push the middle-class narrators/characters in these texts toward an open space of authority, growth, and development, while the working-class figures are moved closer toward isolation and restriction, or a space in which they can only signify in terms of their excessive surplus desire that prevents any empathy between them and the reader. In Pat Barker, despite her earlier working-class-based novels, her thoroughly canonized *Regeneration* trilogy will be read as a body of work that seeks to recuperate and reconstruct a bourgeois subject for a postmodern world in the form of Rivers, while eliminating any trace of a class-based modern subjectivity. With Ian McEwan I will be concerned with how *Saturday* and *Atonement* place Baxter and Robbie Turner into positions whereby they occupy an awkward textual space that is both central and yet marginal to the narratives and are finally excluded altogether. McEwan's novels leave us clearly lined up against these figures, while drawing us into ideological and emotional empathy with the authorial middle-class narrative voices of Perowne and Briony. In Ishiguro, while the content of the novel centers on the lives of the working-class Stevens and Miss Kenton, it does so to dismantle the working-class Stevens, presenting him as passively and naively cooperative with the machinations of power. Disempowering Stevens, the novel's form similarly draws the reader into identifying with bourgeois positions of authority and knowledge. In the case of all three authors, I shall also explore how critical readings of these novels serve to reinforce, rather than challenge, their ideological foundations.

Chapter Two deals with Zadie Smith's *On Beauty* and Will Self's *The Book of Dave* to look at how two seemingly diverse novelists, despite their race and gender differences can reach startlingly similar conclusions when we examine their novels in terms of class. While Smith has openly paid homage to Forster's *Howards End* in her novel, the conclusion that she draws from this parallel shows that despite the postmodern identity politics in the novel, problems of class remain unchallenged. Unlike Forster, who insisted on making Bast as central to the narrative as his ideological limits would allow, in Zadie Smith, the elimination of her Bast figure, Carl Thomas, as well as the treatment of the working-class Howard Belsey, clearly reveals the texts' failure to fully confront class conflicts. Similarly, in *The Book of Dave*, Will Self offers us a text in which the humor emerges, as in Amis's *Money*, from having a working-class protagonist who simply cannot and must not be taken seriously. At a time of supposed classlessness and multiculturalism, Will Self's choice of a white working-class cab driver who is overtly racist, sexist, and homophobic clearly establishes how this novel wants to replace the working class, moving them back into a space whereby they can be safely defused. The idea that Dave's angry rants in the present would go on to form the basis of a future religion reverberates through the novel's double sense of mockery and panic, and finally, the bourgeois norm is reestablished when Dave is killed off at the end of the novel, while the middle-class father and son, Carl and Cal Devenish, are reunited and inherit the future. In both texts, the authority of the narrative voice ensures that we remain at a safe distance from the working-class figures in these novels, aided by a paradoxical mixture of mockery/humor and fear/disgust.

Chapter Three focuses on the work of Martin Amis, Peter Ackroyd, and Hanif Kureishi. Despite critical attempts to position Amis as writer who is either somehow "above" class altogether or one who is actively deconstructing and moving us "beyond" the limitations of class, it is plain that in *Money*, the working-class protagonist John

Self is clearly positioned as a figure of contempt and disgust who is finally ejected from the space of the novel for his attempts to raise himself above his station. The novel, despite its formal experimentation, not only reasserts the authorial position of the traditional middle-class author in the shape of "Martin Amis" who appears in the novel, but also manages to express and suppress the anxieties of confronting an expanding working-class population during the 1980s. Peter Ackroyd's novels have been quickly absorbed into the canon, and his work is easily blended into the postmodern world of play, forgery, historical slippage, and fragmented subject positions. However, the question of class is something that is easily elided in his work. Focusing on *Hawksmoor*, the chapter will examine how Ackroyd's work is concerned with erasing any trace of historical ground upon which a dialectical subject could be raised, and that his particular approach to postmodernism produces a textual field in which class is eliminated in favor of a classless "spiritual" rebirth that transcends the troubling particularities of history. Despite criticism's desire to position Ackroyd as "radically anti-referential and anti-mimetic" as Julian Wolfreys would claim,[90] his work is clearly driven by an ideological desire to eliminate the real and place any kind of working-class subject beyond reach, leaving us with only, as Jameson has said of postmodernism, "a semblance of historical verisimilitude."[91] The current way of reading Hanif Kureishi (as with Zadie Smith), is to assert that his work offers radical ways of rethinking identity and consciousness in a fluid postmodern global culture that has no need for old models of subjectivity and agency. However, reading Kureishi's *The Black Album* and *The Body* I will argue that such a strategy fails to read these texts "against the grain" and instead merely replicates the erasure of the working-class subject at the level of ideology as we are presented with two novels in which middle-class subjectivity is at the center of the narratives. This chapter will look at how a similar pattern is at work in all three novelists whereby any historical ground must remain out of reach if (bourgeois) subjectivity is to remain "free." What we see in Kureishi's work is thus a reworking of the same problems in Amis and Ackroyd whereby class exists and can be imagined only as an impossible subject position, while retreating ever further into postmodern models of the subject which as the texts themselves make clear, cannot solve the contradictions that class divisions produce.

Chapter Four takes up the questions surrounding class and realism in the contemporary novel. Andrezj Gasiorek has suggested that what we see in the postwar novel is an end to the binary struggle between realism and experimentalism, which has been replaced by a plurality of "realisms."[92] Dominic Head develops this by suggesting that "the greater proportion of [postwar] serious fiction" has been written with a "dependence on some version of social mimesis" and feels that the continuation of this tradition in Britain "is a marker of the topical expansion of the novel in Britain." For Head, echoing Finney, the continued survival of the realist tradition emerges from Britain's greater "social diversity."[93] This chapter will set out to critique this assertion by arguing that the contemporary novel has resorted to realism not so as to open up questions of "social diversity" but rather to preserve the introverted bourgeois novel while providing an ideological appearance of plurality and diversity. Looking at the work of Graham Swift, Jonathan Coe, and Alan Hollinghurst the chapter will examine how realism has been reconfigured by postmodernism in Britain and how, despite the appearance of a mimetic grounding in the political milieu of contemporary Britain, these authors have managed to continue a tradition whereby the middle-class novel maintains an aesthetic form that ensures the erasure of any dialectical critique of class while appearing to offer it up for critical scrutiny through the supposedly "transparent" and "impartial" lens of realism.

Chapter Five examines the representation of class identity in British cinema and television from 1979 to the present. Drawing on conclusions that have been raised throughout this book, I will examine cinema and television during this period so as to map some of the contours that have seen class being reshaped for the British viewing audience. There is not enough space in this present work to deal adequately with the vast range of works from 1979 to the present in television and cinema but I have taken what I feel are some central texts and issues to draw out the lines of thought that have emerged from the preceding chapters. To this end I have focused on Art cinema (Mike Leigh, Peter Greenaway, and Derek Jarman), moving on to Mainstream Cinema looking at such texts as Stephen Frears' *Dirty Pretty Things* (2002) and *Harry Potter,* while finally turning to television by examining *I'm Alan Partridge*, and *The Office*, as well as *The Amazing Mrs. Pritchard* and *Life on Mars*. This chapter examines how class has been staged, recreated, and elided from Thatcher to Blair and will assess the extent to which class concerns have been morphed into abstractions of identity and the fulfillment of personal desires.

Chapter 1

"Unworkable Subjects": Middle-Class Narratives in Pat Barker, Ian McEwan, and Kazuo Ishiguro

History is what hurts...

—*Fredric Jameson*[1]

Class is a communist concept

—*Margaret Thatcher*[2]

John Brannigan recently argued that the psychic disturbances in Pat Barker's *Regeneration* trilogy and the subject's concomitant "haunting" by history are "a constituent element of modernity."[3] However, I would argue that this splitting cannot be separated from the question of class. This chapter examines how Barker, McEwan, and Ishiguro produce representations of working-class subjects that expose how the modernist subject is at odds with contemporary desires for a postmodern classless subject. I will examine how Pat Barker's Billy Prior from the *Regeneration* trilogy, Ian McEwan's presentation of Baxter in *Saturday* and Robbie Turner in *Atonement,* and Kazuo Ishiguro's Stevens and Miss Kenton in *The Remains of the Day* all open up questions of class to the tensions between modern and postmodern subjectivity: tensions that are always resolved favorably for a "postmodern" middle-class protagonist and unfavorably for the "modern" working-class subjects.

Pat Barker CBE

In a 1992 interview with Rob Nixon, Pat Barker admits that she originally began writing "short, *middle-class* novels which weren't published."[4] After many rejections, she gave up writing for the market and decided to write for herself: the result was the early social realist novel *Union Street*. Angela Carter, who was Barker's tutor at the University of East Anglia, showed the novel to Virago who then decided to publish it.[5] After writing three of these working-class feminist novels centered on the hard lives of working-class women in the North of England, she says that she felt pigeonholed as a feminist writer: "I felt I had got myself into a box where I was strongly typecast as a northern, regional, working-class, feminist—label, label, label—novelist."[6] In the highly successful *Regeneration* trilogy, her focus shifted toward the male and middle- to upper-class world of the First World War officers. While critics have gone back and examined Barker's early work in the light of her later success, these early novels are not as heavily canonized as the *Regeneration* trilogy. Although there is a political and aesthetic split in her oeuvre, many critics assert that there is no disjunction, and that what we see in Barker's work is a unified field that doesn't switch gears, or abandon its earlier politics, but that in fact we see a "deepening" of her concerns. This argument is made by Lynda Prescott who aims to show that the "critical division between Barker's earlier writing" and the later novels, which are seen as "transcending the sociological limitations of the working-class female communities"[7] is a "spurious kind of division."[8] This critical position is valuable in that it reveals how working-class literature can be consumed by the canon, not as "Literature," but as books about the working class, and that it also made Barker feel trapped, like the usual working-class protagonist trapped in her town, her job, or her family. Once she abandons social realism and her working-class protagonists, Barker presumably felt "free" to no longer be a "feminist" who writes "working-class" novels, but an author. It is at this point that we see Barker fully permitted to join the canon, and her work is then praised for its "depth," "complexity," and "humanity." The work is now attached easily to the labels "masterpiece" but since these are bourgeois labels (as opposed to labels like "working-class feminist realist"), they supposedly no longer leave Barker feeling trapped "in a box." Barker points out that most of the publishing houses that read the early working-class novel *Union Street* rejected it, because "Frankly, this is too bleak and depressing."[9] It is certainly worth noting then that a *working-class* novel about a few women is "bleak" and "depressing" but a *middle-class* trilogy about the pointless slaughter of thousands that ends with the working-class Billy Prior being sent back to the Front to die as the denouement is "an inspiring book" (The *New Yorker*), which is "formally superb" (A. S. Byatt), and which "lifts the reader up" (Fay Weldon) through its "intellectual nuances" (The *Sunday Times*) and "formidable energy and integrity" (*London Review of Books*). The trilogy is thus not "bleak and depressing" like feminist working-class novels: *this* work becomes "one of the richest and most rewarding works of fiction of recent times" (The *Times Literary Supplement*).

It is clear that there has been a breach between the early and later Barker which is why literary critics will go to such lengths to show that there has not. This idea that Barker's oeuvre is an organic whole reappears in Sarah C. E. Ross's essay "Regeneration, Redemption, Resurrection: Pat Barker and the Problem of Evil." Ross argues that whereas Barker's early theme is the problem of domestic abuse, and economic, class-based evil (which victimizes both men and women), in the war novels this has not been abandoned but has been expanded to include the evil of war and what it does to men (and women). What is startling then, and what is relevant to our discussion of class, is the way that Barker's work has been so thoroughly canonized and placed onto school and college syllabi once the works move away from a direct treatment of the working class, and instead focuses on the middle-class concerns that are voiced by Rivers across the entire trilogy. Once Barker is seen to have "matured" into a bourgeois writer, then her work can be easily canonized, and while the earlier works cannot be dismissed, they are retrospectively framed as a form of juvenilia, a sketch for the "fully developed" themes and "Art" of the *Regeneration* trilogy. If, as Ross says, the novels are all of a piece, then surely the earlier novels would have become classics, or would have been taught, assigned, read, filmed, and studied in the same way that *Regeneration* has. If the novels are ideologically parallel, as Ross asserts, then why is it that the *Regeneration* trilogy has had an appeal far wider than the others? Is it because it is "better" or more "mature" or more "developed"? Clearly, the reason, I would argue, is because the trilogy articulates and resolves essentially middle-class desires and anxieties.

Ross quotes Margaretta Jolly, who, she says, "correctly identifies, 'a maturing, rather than a rejection' " of Barker's earlier concerns.[10] Using Prior as the link back to the earlier novels, Ross says that the treatment of Billy Prior in the trilogy is the opportunity for "Barker's extended exploration of the function of class, gender and male sexuality" (135). Ross says that Prior is "fractured" by his split sympathy and since he is not at home with his own people or with the upper- and middle-class officer ranks (into which he has been promoted), he "splits into Jekyll and Hyde personalities" and tries to assist his working-class antiwar friends but finally "betrays them" (135). Sadly, this is all we get on Prior from Ross's analysis and the bulk of Ross's essay drifts into a discussion of Rivers. After all it is Rivers (and not Prior) that ponders Abraham and Isaac's sacrifice; it is Rivers (not Prior) "who is Abraham," and whose job, is "restoration." It is the brave Rivers, not Prior, who "looks into the abyss" and it is the "complex" Rivers, not the split Prior who is "deeply humane." In fact, Billy Prior is even dismissed by Ross as being unable to read Rivers: Rivers, we are told "is more than the empathetic strip of wallpaper Billy Prior accuses him of being." Finally, it is the middle-class Rivers who has the depth of character to suffer the "conflict between his belief…and his horror" (137).

The trilogy is thus being celebrated not for the troubling disruptive things that it says about class, but for the ideologically supportive narrative that it offers for the bourgeois subject. Having spent the bulk of her essay on the middle-class Rivers, Ross's essay slips back to her opening remarks about how political Barker is, and the result is a conclusion which asserts that what we see in Barker is not a break from her earlier working-class (relatively ignored) novels to her later (highly praised) middle-class novels, but instead, says that "socialist feminism and conscientious realism, are in Pat Barker's case, aligned in one novelistic trajectory. Rather than a shift in focus, an unflinching view, ever broadening, is discernible in her fiction…" (140). Interestingly, this socialist politics seems to be absent from Ross's conclusion, as what Barker offers us, according to Ross, is not socialism or even working-class feminist politics but "resurrections of the human spirit" (140). Like the fifteen meter high sculpture of Christ that Barker speaks of in *Double Vision*, Ross feels that Barker's work makes it clear that "in history and across time, full regenerations may not be possible, but precarious redemptions, resurrections of the human spirit, are possible in individuals and in communities, and are representable in art" (140). These platitudes can be smoothly absorbed by bourgeois culture and so derail any need for a political transformation of society. Once the "depressing" politics of the earlier working-class novels has been abandoned then the canon can readily celebrate Barker's work that now holds out the joyous ideological hope that "resurrection and redemption," but not revolution, are possible. John Kirk is surely correct in suggesting that a novel like Barker's *Union Street* certainly "eschews some of the ideological strategies associated with the bourgeois realist text"[11]; however, the *Regeneration* trilogy operates in the opposite way, as it clearly provides a narrative space of growth for the middle-class Rivers and a closing off of possibilities for the working-class Prior.

John Brannigan in his 2003 essay on Barker entitled "History and the Hauntological Imagination" rehearses the usual argument about ghosts and haunting in Barker.[12] The argument is also repeated by Nick Hubble, writing about Pat Barker's *Regeneration* trilogy.[13] While it may be theoretically fashionable to talk of ghosts, I feel that this desire to exorcise the ghosts of modernity is highly problematic. Hubble's 2006 essay is clearly haunted by Brannigan's 2003 essay and in circulating around discussions of Freud and ghosts they both seem unable to move their analysis forward. Brannigan opens with a discussion of Freud's essay on the Uncanny in which Freud encounters "himself" in a mirror on a train. This encounter with one's double becomes for Brannigan the signature moment in Barker whereby all of her main characters experience this moment of meeting another self, or a past self, or an Other. Brannigan's argument will show that these haunting doubles are "signs of crisis in scientific (or more accurately psychoanalytical) modes of knowledge" and that haunting "is a constituent element of modernity."[14] Brannigan asserts that Rivers tries to deal with the patients he encounters using a barrage of "skilful rational examination" but that despite his reliance on Western metanarratives of psychoanalysis, in the end "his own experiences of the hauntological in Melanesia defy his attempts at rational explanation and serve to disturb the stability of his distinctions between appearance and reality, illness and sanity. . . ." The result is that the trilogy thus stages "the crisis for modern rationality." Rivers realizes that he is both an instrument of social discipline (he returns Prior back to health and back to the Front) and, like Ross's use of a Christian resurrection, Rivers becomes in Brannigan, an instrument of "salvation" for his patients.[15]

But what Brannigan never gets around to mentioning is how these various positions of authority, control, and submission in the novel are all rooted in class structures. While ghosts show up at bedsides and in nightmares, the real ghost that is haunting the trilogy (and the criticism of it) is class. Rivers's class position is clearly a middle-class position, as he does not share a working-class background with Prior, nor does he identify with the upper-class logic of the war machine of businessmen and politicians. Significantly, in the struggle between Prior and Rivers, for all of the discussions of hauntology and

Derridean notions that "the past as such is a perpetual palimpsest"[16] it is clear that Rivers is meant to be our central concern (as we saw in Ross's criticism), and by the end of the trilogy it is Rivers that will have his powers of visualization restored, while Prior, powerless to the last, will be sent back to France to die a pointless death in a meaningless war.

If we follow Žižek, all of the trappings of the First World War in the novel are a red-herring (albeit one that gives the game away by being an image of thousands of working-class men being buried under piles of mud) that distracts us from the need to see a very simple narrative desire: the repression of the working-class subject Prior and the glorious rebirth of the bourgeois subject: Rivers. Brannigan points out that Rivers's modern rational self is challenged and undergoes a transformation, yet such a "transformation" is denied to Prior and his class. Brannigan quotes Michel de Certeau in terms of how haunting operates, but the passage cannot be separated from how questions of class are repressed by bourgeois ideology: "[Any] autonomous order is founded upon what it eliminates, it produces a 'residue' condemned to be forgotten...But what was excluded re-infiltrates the place of its origin—now the present's 'clean' place. It resurfaces, it troubles, it turns the present's feeling of being 'at home' into an illusion...."[17] Brannigan's argument is that Barker is revealing how modernity (including that central social science of modernity, psychoanalysis), cannot hope to fully repress the past. But paradoxically, while Rivers may worry briefly that he is silencing his patients by curing them, Prior is nevertheless sent back to the front to die. The reader is meant to empathize with the troubled doctor who is transformed and grows inwardly, while the narrative clearly prevents any empathy with the sexually obsessed class traitor, Prior. Thus paradoxically, the novels reinforce the ideological structure of the war by leaving us with only two possible outcomes: working-class sacrifice and bourgeois redemption.

Brannigan concludes by saying that due to his Melanesia experience, Rivers is now in "the land of the living dead, like all his patients."[18] Yet the difference is that unlike Prior and the dead, Rivers is not dead, and unlike Prior, he lives to tell the tale. In this sense we are circulating in the same terrain laid out by Virginia Woolf in *Mrs. Dalloway* in which the shell-shocked First World War veteran Septimus Warren-Smith dies by "sacrificing" himself on the iron railings, while Mrs. Dalloway goes on to have her evening party.[19] In this sense these novels work not so much to "regenerate the past" as

Brannigan says, but only repeat it.[20] The narrative thus "regenerates" the troubled bourgeois subject who in our own historical moment must be reshaped and remade to align themselves with postmodern models of subjectivity: the working class qua working class cannot be regenerated and so are removed. As Brannigan states:

> [T]he dramatic return of Rivers's powers of visualization represent also a "traumatic shift in historical consciousness" in which England moves from a modern consciousness which centered around moving "progressively towards healing" and into a postmodern consciousness of "loss, absence and otherness."[21]

In this sense, Brannigan sees the trilogy as confirming a postmodern desire for otherness, difference and the endless palimpsest of history, and a rejection of teleology and modernism. While Brannigan reads the novel as a farewell to modernity, the class division between Rivers and Prior is distinctly a problem that has its roots still firmly planted in modernity. In this way the *Regeneration* trilogy is attempting to exorcise the specter of class that is haunting contemporary British society. We are still not in a place whereby a canonized novel can leave us with a *working-class* protagonist who undergoes a "dramatic return" in their powers of visualization that would signify a "shift in historical consciousness." Prior experiences no redemption and his death brings about no shift in working-class consciousness.

Nick Hubble goes through the same arguments about haunting in Pat Barker, and the opening section of his essay is clearly marked: "The Ghosts of Modernity." In this essay, he wishes to make the point that her fiction deals with "the repressed elemental forces straining against the constructed meanings of modern reality" and that "the characters in her later fiction can see in more than one world and sometimes cross the borders between these domains."[22] In this sense, as with Brannigan, we are in a Peter Ackroyd-esque world in which we are all at some kind of historical ice rink in which everyone is slipping and sliding while drifting in and out of overlapping time zones. This fluidity, so beloved of postmodern critics, at times makes rather large claims for what the trilogy is doing. For example, Hubble says that "*The Ghost Road* eliminates hierarchical values by going beyond the boundaries of modern cultural representation."[23] This postmodern truism is repeated by Lynda Prescott who says that in Barker we see a "crossing and blurring of boundaries" and that her work "tends to dissolve the barriers between past and present."[24] In what ways is the reader being taken *beyond* hierarchical values when this final part of the trilogy ends with Rivers (middle-class, educated) alive and regenerated, while Prior (bisexual and working class) is killed off?[25] How can this be a "collective act of regeneration" when it only concerns Rivers, and when the largest "collective" is the thousands of doomed working-class soldiers for whom no regeneration is possible? The idea that the "ghosts of modernity are allowed to depart in peace" (i.e., Prior and his class) is also unintentionally apposite, because, as with Brannigan, the desire in the novel is to kill off the modern-class bound subject and replace it with a postmodern subjectivity that is so slippery that no purchase can be made on it.[26] Ironically then, Hubble clues us into how Prior (and his troubling working-class position) is again the "ghost of modernity" that must be removed if the bourgeois subject is to be liberated. As with Brannigan's reading, the ghost of class and the question of modernity are what the text exorcises, while restructuring and resurrecting the middle-class subject through Rivers. The dynamics of the novel are right here with their names: Prior is a preexisting condition, something before our own historical moment, he was there before, and is the thing that must be removed/erased and overridden. Rivers, on the other hand, is in flux and will keep moving and thus will survive, like the class to which he belongs, which will always be a plural and fluid moveable present. In Pat Barker's *Regeneration* trilogy, the bourgeois subject has thus been successfully reattached and linked to a postmodern vision of history, while the working-class subject is disconnected from history and sent back to the land of the dead. Paradoxically, the working-class subject has not been eliminated or absorbed into a classless society but simply killed off, rejected, and repressed. This is the ghost that then haunts our every action, and it is still there on every page of the British contemporary novel, calling out to us, asking to be heard.

Toward the end of *The Ghost Road,* Billy Prior is writing what will be his final diary entries and he reflects on how British institutions and class power is what has brought him here, while the officers, like Rivers, are safely back in England. The diary entry refers to words and the way that those words remain, like Prior's diary, long after the dead have gone, to remind whoever reads them of the class war that is continually being fought and lost in Britain:

> Little words that trip through sentences unregarded: us, them, we, they, here, there. These are the words of power, and long after we're gone they'll lie about in the language, like the unexploded grenades in these fields, and any one of them'll take your hand off.[27]

Interestingly, this powerful comment is not where the novel closes, instead, the novel ends with the comforting and reassuring cleansing of all of the "ghosts," that like Prior, have been troubling Rivers throughout the novel. Rivers is "struggling to stay awake" at the night nurses' station in the Empire Hospital when the ghost of Njiru comes to him, "attended by his shadowy retinue." Njiru says "Do not yearn for us, the fingerless, the crippled, the broken. Go down and depart, oh, oh, oh." Having said this, Njiru and his retinue, like ghosts of the working class, can then safely disappear from the now cleansed and regenerated bourgeois world as "the brown face, with its streaks of lime, faded into the light of the daytime ward."[28]

Ian McEwan CBE

Opening up a copy of *Atonement*, the reader is struck by a barrage of compliments from both sides of the Atlantic, attesting to the excellence of McEwan's *Atonement*: "A work of astonishing depth and humanity...It is rare for a critic to feel justified in using the word 'masterpiece,' but [*Atonement*] really deserves to be called one" (The *Economist*). The *New York Review of Books* feels that McEwan can do "more or less anything he likes with the novel form." The *Wall Street Journal* applauds his "psychological insight," while the *Guardian* praises the novel for hauling "a defining part of the British literary tradition up to and into the 21st Century." The *New York Times Book Review* describes it as "compassionate." *Esquire* feels that "McEwan could be the most psychologically astute writer working today, our era's Jane Austen." The back cover informs us that the novel was selected as Best Book of the Year by *Time*, The *Washington Post Book World, Boston Globe, Chicago Tribune, Village Voice, Entertainment Weekly, San Francisco Chronicle, Atlantic Monthly,* and *Seattle Times*.

Given such a wide range of critics who all agree on the novels "excellence" and are thus "for" literature, it would be ludicrous to challenge such a chorus of praise. But what if we stop for a moment and instead of assuming that literature is somehow with "us" and against any kind of nasty "ideology," what if we adopt Raymond Williams's position for a while, just to see what emerges. What if we, as literary critics, decide to stand "against literature"? What critical positions are now available to us, and what would "literature" look like from such a position? What stops us from simply stepping back from literature for a moment and instead of assuming that literature is somehow always on "our" side (or on the side of literary theory) or the interests of large sections of society, what if we consider that perhaps literature is not so much what enables us to see through ideology to become "more in sympathy with the vulnerability of the human heart" (*Sunday Times* on *Atonement*) but that instead it is thoroughly ideological and may actually stop us from seeing certain things. To the extent that any novel is praised so highly is surely an indication of how effectively it manages, not to tell any kind of "truth," but to resonate and ring true with preexisting ideological structures of feeling. The praise for *Atonement* is thus indicative, not that the novel somehow challenges a bourgeois worldview that literary critics wish to subversively propagate, but it is indicative that it contains highly charged ideological content that bourgeois culture is eager to reinforce and disseminate.

If it is possible to seek out the bourgeois ideology that sneakily lies buried within Evelyn Waugh, or Virginia Woolf or Ezra Pound, why does this chorus of disapproval, so easily engaged in by a host of academic literary critics, fall into silence when confronted with our own living writers? Why can't we explore McEwan as an author whose work reveals the bourgeois ideology of our own moment? Are we disturbed by the idea of being "against literature" that, in turn, would somehow mean being "against" McEwan?

I would like to therefore move aside this critical chorus of approval of *Atonement* and treat it as a thoroughly ideological work of literature that reinforces notions of literature, class, and authorship and which thereby reinforces rather than deconstructs a dominant worldview of the bourgeoisie. John Yardley of the *Washington Post Book World* says of *Atonement* that McEwan has told a story "that reaffirms in every syllable our need for storytelling and its own transformative power...." But who exactly is this "us"? If this was a novel written by an African writer and was set in Africa, would a white reader feel included by this "us" on the back jacket? Would a lesbian reader feel included if "us" was on the back jacket of *Wuthering Heights*? Obviously not, yet this novel by a white middle-class male author about white middle-class people can easily pass itself off as the universal condition, and thereby the "us" (functioning ideologically) is meant to include "everyone."[29] So, if as a working-class critic, I do not feel included in this "us" then the novel shapes itself up very differently and when we read as a working-class subject, the textual landscape shifts and different shadows and lights emerge across the terrain.

Let us look at how current academic literary criticism deals with *Atonement*. Although the rhetoric is more restrained than in the newspapers, there is still the sense that McEwan can tell "us" the truth, a "truth" that the rest of us, blinded by ideology, cannot see. If the journalist Yardley feels that McEwan has told a story "that reaffirms in every syllable our need for storytelling and its own transformative power" so, Brian Finney repeats this in academic vocabulary: "In the first place, when novelists force us to understand the constructed nature of their characters, they invite us simultaneously to reflect on the way subjectivity is similarly constructed in the nonfictional world we inhabit."[30] Moreover, he says that

> [t]o complain about the metafictional element in the book is to fail to understand that we are all narrated, entering at birth into a preexisting narrative which provides the palimpsest on which we inscribe our own narratives/lives. McEwan's foregrounding of the metafictional element compels the reader to face the extent to which narration determines human life (79).

Therefore, the literary critic reasserts that the strong novel can make the weak reader "face" something and instead of "us" failing to understand something (because we are blinded by ideological demons) the novel, in its genius, and its brave struggle for the truth, breaks through with its power (described by many reviewers as some version of "magical") and passes on a vital humanist lesson: that "we" are all narrated: a fact that "determines human life" (79). Surely this is a narrative in which literature (and the critic) is given all the good parts. It leaves the reader, like some ideological damsel in distress, waiting to be rescued from ideology by literature. More importantly, in contemporary British society some people's lives are literally narrated by the authority of others, just as Robbie Turner's life is narrated by Briony in *Atonement,* so that what actually "determines human life" in contemporary Britain is class: some are born to narrate, others have narration thrust on them.

McEwan has said that he looks "on novels as exploratory, forms of investigation, at its broadest and best, into human nature" (76). But surely it is clear to any literary critic over the past thirty years that human nature is not peered into by the author like a person staring into a jar, and that novels are not (despite the quasi-scientific/Naturalistic novels use of "forms of investigation") objective exercises but are thoroughly ideological spaces in which human nature is "produced" out of the available ideological raw materials.

What of the plethora of intertextual references that are scattered throughout the novel? Finney argues that all of the references to literature in the novel are either postmodern "ironic" references or are examples of Derridean "intertextuality" (74). Praising McEwan's use of metafictional narrative strategies in *Atonement* Finney continues: "In this sense, the use of metafiction in the book serves to undermine the naturalization of social and economic inequalities that especially characterized British society in the 1930s" (74). For Finney, the novel is therefore "from beginning to end concerned with the making of fiction" and that in some circular way, the novel shows how fiction can be "damning" or "redemptive": as Briony Tallis will use "fiction" to make "amends for the damage fiction has induced her to cause..." (69–70). Finney, eager to make McEwan into the hero, shows how the intertextual references make the novel open, honest, and healthy, while any tendency to classical realism is rejected as unhealthy and secretive. The more McEwan's text foregrounds its status as fiction, paradoxically, the more real it is: the references "throughout the book [serve] to undermine the classic realist mode of narration" thus "forcing the reader to take note of the presence of a self-conscious narrator" (70–71).

Such a maneuver places the novel somehow beyond ideology, while literature is given an unlimited power to expose the truth that ideology wishes to hide. But what if the book is not undermining/exposing anything? What if the text's metafictional strategies are, in themselves, ideological? What if the text's self-consciousness conceals rather than reveals as we assume? If it is the former then shouldn't we be "against literature"? It would seem not, as these unquestionable truths about metafiction are something that "we" are meant to see as True. As Finney points out "Patricia Waugh argues [that] 'Contemporary metafictional writing is both a response and a contribution to an even more thoroughgoing sense that reality or history are provisional: no longer a world of eternal verities but a series of constructions, artifices, impermanent structures.'"[31] McEwan's use of metafiction is now reinforced by Finney and Waugh who inform us that the real world outside of McEwan's novel is undergoing precisely what McEwan is identifying. But while these truths may be ideologically appealing to some sectors of society, surely they are shocking to others. Surely, we are aware that there is certain politics behind the desire to abandon those grand narratives. So once again, I think we can see that McEwan's novel is being praised, not for challenging any ideological orthodoxy but for reinforcing ideological frameworks that appear truthful to "us" (the middle classes) at this moment in time. Novels, as Pierre Macherey has made clear, are not something that simply reveal ideology to us in a raw form, nor can they totally conceal it: what we see in the novel form is the "false resolution of a real debate."[32] In this sense, how can we read *Atonement* against the ideological current that it wants to establish, and see it as an ideological resolution of real conflicts?

Finney feels that the coda of the novel "suggests the way fiction can make visible the inequalities in society that ideology works to conceal."[33] But Macherey would suggest that the novel is actually struggling not to make visible, but to hide ideological gaps and fissures, but since it cannot do it successfully, they slip out in various aporias and gaps. But in Finney's analysis, the novel, in the hands of an author like McEwan, has become more powerful than ideology and can cut right through it and expose the harsh realities underneath, while the novel is now actively (rather than inadvertently) exposing harsh truths that ideology would rather keep locked up. But as we have seen, the lesson that the novel taught us was that "we are all narrated" and that narrative, as Finney said, "determines human life." If this is the truth that fiction's power can uncover, what was the ideological message that we would have been blinded by had it *not* been for McEwan's masterpiece: Was it that we are *not* narrated, or that narrative does *not* "determine human life"? Why would "ideology" (as Finney said earlier) wish to (a) propagate such an idea or (b) wish to conceal it? Now that this truth has been "revealed" by the "powerful masterpiece" where does that leave us? Do we feel as if we have "seen through" ideology? Is this truth something "troubling" for bourgeois ideology or is it actually comforting? Will this truth destabilize the institutions of "Literature" and "Criticism" or reaffirm them?

One place to begin reading this novel against the grain is by looking at the way in which Briony is read. She is treated by all reviewers as somehow not McEwan, she is the foolish young girl who, in misrepresenting Robbie and Cecilia then atones for that crime and its guilt by rewriting their life so that while it ends tragically in reality they can live forever in fiction. This is then the atonement of the title, and this is why we must have the Coda to the novel (which some critics felt was a postmodern sleight of hand) making it clear that the novel we have just finished, a la Proust, or closer to home, Karim in *The Buddha of Suburbia*, is Briony's text. Unlike her former, rigid self that loved to bring order out of chaos, as an adult writer she is now flexible and aware. In a sense, she goes from a metonymic realist where signifiers and signifieds must match to a metaphoric modernist with a penchant for linguistic play. This is the standard way of reading the novel. As Finney remarks, Briony has "finally learned how to imagine herself into the feelings of others...."[34] And that even though she "mistakenly cast them in a story that totally misrepresented them" as an adult "Briony's novel is her literary attempt at reparation for the damage she inflicted as a child." As a result, by the end, we witness Briony's "painfully acquired honesty."[35] This all seems very neat and settled. Briony goes from a closed, rigid, narrow-minded middle-class person to one who is an open, empathetic, middle-class person. Having become self-aware of her guilt, and having punished herself by rewriting Robbie and Cecilia's life she has atoned and is now, like Pat Barker's Rivers, deserving of our sympathy. Surely, it is this kind of a reading that leads reviewers to say how the novel makes them "starry-eyed all over again on behalf of literature's humanizing possibilities."[36]

But why do we separate Briony from McEwan? Why do we assume that McEwan is not Briony? If we read Briony as McEwan (in the same way that McEwan can be read as Perowne in *Saturday*), the political unconscious of the novel is made available to us and the class dynamics of his work begins to materialize. It is clear that *Atonement*, by silencing and killing off the working-class Robbie Turner suffers its own textual guilt. Terry Eagleton came to the same conclusion in a review for the *Lancet:* "it is not hard to read this novel as McEwan's own atonement for a lucrative lifetime of magnificent professional lying."[37] The sympathy that is evoked for Briony for indirectly killing Robbie by the end of the novel is sympathy that is unconsciously being directed to McEwan: we forgive her, we forgive him, we forgive ourselves, and the tradition of literature can continue, modified gently by a degree of self-consciousness while remaining ideologically intact.

While Briony watches Robbie and Cecilia at the fountain in Part One, she says that "None of these three was bad, nor were they particularly good. She need not judge."[38] This is the 1999 Briony speaking, someone who, having written the entire novel, is now in a position of open-minded flexibility. She goes on to confess what has been her lifelong guilt and its reparation: "...above all, it was the failure to grasp the simple truth that other people are as real as you. And only in a story could you enter these different minds and show how they had an equal value. That was the only moral a story need have."[39] This rings true with McEwan's remarks on the September 11 hijackers: "If the hijackers had been able to imagine themselves into the thoughts and feelings of the passengers, they would have been unable to proceed...Imagining what it is like be someone other than yourself is at the core of our humanity."[40] The adult Briony who has learnt from her mistakes also echoes McEwan in terms of her style as she finally develops an "impartial psychological realism," and her "fiction was known for its amorality."[41] Finney would agree, imagining what it is like to be someone else "lies at the core of McEwan's fiction and explains its apparent amoral stance" moving on to praise McEwan's "non-judgmental precision."[42] The novel, in its own self-conscious way is even aware that we will see the link between McEwan and Briony, and so it raises the issue early on: "the reader was bound to speculate that she was describing herself."[43]

So, if we read the novel as a tale of McEwan's own guilt and desire for atonement, rather than just that of a silly girl who must learn her lessons, then the novel's crime of repressing Robbie is not just a fictional one. But it is a crime that takes place in literary history, the crime of McEwan's own pen, which pressured by form, genre, style, and the class ideology in which he participates, has constantly served to undermine the working class. Briony's guilt over Robbie's jail time and meaningless death is McEwan's historical guilt as a bourgeois author, who, try as he might, cannot fulfill his own stated aim of "imagining what it is like to be someone else" as neither he nor Briony can enter into Robbie's consciousness, or tell his story from within, not through lack of desire, but due to ideological constraints, rooted in class, that McEwan/Briony cannot circumvent. In examining Cecilia's letter to Robbie in which she explains that it was probably Danny who was the real rapist, Finney points out how McEwan "subtly suggests the invidious nature of a class system that permeates even those seeking to reverse its effects...."[44] I would agree, but I would add that Briony's problems can also be McEwan's.

It is clear from the outset that class is at the heart of this novel but it is being dealt with in such a way that our concerns shift not toward a system of exclusion that sentences one person to jail and then, like Barker's Prior, sentences them to death, but instead the focus shifts to Briony's consciousness. As with the tradition of the bourgeois novel, it is the bourgeois protagonist who becomes the readers' concern, and as with Rivers, it is *her* growth that concerns us, it is *her* consciousness that envelops us, and it is *her* pain that we are to feel. We could say that she does spend a large amount of her novel showing us the painful struggles of Robbie at Dunkirk, but once we reach the Coda we realize that this was not his narrative at all, but once again is absorbed back into her production and belongs to her: what Robbie "feels" is always already the property of the middle-class author. The changes that she undergoes reveal that she has "grown" and "painfully" learned her lesson, and that the bourgeois subject has been challenged, tested, and reaffirmed once again by the novel.

Lest we think that Briony is the evil bourgeois we are given Paul Marshall as the stereotyped ugly middle-class "warmonger" to whet our appetite and to distract us.[45] Marshall is so obviously vain and horrendous that he comes across as the stock villain and McEwan makes him the person who brings up the issues of factories and unions and "disputes about overtime rates" and tells us that the "sullen" union members needed to be "coaxed like children."[46] These discussions of work and class are seen as ugly and intrusive in the polite bourgeois Tallis household, and McEwan pushes our dislike of him by having Cecilia say that he is "unfathomably stupid" and has what looks like "pubic hair" coming out of his ears.[47] It is as if McEwan/Briony were saying "See, I am not bourgeois, look at what little sympathy I have for this ugly horrid man." This leaves us free to see Briony as the norm, like "us" who, for all of her faults, can finally change, and like Dickens' Scrooge, by the end of the text will be a softer, gentler author, who deserves not only our respect, but also our praise.

So what about Robbie? We know that his mother is Mrs. Turner, the "charlady" for the Tallis's home, and that having won a grammar school scholarship he then goes up to Cambridge University where Jack Tallis pays for his education, which Emily feels was "meddling."[48] Robbie gets a first in literature (while Cecilia gets a third) and wishes to go into medicine. He rolls his own cigarettes, which is dismissed by Briony as simply "a hangover from his Communist Party time—another abandoned fad...."[49] We also learn that he has "no known father."[50] Even in Finney's standard reading of the novel, the question of class rises to the surface, as it is also there on the surface of the novel, as he says, "the difference in social class accounts for the early misunderstanding between Robbie and Cecilia."[51] This does not amount to reading the novel against the grain, or reading the texts political unconscious, but it does establish that the novel is rooted in the problem of class, something which the novel is both aware of and unable to fully resolve. For both Briony and McEwan these tensions and ideological conflicts exist in the real, but can only be resolved at the level of the novel. In this sense McEwan and the elder Briony are no different from the younger Briony who always insists on using her writing to impose her order on the real: "Her passion for tidiness was also satisfied, for an unruly world could be made just so."

She continues: "A love of order also shaped the principles of justice, with death and marriage the main engines of housekeeping, the former being set aside exclusively for the morally dubious, the latter a reward withheld until the final page."[52] Strangely, even though she has supposedly put away childish things and learnt to step into the feelings of others, this brutal textual economy is adhered to in the mature novel that she writes. Briony, thinking about the Quincey's divorce decides that it is something that she cannot write about in that "she did not regard it as a proper subject, and gave it no thought . . . it belonged in the realm of disorder."[53] Robbie's class position in the Tallis household (he is both inside and outside the family) means that he too is not a "proper subject" and so must, like divorce, be sent out of the novel, only to return once he has been rewritten. History, like Briony, will dispense its "principles of justice" and death will be given to Robbie for being "morally dubious" while providing a fictive "marriage" for Robbie and Cecilia. In this way, having atoned for its own class guilt, the "engines of housekeeping" ensure that the economy of the novel remains undisturbed.

McEwan's *Saturday* makes these questions of class much more visible. In an interview in the *Guardian*, McEwan says that the reason that people were angry at his portrayal of Perowne was because "People felt very uncomfortable because I painted this exaggerated version of themselves, really. Henry is really the fat contented western man, they themselves are fat contented western people. And it was a mirror, in a sense, like Caliban's mirror, and it made people feel enraged . . . that was always the premise . . . [Henry] is not me."[54] Why would McEwan be excluded from this critique, why are all of his readers "fat contented westerners," while McEwan is not?

In an interview with Ian McEwan published in the *Believer*, Zadie Smith tells us that she did the interview in McEwan's house, which is Dr. Henry Perowne's house in the novel *Saturday*, "a lovely Georgian townhouse that sits in the shadow of London's BT Tower."[55] This parallel between Perowne and McEwan is important because it stresses the way that McEwan is Perowne in the same way that McEwan was Briony, while in this novel Briony's craft of the writer is replaced by Perowne's craft of brain surgery.[56] The middle-class position of the narrator has also remained the same: as Tew and Mengham point out, in *Saturday* there is "an unembarrassed and confident investment in male middle-class identity" (xiv). In an interview with *Der Spiegel,* McEwan was asked if Perowne's sarcasm toward the antiwar movement in the novel echoed his "own ambivalent views on the matter" to which McEwan answered "Yes, it does."[57] These various comments are used not simply to expose Perowne as McEwan but to help us in reading the novel as a text that directly draws on the anxieties and contradictions of McEwan's own historically situated class position. The class concerns that Perowne has, while not a reflection, are certainly a mediation of McEwan's own middle-class anxieties, and how those anxieties are resolved in the novel is of concern to us.

Saturday is openly concerned with terrorism and the specter of September 11, and a large majority of the reviewers take these concerns as the main focus of the novel. Far from being outraged, the "fat contented western" media adored the novel. The *New York Times* described it as "one of the most powerful pieces of post 9/11 fiction yet published," while Christopher Hitchens in the *Atlantic Monthly* says that the novel shows us "that civilization and culture and the life of the mind, fragile as they seemingly are, nonetheless have a resilience that can outlast barbarism."[58] Other reviewers are eager to turn the book into expressing a zeitgeist: McEwan shows us "how *we* live today" (The *New York Times,* my emphasis) and the novel shows us "both the comforts and the anxieties of the world *we* live in right now" (*Vogue,* my emphasis). I would like to stop and ponder what the use of "us" or "we" or "our world" might mean at this juncture, but I will pursue this line of thought by drawing out the ways that for all of its surface sense of dealing with "terrorism" and major international events, this framework is soon abandoned and replaced by the mundane issue of an argument with a white working-class man after a small car accident in which no one is even injured: the "terrorism" at the heart of the novel comes not from the forces of Islamic jihad but simply from one white working-class man: Baxter.

The novel opens in the midnight with a naked Perowne standing looking out of the large French windows of his London townhouse at a burning plane coming into Heathrow. Tew and Mengham suggest that "Perowne's nakedness conveys mankind's vulnerability...Perowne's notion of a penumbra of fear and uncertainty signifies a more general perspective, a post-millennial vulnerability and unease."[59] However, while Perowne may feel a postmillennial unease and vulnerability it will soon be apparent that the working-class yob Baxter is not allowed to feel any such generalized unease. Since Baxter will be the source of fear in the novel, Perowne's unease is clearly a class-based unease, not one that can be generically applied to "mankind." After all, Perowne is not going to meet Al-Quaida on this unlucky Saturday, only an uneducated and violent working-class male.

Even though the novel is set close to the invasion of Iraq, it is unable to access this narrative of the West's violence, in the same way Perowne, off to play squash, cannot access the streets that he wants to due to the crowds and since he does not want to deal with the rally he drives into the side streets where he meets Baxter. Perowne instantly dislikes Baxter and yet in the course of the novel Perowne will save him and, as with Briony Tallis, the implied reader is meant to praise Perowne for the depth of his humanity as he bravely and humanely reaches across the gulf of class, something that the ignorant Baxter would never do. In *Atonement* Robbie is killed, but thanks to Briony's skills he lives in fiction and in *Saturday* thanks to Perowne/McEwan's skills as a surgeon/writer, Baxter is also permitted to live. In *Saturday,* the real issue then is not Iraq, or terrorism or WMD or the lies of the British and American establishment. These are just diversions or screens, that in some way are necessary to cover over what the novel really wants to deal with which is the troubling problem of class. If this novel does reveal how "we" the bourgeoisie live now, then it does so by drawing in and expelling the working-class character, allowing the self-generated bourgeois male to carry on as before, challenged but finally stronger, and with his class dominance firmly reestablished. Moreover, having a novel in which Perowne is the sole controlling voice, "we" readers, whatever our own class position, are forced into reading the text through Perowne's consciousness.

The novel is also framed by the strange case of Andrea Chapman, which on first reading, seems like an aside, something just to show us Perowne at work. But Andrea Chapman also returns at the end of the novel and I feel that her change is also a significant ideological element in the novel and operates as a counter to Baxter. When we first see Andrea Chapman, we are told that she is a "problem patient" who takes drugs, shoplifts, and "hates authority." She is fourteen and has moved to England from Nigeria, and she is now at a comprehensive school in Brixton and has quickly taken to the "the values [of] the street."[60] The vicar/uncle who takes care of her is worried that a tumor is pressing down on her brain, making her violently aggressive and generally out of control. Perowne feels that her violent behavior has nothing to do with the tumor, as it is "remote from the frontal lobes." Significantly, it is only the American doctor, Jay Strauss, who has any luck in bringing her "into line" (Ibid). Perowne operates on her tumor and she is forgotten until the novel is almost over and Perowne, having seen off the threat of Baxter, visits Andrea in the ward. The change is almost miraculous. The first thing he notices is a "reading light" over her bed and she is "sitting up writing in a notebook." She is now transformed by the operation (and McEwan's language) into an "African queen" and thanks to the bandage that Perowne "wound round her head yesterday" she has a "dignified sepulchral look." Perowne is amazed at her change: "Her change in manner, her communicative warmth, the abandonment of the hard street talk, can't simply be down to her medication, or tiredness. The area he was operating in, the vermis, has no bearing on emotional function" (267). Her change is a scientific mystery, even to Perowne, and he decides "whatever's changed in Andrea Chapman's life is written down in her notebook" (268). She has decided that she wants to be a "brain surgeon" and also has a crush on his colleague, Dr. Browne. The staff also agree that this new "self" that Andrea has woken up with is preferable: "We love her like this" (270). This miraculous change in Andrea from angry street teen to pliant, career minded soppy love struck girl, is rather striking, and while it is obviously ideological in terms of changing a whole segment of society, drawing them into a safe, content citizenship, what is fascinating is that such a miraculous transformation is not permitted for the working-class Baxter. Whereas Andrea changes utterly, Baxter, even at the end of the novel, is still seen as an "unpickable knot of affliction" (282). Unlike Andrea, who can be unraveled by this narrative, Baxter cannot. He remains a stubborn problem in the novel, and sadly "the head bandage doesn't ennoble Baxter the way it did Andrea" (270). While Andrea only has a tumor, Baxter has a "disease" and his condition at twenty-five years of age is "hopeless" and has an "unmendable brain" (263, 270).

Like Barker's divided Prior, Baxter, like a kind of working-class Al-Quaida, becomes the real invasion of terrorism, and yet he is never treated like an adult: he is "like a greedy child" and an "excited child," whose trust is "childlike" (232–235). Daisy's hypnotic capture of Baxter's mind with Matthew Arnold's "Dover Beach" at the end of the novel is like "entrancing a child" (229). His steps are like an "ill-rehearsed children's ballet" and he "looks small" and is "small faced" and "immature" (88, 90, 227, 264). Paradoxically this weak child/monkey also becomes the "lord of terror" (231). From here the working-class "child" is then blurred into Saddam Hussein, whose "organising principle was [also] terror" (72). Baxter and his friends Nark and Nige are also the only characters in the novel who are given animal qualities. While Baxter is seen as a monkey and Nige as a horse, both are described as looking like "deer disturbed in a forest" (84). Baxter has a "general simian air" (88, 271) and "a monkeyish air" (214) and Nige's character is known to us only as the "horse-faced fellow" (85), with the "long mournful face of a horse" (84). What the novel has shown is that while Andrea, like Baxter, is a threat to the British way of life, she can be changed and accommodated. She can be drawn into an image of a new Britain insofar as there is a colonial discourse of orientalism that can be used to position and "speak" her and so she can be safely integrated into bourgeois society by the end. The working-class Baxter on the other hand remains obscene: stranded in the real where he cannot be fully rejected or fully absorbed.

More importantly, Baxter's "disease" (some form of Huntington's disease) which he got from a previous generation of working-class males ("Your father had it..." [95]) positions Baxter's condition as historically and congenitally fixed, and since the disease affects Baxter's mood swings, his seemingly class-based love of aggression and violence thus becomes a biological condition. Hence, this working-class child-monkey, who is also the "lord of terror" in Perowne's words, is who he is, not because of any sociopolitical categories or any educational policy or even poverty: quite simply, and with no guilt attached, it is biological. As a result, Baxter is fixed, static, unlike all of the other characters in the novel. Everyone in the novel is an artist, or a creator of some sort, everyone is working on something, whether it is Theo with his blues, or Daisy with her poetry or her pregnancy, or the old Thatcherite grandfather/poetry mentor John Grammaticus, or even Perowne whose surgical skills McEwan compares to the skill of writing. Even Andrea in her hospital bed with her notebook is a writer. In short, everyone works and is productive: except the one *working-class* figure: Baxter. So while "we" are cultured and work and are productive, "they" are unproductive, and useless, or as Rosalind, Perowne's wife says of Baxter, he is simply "meaningless."[61] Paradoxically this meaningless figure is also "at the centre of their ordeal."[62] So for all of its flexibility in other areas of the novel, the presentation of Baxter is firmly rooted in very rigid constructions. Baxter is, according to Perowne, "biological determinism in its purest form" (94). His class position and his nature is not due to environment or education, it is due to individual chemistry: "Chromosome four. The misfortune lies with a single genes...." All Baxter has to look forward to is either "psychiatric prison" or a "meaningless end" (94, 223). Baxter's "impulsiveness, poor self-control, paranoia, mood swings, [and] depression balanced by outbursts of temper" in short, all the markers of his class position, are simply aspects of biology, which unlike social categories, cannot be changed: "It is written. No amount of love, drugs, Bible classes or prison sentencing can cure Baxter or shift him from his course. It's spelled out in fragile proteins, but it could be carved in stone, or tempered steel" (217). If we are perhaps not convinced by this argument, the novel also preempts our doubts when we see that even "Perowne can't convince himself that molecules and faulty genes alone are terrorising his family...."[63]

Perowne and Baxter share a dislike of the antiwar movement, but Perowne is dismissive of any kind of social intervention, especially the kind that would alleviate poverty. Perowne, thinking of Baxter, muses on the reasons for all of the working-class dropouts that he sees. Once again, while the *multicultural* "men and women of various races" in London are magically "unoppressed" and "at home in their city," the likes of Baxter are a disease that nothing can cure (281). Baxter, Nige, and Nark, the white (un)working class, have slipped into the realm of the Victorian undeserving poor and their social position is both impossible and yet biologically determined. As Perowne tells the reader: "It can't just be class or opportunities—[it is] written in code, at the level of molecules...No amount of social justice will cure or disperse this enfeebled army haunting the public places of every town...all you can do is make them comfortable somehow, minimize their miseries" (Ibid). This rather inflexible attitude toward what is now generally referred to as the "underclass," hardens elsewhere in the novel: "...these last few years what's now called the culture has changed. The medical staff have had enough. They want protection. The drunks and loudmouths are thrown out onto the pavement by men who've worked as bouncers and know their business: It's another American import, and not a bad one—zero tolerance" (251).

Baxter, unlike anyone else in the novel, including Andrea Chapman, remains almost wholly unknown, even though the entire novel orbits around this lost son. Baxter's brain is an unknown space that science can do nothing to help and cannot penetrate. Perowne recalls a memory of being in Rome for a symposium and how the mayor had given them a tour of some beautifully decorated hidden rooms but robbers had drilled a hole in the wall to get in and steal the gold leaf. Perowne thinks this is a valid simile for his profession: drilling through the skull to get at the inner workings of the brain. Sadly, the mind remains unknown: "If only the mayor was right...that penetrating the skull brings into view not the brain but the mind. Then within the hour he, Perowne, might understand a lot more about

Baxter; and after a lifetime's routine procedures would be among the wisest men on earth" (249). This comment reveals how Perowne sees Baxter's mind as an unknown territory. Strangely, since the whole novel is conducted through the consciousness of Perowne, we readers are left with no doubt that Perowne's mind is fully open to us, while as readers, Baxter's mind is beyond our understanding since the novel never hands him the space to narrate himself into being. Paradoxically, Perowne also says later that Baxter's brain (albeit not his mind) is well known to him: "He can easily convince himself that it's familiar territory, a kind of homeland...as known to him as his own house." Perowne also places his "faith" in science, and knows that "in years to come, the coding mechanism will be known...the brain's fundamental secret will be laid open one day" and the mystery of consciousness will be known to all: "the secret of consciousness will be revealed...that's the only kind of faith he has. There's grandeur in this view of life" (262–263). Presumably though, Baxter's working-class mind will remain terra incognita, since Perowne goes to great lengths to remind us of the "hopeless condition of this particular brain" that is "unmendable" like a "broken china-doll's head clumsily repaired" (263).

If surgery cannot save the day, then it would seem that literature can, as at the end of the novel Matthew Arnold's "Dover Beach" comes to the rescue, and saves the bourgeois family from Baxter's irrational violence. Daisy, naked, on the verge of being raped by Baxter, recites the poem from memory, causing a sudden shift in Baxter's mood, and although we might find it odd, Baxter finds "nothing extraordinary" in suddenly shifting from "lord of terror to amazed admirer" (231–232). The moment of crisis has been averted that thus allows Perowne to distract Baxter into going upstairs to look at some medical journals, only so that he and Theo can then push him down again, and as he falls so Henry Perowne thinks he sees in Baxter's eyes a look of "betrayal" (236). The cracked skull that he inflicts on Baxter is then repaired by Perowne himself. Yet while Matthew Arnold saves the Perowne family (as Baxter says, "They look after their own don't they?"), the poem does nothing to help Baxter (234). The poem is here used as a kind of poetic tazer gun that zaps the unsuspecting working-class suspect, causing a change in his mood from active threat to passive drone, but not raising *his* consciousness. Literature is effectively used as a tool of control, not as a tool of liberation, other than to liberate the bourgeoisie from the dangers of the working class. Are we to assume that the novel as a whole is meant to have the same effect on a working-class reader as "Dover Beach" has on Baxter? If we look at the historical context of "Dover Beach," the ideological elements of this novel begin to come into focus. Andrew Sanders points out that written in 1867, the poem registered not a general human malaise, despite its use of Sophocles to muddy the waters, but it is the lament of the Victorian bourgeoisie in the face of a rising tide of political radicalism after the passage of the 1867 Reform Bill that extended the franchise to larger sections of the male working-class population that had been granted under the limited 1832 Reform Bill. The melancholy of the poem therefore comes from "the sapping of the political status quo and of the stable foundations of bourgeois culture."[64] The passage of the 1867 Reform Bill was troubling for liberals and conservatives in the period as they felt it "opened the way to a future mass democracy [in which] the masses posed a threat to the present workings of democracy."[65] The fact that McEwan uses this poem to defuse Baxter's threatening behavior is truly extraordinary. Although the poem registers a moment of panic for the bourgeoisie, it was surely a moment of great joy and a cause for celebration for the Victorian working classes. The literary canon does not record the pleasure of that grand achievement, but it has preserved the bourgeoisie's sense of loss, and that loss for them as a class, is turned, via Arnold's use of Sophocles, into a universal loss in which the implied reader can only empathize with the embattled bourgeois subject. The poem, lamenting the state of the bourgeoisie that felt it was on the verge of being swept away by the working class, is used by McEwan as a talisman of how high-brow culture and universal goodness and "truth" can avert the literal destruction of Perowne's bourgeois family. Writing of Arnold's *Culture and Anarchy*, Andrew Sanders says that the text playfully divides British society into three classes: "Barbarian 'aristocracy,' a 'Philistine' bourgeoisie and an unlettered 'Populace' " and that none of these classes "upholds a truly refined culture which could withstand further decay in the political...order."[66] Sanders remarks that in the end, *Culture and Anarchy* "enforces peace by effectively suppressing the inconvenient and the disruptive": a sentiment that would apply equally well to *Saturday*.[67]

McEwan has said that what saves us as moral beings is our ability to step into the thoughts and feelings of others, yet this novel, like *Atonement*, fails to do just that. Terrified by its own fears of "infection from the public domain," it desires to remain safely immunized within the consciousness of Perowne's mind.[68] We see the world through his mind, which seems wholly accessible, and he puts his faith in the power of science to dig down into the inner workings of consciousness, while Daisy puts her faith in literature.[69] Despite this faith in science and literature, the novel itself is powerless to enter into the consciousness of Baxter as he remains a closed book even to a writer like McEwan. True, we could argue that the novel gives us access to the bourgeois mind, but literature has always done that. The novel uses Baxter as a challenge for Perowne to test his status as a bourgeois subject, only to reaffirm it at the end as the reader experiences the joy of what Perowne calls the "resumption of normal existence."[70]

Repeating his notion about the September 11 hijackers, McEwan has spoken directly of how the genre of the novel operates:

> The novel is supreme in giving us the possibility of inhabiting other minds...It's developed these elaborate conventions over three or four hundred years of representing mental states...so in that sense, yes, I think that "other minds" is partly what the novel is about...the main tool of that investigation has to be to demonstrate, to somehow give you, on the page, the sensual "felt" feeling of what it is to be someone else...the novel is supreme in giving us that sense of other minds.[71]

Yet for all of this, in *Saturday,* when Perowne fills out Baxter's hospital report there is nothing to say, "known as Baxter...est. age plus/minus 25. All the other personal details he has to leave blank."[72] So, even with four hundred years of elaborate conventions, working-class subjects are just too hard for the novel to deal with. Unlike the other major figures in the novel, including Andrea, who are all "fully qualified to exist," Baxter, is a dense, unworkable subject who remains "an unpickable knot of affliction."[73]

In both *Saturday* and *Atonement* the Briony/Perowne/McEwan figures appear quite content with letting the narratives they have created protect them from the real, rather than forcing a confrontation with it. Significantly, in both novels the notion of "immunity" is used to signal this "padded privacy" that the novels retreat to.[74] In *Saturday*, Perowne is angry at one point that television is "invading" his home: "Isn't it possible to enjoy an hours recreation without this invasion, this infection from the public domain."[75] In this novel it will not be television, but Baxter who is treated as the threatening "infection" who invades from the outside, bringing the world of mass culture with him, traipsing its muddy feet across the expensive carpets of Fitzrovia. Luckily, by the time Baxter has been expelled from the house and safely arrested, Perowne is immune: "the house is big, seven thousand square feet...he's a king, he's vast, accommodating, immune...."[76] In *Atonement* Briony feels the same as Perowne: "Only when the story was finished, all fates resolved and the whole matter sealed off at both ends...could she feel immune."[77] It seems that McEwan is anxious that his novels are not contaminated by the intrusive infections brought by the working-class characters that he invites into his novels (only to violently exclude them).[78] In this way, the novels function like classical comedy in which an element is deliberately introduced to disrupt the harmony of the bourgeois world, and then on its removal, "we" all breathe a sigh of relief that "our" world has returned to "normal." Unfortunately, not all readers are "we," some of "them" are "us" and disappointingly the novels on this occasion also seem to have suffered from an ideological failure of imagination and are unable to enter into the minds of the working-class subjects Robbie and Baxter.

Kazuo Ishiguro

Fredric Jameson has said that New Historicism is

> a return to a pre-theoretical procedure, whereas it also...proves to open up a whole post-theoretical set of operations that retain the discursive conquest of a range of heterogeneous materials while quietly abandoning the theoretical component that once justified that enlargement, omitting the transcendental interpretations that had once seemed to be the very aim and purpose of homologies in the first place.[79]

The result is that New Historicism can have its cake and eat it at the same time: "We will therefore describe the New Historicism as a return to immanence and to a prolongation of the procedures of homology which eschews homology's theory and abandons the concept of 'structure.'"[80] In this sense, Jameson sees New Historicism as a brilliantly executed performance but one which finally lacks an overarching critique of the structures of capitalism. As Jameson points out: "Whence, in the most successful of such artifacts, that sense of breathlessness, of admiration for the brilliance of the performance, but yet bewilderment, at the conclusion of the essay, from which one seems to emerge with empty hands—without ideas and interpretations to carry away with us."[81]

This kind of New Historical postmodern performance is highly visible when it comes to criticism of Kazuo Ishiguro. If we look at

The Remains of the Day, a work centrally concerned with the inner and outer life of a working-class male and to a lesser extent a female one too, criticism seems to be able to probe the deepest shallows of the text engaging in "radical" readings of the novel and its concerns with a postmodern/postcolonial subject while somehow failing to touch on how the novel mediates contemporary ideas about labor, alienation, and the working class.

Ishiguro's writing seems to initiate an almost automatic response on the part of the critics, which is to place his work straight into the safely cordoned off area of "the post-colonial." Why his work elicits this response is in part due to a kind of containment strategy whereby the problems of class that Ishiguro does open up can be safely closed off or reassigned to a different cultural register. For example, Richard Bradford in *The Novel Now* places Ishiguro in a chapter entitled "The Question of Elsewhere" while in Lane, Mengham, and Tew's *Contemporary British Fiction* he gets pride of place in Section IV: "Pathological Subjects." Dominic Head places Ishiguro into his "Multicultural Personae" chapter, while Brian Finney, following John Carey, focuses on Ishiguro's "fusion of memory, imagination and dream...."[82] Although there is no denying that effective readings come out of seeing Ishiguro through a postcolonial lens, I fear that this framing, while it makes a whole range of utterances possible, also silences others. Even though Japan was never part of Britain's empire and Ishiguro left Japan when he was six, these facts have not prevented critics from reading him as a postcolonialist. Since Ishiguro's Otherness is written on his body, the postcolonial concerns tend to obscure all other considerations, including the issue of class. Ishiguro has said that Stevens from *The Remains of the Day* is a "good metaphor for the relationship of very ordinary small people to power" but critics do not seem to treat it as a novel about class directly, but insist on seeing it as containing important messages about colonial identity and psychological and emotional/national repression.[83] Even though it is essentially a realist novel about the lives of two working-class people over a twenty-year span, the sense that the novel may be engaging ideologically with middle-class perceptions of work, class, labor, and exploitation seems to be outside the critical radar. Paradoxically, while postcolonial critics may wish to side with the subaltern and the marginal voice, in this case Stevens does not become a celebrated marginal voice but is transformed into a target of criticism. In nearly all of the criticism on Ishiguro, Stevens is blamed for the problems he finds himself caught up in. In Bradford, we are told that the problem is

"Steven's inability to move beyond his class-obsessed script of expectations..." while Stevens's "failure," is that he "immunizes himself from the [real world]."[84] In Dominic Head, Stevens becomes a "devastating portrait of repressed Englishness and an exploration of those national characteristics that must be expunged before an authentic post-nationalism can emerge...."[85] In so far as Stevens suffers from being "fixated with the past," it is then this "obsession" with history that must be "expunged" before an "authentic" (classless) national identity can emerge.[86] As in Pat Barker, what we are witnessing is the bourgeois desire to exorcise the ghosts of Modernity and the past. What we are beginning to see takes shape in the criticism here is that the working-class Stevens is being made to take the blame for a national problem, and that it is *his* failure to let go of the past, and *his* identification with an outdated form of ideological rootedness that constitutes the tragedy of the novel. As Head points out "Stevens's true allegiance...is to the era of Lord Darlington...and the almost feudal pre-war class structure it represents."[87] It is important to note that the novel offers us the effete upper-class figure of Darlington and the working-class Stevens as if they were on the same plain. The middle-class bourgeoisie are absent and I would argue that the reader of the novel is positioned as the (invisible) bourgeois figure that stands above and outside of the novel and is able to judge and condemn both Stevens and Darlington. Significantly, the only other figure that would come close to occupying this middle-class subject position is the wealthy "classless" American, Farraday. So, in effect, while the reader is placed in a position somehow magically outside of class and its feudal limitations, Stevens (like Darlington) fails to do so and can be condemned for being unable to adjust and move beyond the limitations of a class society. It is thus Stevens's false consciousness that is preventing Britain from developing an authentic identity: it is what Dominic Head calls his "emotional retardation" that is holding everything back.[88] Given that the novel was written under a Thatcherite period marked by an ideological shift away from class toward a supposedly classless society, it is interesting that Stevens come to embody the figure that resists a dominant ideological shift and is made to suffer and pay the price for holding onto the past and his class position within it.

Stevens's sense that he must hold on to class distinctions, even if it means he will not be emotionally fulfilled, creates a space where the implied bourgeois reader can drift into a free space of postmodern classless identity and emotional fulfillment, while Stevens becomes the sad "repressed" anachronism who, unlike us, is unable to read history. The "fallible perspectives" of the narrator means that while Stevens is blinded by his own ideological limitations, the reader, in the act of reading, is given the impression of being lifted beyond the limitations of class.[89] Frederick Holmes feels therefore that Ishiguro's characters always suffer from an "inability to come to terms with the historical traumas of the Second World War...."[90] Moreover, Holmes feels that Ishiguro explores "the personal and collective damage caused when people internalize a national ideal that entails the denial of their own emotional needs."[91] In this sense, there is a simple binary between an adherence to an empty and meaningless category of class on the one hand or the fulfilling freedom of personal desire on the other. This also makes the novel and the film a satisfying ideological narrative in that any preoccupation with class and older ways of thinking about history can be dismissed as an emotional cul-de-sac that cannot satisfy the fully released libidinal drive of the fluid and "free" postmodern classless subject. The way the novel operates also means that we are not expected to empathize with Stevens, but merely to pity him, while being actively disgusted with Darlington. Unlike the libidinally charged reader who manages to wake up from the nightmare of history, Stevens is trapped by it and can blame no one but himself.

This sense that Stevens is to blame for his condition is repeated across the critical terrain. Cynthia Wong restages the usual positions that are available. She follows Kathleen Wall in suggesting that Stevens is both an unreliable and a reliable narrator, and that he is both a "conspirator of the failures now present in his life" and a "victim."[92] The overall result, following Meera Tamaya, is that Stevens now stands in for English history itself: "the tragic truth of his past [is] a truth inextricably bound up with the history of his country." Moreover, they even go so far in their criticism of Stevens that he becomes as slippery and sneaky as his Fascist sympathizing boss, Lord Darlington. Wong approvingly quotes Tamaya's "clever" analysis of how Stevens tricks us into accepting his version of the past: "...the intimate tone of the narrative beguiles the reader into a curious complicity with Stevens' point of view; this enables one to empathize with Stevens even as the butler is completely taken in by Lord Darlington."[93] It is his "shameful" past, which is the reason for this "duplicity" that results in a novel of "loss, shame and regret."[94] In this way the novel is easily cleansed of its class dynamic by reducing it to a psychological portrait of repression and self-deception. While lip service may be made to historical or national parallels, the readings never pull free from a psychological and individualized level.

The other way that the novel is shielded from considerations of class is paradoxically by flooding the reading with historical specifics, after all, as Jameson points out; such new historical approaches always raise the specter of history only to exorcise it. John P. McCombe's "The End of (Anthony) Eden: Ishiguro's *The Remains of the Day* and Midcentury Anglo-American Tensions" strikes me as a textbook example of the problems that Jameson is addressing and which continue to distort discussions of the contemporary novel.[95] McCombe establishes his concerns by drawing on the usual framing of Stevens's "personal concerns" being "inextricably bound to the political and social climate that surrounds him" and that "Stevens' narrative connects the personal to the political."[96] McCombe admits that Stevens's personal narrative can also offer us insights into history that are often hidden by colonialism or gender or, "in Stevens's case, by an unyielding class system" (77). While this sounds promising, the analysis soon drifts into a detailed recounting of the historical events touched on in the novel. So instead of the focus on psychology and repression, as in Wong and Tamaya, we are now treated to in-depth discussions of Suez and Nasser, the policies of Anthony Eden, the place of American loans and the place of Israel, as well as the German attack on Norway in 1940 and the role of the International Monetary Fund. Although this historical framing is interesting it seems to silence the novel, flooding it with a kind of newsreel white noise in which the novel seems to take a backseat. When the smoke clears, we are back where we always are with critics of this novel, as the real problem is that "Stevens' colonialist ideology is his belief in the benevolence of the father figure" (83). So, once again, the real issue is Stevens's failure to be a man and confront his false consciousness, as he is weak and would prefer to be a dupe. Like Baxter in *Saturday*, Stevens in this reading is also not even an adult, as he has a "childlike trust in Darlington" (Ibid). Moreover, McCombe's desire to find guilty links between history and Stevens is sometimes stretched to the breaking point:

> In the Merchant Ivory-Jhabvala film adaptation of *Remains*, when Stevens borrows his employer's car for his motor journey to the West Country, the vehicle is an aging German-made Daimler, a choice that links Stevens' worldview to aspects of Nazi ideology, particularly its malevolent paternalism and belief in rigid hierarchies. (88)

Hence Stevens, the working-class butler, now has a worldview shared by Hitler and Goebbels simply because the movie uses a Daimler instead of the Ford that appears in the novel. In the same way that the working class Baxter is equated with that "lord of terror," Saddam Hussein, in *Saturday*, so here the working-class butler Stevens is now being cordoned off as a Nazi sympathizer who is all the more dangerous for being an *unconscious* sympathizer who loves Darlington/Hitler as a stern father who will tell him what to do. Again, we are back to Stevens the fool, the dupe, the failure who cannot read himself clearly and is weighed down by an outmoded desire to hold on to a class system.

The real concern I have with these kinds of readings is that they seem like a distraction from the novel's ideological tensions. This problem can be summed up in the way that McCombe talks about Stevens's interest in the radio. After saying that there is really no need to locate "the actual radio program" that Stevens would have been listening to, he asserts that nevertheless "Stevens listens to the radio not only because of his professional obligations but also because the narrative once again reflects its historical moment" (93). This remark presupposes an odd kind of Marxist reflection model in that the novel is *not* reflecting the moment of the novel's production, that is 1989, but is somehow accurately reflecting its *fictional* moment of production: 1938–1956. The real issue here then is that the present, the actual moment of the novel's production, 1989, is elided. In both cases, whether the criticism moves into the Wong, Tamaya, and Head camp and places the novel within some kind of postcolonial/psychological reading, or whether the critics recreate a simulacra of 1956, like McCombe, and gently slide the novel into place, the result is the same: the novel is prevented from interacting with its own moment of production, and questions of class are easily bracketed off and evaded.

Following this New Historicist path means that McCombe's conclusions become somewhat strained. Using this historically parallel reading, what happens in history has to be *directly* reflected in the novel. For McCombe it works this way: "By the end of the 1950s, a cultural (and political) détente between Britain and the US emerged, and by the end of *Remains*, Stevens also seems to rethink his apathy toward America (and Americans)" (96). It is true that this reading is counter to the usual reading of Stevens as a failure, but now, rather than the usual argument of England's weakness being equal to Steven's weakness, now, in just the same way that England has somehow "matured" from 1936 to 1956 so Stevens has also grown and "matured." In the same way that Darlington felt that Roosevelt had taken "a few bold steps on behalf of his people" so Stevens has also taken "relatively bold" steps toward maturity by the end of the novel. By 1956 the "American Century" is under way and the rather odd conclusion is that the disempowered Stevens has now "travelled the open road of his own country as the means by which he can finally confront the changes that lie ahead for Britain in the post-Eden era" (97). In either case, we can only read Stevens as a dupe and a failure, or as a child who matures into an adult appreciation of the "changes that lie ahead."

What we now see in the case of Barker, McEwan, and Ishiguro is that these novelists are not simply working on an individual isolated level, but that the parallel treatment of the working class in all three authors reveals that we are dealing with an ideology that works through and is being sustained by the fiction (and the critical perspectives) of an entire class. Hopefully, what is beginning to emerge is something that Fredric Jameson suggested that we look for, and as our knowledge of individual texts becomes transformed what begins to develop are the outlines, not of individual "authors" or texts, but of a historically specific class discourse:

> [we] find that the semantic horizon within which we grasp a cultural object has widened to include the social order [and] we find that the very object of our analysis has itself been thereby dialectically transformed, and that it is no longer construed as an individual "text" or work in the narrow sense, but has been reconstituted in the form of the great collective and class discourses of which a text is little more than an individual parole or utterance.[97]

Chapter 2

"Our Economic Position": Middle-Class Consciousness in Zadie Smith and Will Self

"I'm obviously extremely middle-class now. I'm sitting in a hammock, which is extremely suspect." She lives across the street from the housing project where she grew up and sometimes feels nostalgic for her humble roots.... "That didn't use to happen when I was working-class. And there are vital parts of the culture I'll forever be removed from."

—*Zadie Smith*[1]

...none of us realized our economic position.

—*E. M. Forster*[2]

The current way of reading Zadie Smith and Will Self is to assert that their work offers radical ways of rethinking identity and consciousness in a fluid postmodern global culture that has no need for old models of subjectivity and agency. This chapter argues that such a strategy fails to read these texts critically and instead, for all of their desires to reach beyond such mundane things as binaries and class, Smith and Self fully replicate the ideological marginalization of the working-class subject in their novels. Drawing on her lecture on E. M. Forster that she gave in London in 2003, I will examine Smith's *On Beauty* in terms of its ideological relationship to Forster's *Howards End*. My analysis of Will Self's *The Book of Dave* will reveal how this satirical novel hollows out the working-class subject position in the present as well as in the imagined future.[3]

Zadie Smith

Zadie Smith's *On Beauty* was nominated for the 2005 Man Booker Prize and was described by Michiko Kakutani in the *New York Times* as "a thoroughly original tale." Frank Kermode also puts Smith into grand company, when, writing in the *London Review of Books* he says that what lies behind both books is what "Lawrence called the one bright book of life—a source of truth and otherworldliness and prophecy."[4] This praise for her originality is odd considering that even Smith herself openly acknowledges that the novel is based on E. M. Forster's *Howards End* and therefore has no desire to be original. Her novel takes the narrative framework of *Howards End* and replants his structure in a small Boston college town called Wellington, which is clearly a portrait of Harvard and its environs. Parts of the novel are also briefly set in London. In this chapter, I will explore how Smith's novel attempts to evade the issues of class that she is forced into, both by the logic of her own narrative, and by her dependence on Forster's narrative.

It is clear that Forster's novel is open and honest about its limitations, and the aspiring working-class figure of Leonard Bast in his novel is openly and brutally removed with physical violence. As Peter Widdowson points out: "Leonard has to die to clear the way for his son to be 'Liberal England's' heir untrammeled by the drab reality of his father's life and class; Leonard himself would not fit into 'Howards End/England' but the child brought up in the right environment will.' Besides, Helen could not credibly 'have married a Bast.'"[5] Bast's role in the novel is to provide a space in which Edwardian liberal guilt about class differences can be explored and explained. Henry Turner has described Bast as one of the "mere symbols" that we see in Forster's work, "placeholders on which to hang, in passing, a certain amount of remorse over the system and its expense."[6] In Smith's novel the Bast figure shows up in the form of Carl Thomas, a young working-class African-American who has no formal education and no wealth. The question that needs exploring then is how will Smith, roughly ninety-six years later, deal with the problem of Leonard Bast/Carl Thomas in a postmodern moment where class is supposedly a thing of the past.

Both Forster and Smith went to King's College, Cambridge, and Smith has commented that being at Cambridge meant that she was surrounded by the old ghosts of the literary world ("Byron…and Wordsworth, and everybody on earth" she says) and that being there made her feel "like I was one of them."[7] So, Forster, far from being simply some dead white male, is transformed into a literary father-figure who gives her, in her words, a "gift" and in fact wishes to pay homage to him by basing *On Beauty* on *Howards End*. But apart from the desire to pay homage, what is to be gained through this rewriting? Why is it necessary? What is it about our own historical moment that makes the rewriting of an Edwardian novel resonate with us? One could hope that the novel would take the liberal guilt in Forster and resolve it, or reveal ways in which our own postmodern multiculturalism has answers to questions that Forster in his own period and lacking our "sophistication" was unable to grasp. Sadly, the novel never reaches very far beyond the same Forsterian limitations, and, I would suggest, Smith's version is actually more troubling than Forster's.[8]

Whenever Smith is presented to us by the media, the information we are usually given is that she is of mixed race, with a Caucasian father and a Jamaican mother: the implication being that this racial information is enough to inform us of everything essential. But such an introduction is rather slippery as it fails to inform us of her *class*. Similarly, book jackets laconically tell us that she was simply "born in northwest London" and "still lives in the area" implying that she has somehow remained true to her "roots." If, on the other hand, we were told that her father was a photographer and her mother a psychologist and that Smith did a degree in literature at Cambridge, and is now currently Fellow in Residence of Creative Writing at Harvard, her class profile looks somewhat different.[9] Forster on the other hand was very open about his class position, and rather than trying to hide it, or not mention it, actually foregrounds it to confront the problem of class inequality that he will struggle with in *Howards End*. In "Two Cheers for Democracy" he openly shows that "we none of us realized our economic position. In came the nice fat dividends, up rose the lofty thoughts, and we did not realize that all the time we were exploiting the poor of our own country and the backward races abroad, and getting bigger profits from our investments than we should. We refused to face this unpalatable truth."[10] Forster continues:

> All that has changed in the present century. The dividends have shrunk to decent proportions and have in some cases disappeared. The poor have kicked. The backward races are kicking—and more power to their boots. Which means that life has become less comfortable for the

> Victorian liberal, and that our outlook, which seems to me admirable, has lost the basis of golden sovereigns upon which it originally rose, and now hangs over the abyss.[11]

In essence, the historical and political desire that is Forster's dilemma is still Smith's dilemma. For Forster and now for Smith, the place to look for answers to these class questions is in the personal, not the political. As Forster remarked: "in public who shall express the unseen adequately? It is private life that holds out the mirror to infinity, personal intercourse, and that alone that ever hints at a personality beyond our daily vision."[12]

For Smith, living in a historical moment in which globalization has deepened rather than removed the fissures of class, the same bourgeois hope is once again placed in the plurality of identity politics and the fluidity of "personal relations." For Smith, the links between the two academic families, the Kippses and the Belseys are the parallel to the intermingling of the Wilcoxes and the Schlegels in Forster. The paradoxes that Forster was aware of, Smith is also dealing with, and since in her words, she is "one of them," she turns to him for answers.[13] Smith however suffers from a paradox: while Forster is not ashamed of discussing his own middle-class status, Smith on the other hand is deprived of this honesty by a postmodern sensibility. Admitting that she was a part of any class herself in the first place would smack too much of a master narrative and would severely undermine the novel's desire to suggest that we are all beyond class. Smith's formal solution to this dilemma (apart from moving the setting to the supposedly "classless" America) is for the novel to present itself as being a "classless" text that will range over all subject positions, and settle on none. This is problematical, because without an honest admission of her class position, the authorial voice of the novel lacks any urgency. Forster wears his wallet on his sleeve all through *Howards End,* but in Smith's hands, the class guilt that attached to the authorial voice has been removed. The removal of this guilt in Smith also removes the desire to resolve the liberal crisis that Forster addressed and that is still unresolved in our own moment.

In a lecture that she gave in London in 2003 entitled "E. M. Forster's Ethical Style: Love, Failure and the Good in Fiction," Smith explains why Forster matters. She points out that the "great, human basis of the English comic novel" comes from the fact that the protagonists are "good readers" and as such "encourage good reading from others."[14] For Smith, Forster becomes an ideal because his narratives and his characters are in a muddle:

> His protagonists are not good readers or successful moral agents, but chaotic, irrational human beings. Lucy Honeychurch, Maurice Hall, Helen Schlegel—Forster's people wouldn't stand a chance against Austen's protagonists. Forster's folk are famously always in a muddle: they don't know what they want or how to get it.

Yet this remark is blind to a major issue: the difference between Austen's protagonists and Forster's is surely a historical difference. The unquestioned certainties of class that support Austen's world are destabilized in Forster's own moment, making it hard for the bourgeoisie *not* to be in a muddle. Yet Smith wants us to see Forster's characters as timeless figures, rather than being embedded in their own historical moment: "Forster wanted his people to be in a muddle; his was a study of the emotional, erratic and unreasonable in *human life*" (my emphasis). But this muddle that the characters experience is surely a muddle linked to history and class. Notice how even Smith selects only the bourgeois characters. Only Lucy, Helen, and Maurice can be in a muddle. Why cannot Leonard Bast be included in this list? Working-class characters cannot be in a muddle themselves: it is because of them that the central characters have a moral dilemma. The working classes are the ground on which the middle-class muddle takes place. Forster's characters are like this she says because he "wanted his people to be in a muddle." But I feel that what this phrase actually needs is an emphasis on the word "*his* people" (i.e., those of his own class). The postmodern spin that Smith is giving to this Edwardian problem is that the "muddle had value" and the characters that seemed to know where they were going and were not muddled are "ethically problematic." However, while Smith is valorizing this muddle for its humanist power and goodness, in Forster it is something that his text is actively trying to move beyond: while Smith wants to read the "muddle" as a benign condition of timeless (and yet thoroughly postmodern) lostness, in Forster the muddle is certainly a class-based muddle and unlike Smith, he makes no attempt to generalize it into a human condition. If it were a totalizing condition, then Bast would also be in a muddle, but he is not, he knows exactly what side his bread is not buttered on, and the muddle only belongs to the bourgeois characters who find themselves torn between economic allegiance to those above them and a guilty pity for those suffering beneath them.[15] For Smith to celebrate this muddle as proof of humanist openness and flexibility is simply a way for the contemporary bourgeoisie to assuage their own guilt. For example, in *Howards End* we see the phrase regarding "the anodyne of muddledom"[16]: it is a drug, a painkiller, the muddle is a place to hide from the painful reality of history, not a place of social justice: it is a place to retreat (for the bourgeoisie) not a solution. Significantly, if we read the quote in context, we notice that this muddle is a place that Bast knows nothing of: "He was alive... The anodyne of muddledom, by which most men blur and blend their mistakes, never passed Leonard's lips."[17] Smith therefore slips casually away from the class roots of this "muddle," into Forster's examination of "the emotional, erratic and unreasonable in human life" as she put it. By celebrating the middle-class muddle, she is articulating a plainly postmodern attitude: variety and difference are healthy and any grand narrative or creeping traces of essentialism are bad. The novelist must also learn from this tradition: novelists, she says, must have "educated hearts" to "avoid caricature" and that "There is no bigger crime, in the English comic novel than thinking that you are right." The result is that "we too" (by which she means her class) must be careful not to lose our way if we become dogmatic and certain: "Like them we become existentially flat when we grow morally inflexible and consistent."[18] How does this apply to Forster's "flat" characters such as Leonard Bast or Smith's own flat version of Bast, Carl Thomas? Not surprisingly, the flat (working class) characters cannot develop, and the fully drawn (middle class) characters, while despite being in a jolly terrible muddle (or rather because of it) have the sensibility, or the "fine awareness" to stumble, and fall, and grow. It is *these* characters that magically speak across the class divide and are supposed to be like "us" and that speak to "us." It would seem then that the moral "muddle" is always reserved for the middle-class protagonists, those characters who have already cultivated a "fine awareness" in Smith's phrase.

Zadie Smith realizes that in Forster's work we also see the "conscientious abstainer," figures who, like Cecil Vyse, Mr. Beebe, or Phillip Herriton, are voyeurs in the novels, and act as Forster substitutes. They are usually always unmarried, and uninterested in the romantic affairs going on around them, and are "privately incomed in a world where most people work." As such, these abstainers mirror Forster's own secure financial background as well as his own guilt and are symbolic of his own "ethical failure as a novelist" as Smith puts it, since his financial independence made him feel that "he could not understand the experience of the great majority of his fellow men." Yet, rather than faulting Forster, or being aware that perhaps his own ideological biases might perhaps lead us to think twice about claiming that his novels and his characters function as some kind of timeless Good and Ethical Baedeker to the World, she reinscribes this weakness as a sign of his "genius": "His genius lay in making these failures the basis of his ethics...." If Forster admittedly has a soft spot for his abstainers, it seems clear that Smith also has a soft spot for Forster. I would argue that the flaws in Forster are showing up again in Smith, and while the postmodern scenery and costumes have changed, Smith's desire to pay homage to Forster in *On Beauty* makes it clear that the underlying relationship between author, economics, class, and history has remained unchanged. Hence, Smith's soft spot for the middle-class Kippses and the middle-class Belseys is to be read neither as a weakness nor as a sign of her own ideological biases, but in fact becomes the ethical heart of the novel. It would seem that we have arrived at a position whereby we are to assume that the novel is now ethical *because* Smith has a soft spot for the middle-class protagonists: these people are "our people" and "we" should admire them for being in a jolly muddle.

By rejecting Austen's limited Enlightenment worldview, Forster, as Smith says, "widened the net of his empathy to include people so muddled they barely know their own name..." This ideological muddle, rather than being seen as a way of exploring the contradictions of class at work in Forster, is recuperated as being yet another of Forster's skills on a formal level. The endings of Forster's novels, instead of being moments where ideology cannot successfully contain the contradictions that Forster has engaged, are instead seen as a "deliberate withholding of satisfaction." So, for example, with Lucy Honeychurch, Smith feels that as she moves closer to the good, so the "less morally enthusiastic" she becomes. Rather than seeing Forster in terms of his class and its contradictions, Smith's own class identification and her postmodern desire to move away from any kind of essentialism sees this framework as mirroring, in her words, "the truth of human relations." Smith universalizes this concept in her lecture and addresses the audience by suggesting that "the great majority of us are not like an Austen protagonist": the implication being that us/we are much more like Forster's muddled protagonists. Smith wants us to accept Forster as a "great" novelist who "lets more life in" to the English novel. But what life is being let in when the plot creaks so obviously as the bookcase comes crashing down on Bast at the end of *Howards End*? What "ethical good" does Smith offer us when Bast returns in *On Beauty* in the form of Carl Thomas only to conveniently disappear toward the end of the novel? What is clear from this lecture is that she desires to see Forster as having opened up the English novel by his rejection of any kind of Enlightenment certainty: "Forster's innovation remains: he allowed the English comic novel the possibility of spiritual and bodily life... He expanded the comic novel's ethical space (while unbalancing its moral certainties)." Smith wants us to return simply to a love of "great novels" as they "encourage good readings from others. This is the great, human basis of the English comic novel." So, rather than the fixed positivistic world of Jane Austen's clearheaded rationalist heroines and their firm moral positions, she would rather adopt the Forsterian position in which moral issues are not cut and dried, and outcomes are never clear or clearly demarcated, so that the moral fuzziness of Forster (which was rooted in class) is to become "our" universal postmodern ideal. Yet while the English novel may have been expanded by Forster to include more "spiritual and bodily life," Leonard Bast gets neither from Forster's pen, and Carl Thomas is also spirited out of the novel pretty quickly in Smith's text. Similarly, Smith's use of the phrase "the great, human basis of the English comic novel" surely points us to the great bourgeois tradition of the novel (of which she is now part) as opposed to its classless "human" basis.

Toward the end of her lecture, Smith praises Martha Nussbaum's ethical view of literature: "Great novels show us the worth and richness of plural qualitative thinking and engender in their readers a richly qualitative way of seeing." Smith feels that she can't top this and continues: "My own flag is rather weak in comparison. It says: 'When we read with fine attention, we find ourselves caring about people who are various, muddled, uncertain and not quite like us (and this is good).'" But, surely we should intervene here and ask Smith to read *Howards End* with "fine attention." What does she make of the working-class Bast's removal from the novel's closing pages? Is there something "great" and "ethical" in this moment of Forster's narrative? Smith feels that good novels make good readers and gives them a "deep, experiential understanding of the bond between the ethical realm and the narrative act." This lesson, Smith feels can also be found "in that too familiar homily 'Two sides to every story'...." However, in *Howards End,* as in its doppelganger, *On Beauty,* the two sides of the story are only half of the picture. The Wilcoxes and the Schlegels, the Kippses and the Belseys are all comfortable middle-class positions. What the English tradition has found harder is the difficult third story: the working-class world of Bast, or in Smith, the working-class world of Carl Thomas. In Forster, the Schlegels represent the artistic side of the equation ("the passion") while the Wilcoxes represent commerce and business ("the prose"), and it is these two that must be connected, not the bourgeoisie and the poor. But in Smith's text, eager as it is to move beyond the limits of money and class, we see only two academic families: in essence two passions. The world of prose (economics in Forster's text) is embarrassingly absent from this supposedly all inclusive postmodern narrative, as is any extended exploration of the working classes. It is not impossible to suggest therefore that Forster's text is actually closer to considering questions of poverty and class than the hip postmodern Zadie Smith.

Smith claims, echoing Martha Nussbaum, that Forster's greatness comes from the fact that his work offers us "genuine acknowledgment of the otherness of the other." But is Smith reading *Howards End* with "fine awareness" if, having modeled *On Beauty* on the novel, she feels that Bast's fate is of no concern in her own rewriting? Wouldn't her "fine awareness" make her attentive to Bast/Carl as a way of "caring about people" who are "not quite like us" as she said? Sadly, the working-class Bast, killed off once in Forster, is "killed off" yet again in *On Beauty*. Smith feels that "if you put people on paper... you cannot help but talk of ethics, because the ethical realm exists nowhere if not here." I would agree, but is there not an ethical imperative to move through Forster's class-rooted ambivalence rather than simply celebrating it as some form of updated postmodern antiessentialism or as a timeless humanist tradition?

The postmodern distrust of rigid metanarratives like "class" means that Smith is happy to remove the economic dimension of Forster's novel leaving us only with questions of identity politics and difference. So, the problem of Carl Thomas, as with Leonard Bast, still floats around the novel like a specter of class that, as in Forster, cannot be fully brought into the novel or fully removed from it. In *Howards End,* Henry Wilcox is connected to Bast economically: it is his advice about the Porphyrion company that leads to Bast's economic ruin, and Wilcox is also linked to Jacky Bast sexually. In Smith we are left only with the parallel of Monty Kipps (as Wilcox) having sex with a student. As Carl points out: "You need to hear some truth. All of you people, you *intellectuals*... OK, how about Monty Kipps?

Victoria's pop? You know him? OK. He's been *screwing* Chantelle Williams...."[19] Lacking any economic implications and connections these purely relational shockers have little impact on larger social questions. While Forster's novel aimed to link the personal relationships to the need to create an England that could survive economically, in Smith, the novel flounders at the level of the personal.

Written right after the Liberal landslide of 1906, and before the First World War in 1914, *Howards End* seriously tried to tackle the major crises facing the liberal humanist tradition, and albeit limited, is an honest attempt to reconcile the class tensions that Forster's class sought to unify. However, as Peter Widdowson points out, "although their attack is intelligent and accurate, it does not lead them beyond their own prevailing world-view."[20] In turn, this limited class-consciousness creates formal problems for Forster:

> ...it is the attempt in *Howards End* to create the idea of "community" within the liberal value system, while recognizing the hostile realities of the world it is to "make whole," that causes strains and tensions in the novel itself. A vision of what the world should be, not what it is, has to be imposed on the novel to make it affirmative, and this creates significant tensions when combined with more "realistic" observations.[21]

These tensions arise due to the mismatch between the harsh economics of the Wilcoxes world, and the soft, tender ideals of the Schlegels. However, once the economic dimension has been erased, as it has been in Smith's own historical period, these productive tensions disappear. Smith, having grown up in a world where class apparently no longer exists, or is just not important anymore, desires to use only the husk of Forster's novel: its personal relations. But as Widdowson says, the failures of *Howards End* speak volumes:

> [T]raditional realism was the expression of an assured and self-confident liberal humanist world-view. The primary ambivalence of *Howards End* is its uncertainty of form. It is this tension which confirms its "historical significance," symptomatic as the novel is of the "liberal crisis"—ideological and literary.[22]

In contrast, Smith, with true postmodern fluidity can skate across all subject positions without having anything so limiting as a fixed position, with the result that no liberal crisis (either ideological or literary) is exposed.

Zadie Smith achieves this strangely elusive omniscient narrative by becoming the nomadic postmodern author who is everywhere and yet nowhere. As her reviewers kindly pointed out, the strength of the novel seems to be Smith's ability to ventriloquize across the social spectrum. For Kakutani, in the *New York Times,* Smith possesses "an ability to inhabit with equal ease the point of view of children, adolescents and the middle aged . . . a captivating authorial voice . . . capacious enough to accommodate high moral seriousness, laid-back humor and virtually everything in between . . . ."[23] Frank Rich describes her as a "fearless *outside* referee" (my emphasis) who can "adjudicate the culture wars" while Michael Dirda in the *Washington Post* revels in her "command of every register of English" from "young hip-hop poet to a formal British lord" and that we should all respond with "either gratitude and admiration or a simple wow . . ." The *Boston Globe* chimes in by praising her ear once again: "she can do street jive and breakfast banter as easily as she does the interminable faculty meeting" while the *Atlantic Monthly* feels "she's equally engaging about the inner lives of a teenage boy and a middle aged mother." The *Guardian* states that "from the perfectly nuanced dialogue of young black men to the refined aesthetic wrangling of art historians" Smith can embrace "all the possibilities of language." The *Writer* also succinctly praises her skill in absorbing, like some strange postmodern sponge, everything from "Rembrandt and rap music, Mozart and Eminem with respect for everything along the spectrum."

But if everything is presented equally then nothing is selected, there is no real position in the novel that she cares to hold for any duration. Many of the reviewers point to how the novel is a satire, and this leaves its politics everywhere and yet nowhere in particular. Unlike Forster who was aiming to build connections and shore up crumbling class edifices, Smith is happy to take no prisoners and make everyone guilty of something in *On Beauty.* What makes the work so troubling then is this tension between its apolitical satirical stance, while offering itself as being in touch and politically aware. The novel is apparently a "rollicking satire" (*San Francisco Chronicle*), with a "pitch perfect ear for smugness and cant" (Rich, *New York Times*). It is "satirical, wise and sexy" (Dirda, *Washington Post*), "skewering hilarity" (*New York Daily News*), a "juicy send up" (*The Kansas City Star*) "poking fun at petty jealousies . . . ironic and acerbic" (*The Crisis*) so that "satire becomes miraculously endearing" (*Salon*).

If all positions are mocked, then what ideological position is the novel itself occupying? Terry Eagleton has pointed out how postmodernism's seemingly unlimited sympathy with everything is actually a thoroughly ideological posture and here again is a central difference between Forster and Smith. For Eagleton:

> The classical liberal subject [e.g. Forster] at least strived to preserve its identity and autonomy along with its plurality, though this was never an easy matter; now, in a drastic declension of that process, the subject [e.g. Zadie Smith] of a more advanced phase of middle-class society is compelled to sacrifice its truth and identity to its plurality, to which it then mystifyingly gives the name of freedom. Or, to put the point another way, the strenuously productive self of liberal capitalism is yielding ground to the consumerist subject of a later stage in that same history.[24]

The result is that having "skewered" all subject positions in a "rollicking satire" nothing is left to hang any agency or subjectivity onto. For Eagleton this means that there is "no longer any unified subject in here to whom the liberty in question might be attached. If that liberty involves the dissolution of the unified subject, then it can no longer be freedom at all. All the subject would seem to be free of is itself. We have arrived at a libertarianism without a subject...."[25] This all-skewering satirical antielitist stance is not surprising since at the level of economics it is also indistinguishable from the logic of the market. As Eagleton points out, "the most formidably anti-elitist force in modern capitalist societies is known as the marketplace, which levels all distinctions, garbles all gradations and buries all distinctions of use-value beneath the abstract equality of exchange-value."[26] Yet while it wishes to appear to be antielitist and democratic, *On Beauty* is not equally celebratory of difference, and elements of class and economic position are strangely impervious to the "rollicking satire." Let us examine how the working-class background of Howard Belsey and his father are presented in the novel and also let us consider the place of Carl Thomas and Choo to gain a clearer purchase on this novel's middle-class consciousness.

In the opening of *On Beauty*, the young Christian son of Howard Belsey, Jerome, is visiting at the Kippses and is delighted that they have a different take on politics and culture: "He had liked to listen to the exotic (to a Belsey) chatter of business and money and practical politics, to hear that Equality was a myth, and Multiculturalism a fatuous dream...."[27] The Forsterian parallel is with Helen, staying at the Wilcoxes: "she liked being told that her notions of life were sheltered or academic; that Equality was nonsense, Votes for women nonsense, Socialism nonsense...."[28] Strangely enough, while "Equality" manages to remain in Smith, socialism is dropped from Jerome's vocabulary and replaced with the much more benign category of "Multiculturalism."[29] The historical difference is startling: while socialism would have been a troubling economic threat to the Wilcoxes way of life (and Forster's) "multiculturalism" is not a personal threat to either Belsey's or Kipp's tenure and job prospects (or Smith's). In fact, multiculturalism operates with, not against, the desires of their jobs and the market. In contrast to the practical conservative views of the middle-class African-American Kippses, Jerome (middle class and half black, half white, like Smith herself) sees how "typically liberal, academic and wishy-washy were his own thoughts."[30] But why is Jerome (like a postmodern critic) shaping the culture up as a choice that exists only between either history as "story shaped" as Eagleton calls it, or history as "colorful chaos"?[31]

As with the mix-up over the umbrella in Forster, the introduction of Carl Thomas into the novel comes via a mix up over a "Discman" player at a Mozart-in-the-Park concert. In Forster, we are given a clear amount of time inside Bast's mind. We see his dreams of betterment and his feelings for the future and his frustrations with the present. Despite keeping to Forster in so many other ways, here, at the points where we could be given the interiority of Carl and his background or his thoughts there is only silence. The reviewers made it clear that Smith's genius was that her voice could go anywhere, and she could speak as anyone she cared to lay her authorial pen on, except, so it would seem, the working-class Carl.

The only truly working-class job that does show up in the novel comes in the form of Levi's part-time job working in what is obviously a Virgin megastore: "He wanted to be a part of it. Levi liked the way the mythical British guy who owned the brand was like a graffiti artist, tagging the world. Planes, trains, finance, soft drinks, music, cellphones, vacations...anything with a surface that would take his simple bold logo." Despite being paid "$6.89" an hour ("tough work for bad pay"), he sticks with it since he feels he is part of "a family."[32] A problem arises when the company wants the "family" to come in on Christmas Day and Levi decides to organize a protest. The African-American single parent LaShonda relishes the idea, not of a strike but of some extra money, while "only the white kids had showed up for the meeting" (186). Levi is eager to be the organic intellectual for the store and lead a strike, but Smith undercuts any working-class energies in the novel not only by mocking Levi as naïve and out of touch with the other workers ("only sixteen, living with his parents in the middle-class suburb of Wellington") but also by cruelly mocking the working-class African-American manager of the store, Bailey (183). The extreme ad hominem attack on Bailey seems strangely out of place in a novel that presents itself as being sympathetic to all. Here is how Smith presents Levi's African-American boss, Bailey:

> Bailey was in his late forties; unavoidably a tragic figure to the teenagers working under him. They considered such employment for a man over the age of twenty-six to be a humiliating symbol of human limitation. They also knew that Bailey had worked in Tower Records for ten years before this—this heaped tragedy upon tragedy. And then Bailey was painfully overburdened with peculiarities, one of which alone would have sufficed to make him a figure of fun. His overactive thyroid made his eyes start from his head. His jowls gathered like turkey wattle. His uneven Afro often had a foreign object in it—pieces of unidentifiable fluff and, once, a matchstick. His heaving, saddlebag backside looked distinctly female from behind. He had a tendency towards malapropism so extreme even a gang of near-illiterate teenagers could notice it, and the skin on his hands peeled and bled, the worst example of the psoriasis that also showed up in milder patches on his neck and forehead. (187)

Salon claims that Smith makes us laugh at her characters "even as she envelops them (and by extension us) in her fierce, radiant and irresistible love" (See book jacket). I am not sure where the love is in this presentation of Bailey. Even Forster attempted to present Leonard Bast sympathetically, indeed, Helen will give birth to his child, but in *On Beauty*, Bailey, the only real working-class person in the novel who is presented for more than a few lines, like Kiki and Carlene's servants Clotilde and Monique, could not be presented more unsympathetically. Like McEwan's presentation of Baxter as an animal in *Saturday*, so Bailey also came "blinking into the sun like a cave animal. He had his megastore cap on backward. There was a strong streak of perversity in Bailey, born of his isolation, which pushed him to pursue these feeble eccentricities." Bailey is mocked as being "vaguely autistic" and the reader gets the last laugh when he says that the young store assistants have been organizing "a coop" against him (189).

Bailey is however given a moment to expose Levi's fake street persona: "I know where you're from. Those kids don't know shit, but *I* know. They nice suburban kids. They think anyone in a pair of baggy jeans is a gangsta. But you can't fool me. I know where you *pretend to be from...*" (191). After this exposure, Levi is furious and within minutes he throws off his cap and walks out of his job and is soon "back on the streets in his own clothes" (192). Now whereas Leonard is soon starving and begging from relatives after losing his job, Levi has nothing to worry about, he is still a minor and only needs to go home to his middle-class home and his excellent education at Arundel. However, Smith seems to want the event to seem serious: "an impulsive decision...now the consequences caught up with him" (Ibid). But what are the consequences? What about the consequences for LaShonda or even for Bailey: this supposedly all-inclusive multicultural novel has no answer. The "consequences" for the middle-class Levi are typically shallow and inconsequential: "no money to escape Wellington on Saturday night, no chance to dance with all those kids, all those *girls* who didn't give a fuck who Gram-ski was..." (193).

Within minutes Levi falls in with Choo selling illegal CDs and DVDs on the street: magically transformed from the mundane working-class Bailey, *these* salesmen are hip, cool, and thoroughly postmodern:

> Their display was so magnificent....They struck Levi as splendid beings, from quite another planet than the one he had been on only five minutes ago—spring-footed, athletic, carelessly loud, coal-black, laughing, immune to the frowns of Bostonian ladies passing with their stupid little dogs. Brothers. An unanchored sentence of Howard's from his morning lecture—now floating free of the tedious original context—meandered in Levi's consciousness. *Situationists transform the urban landscape.* (194)

Levi is drawn to these men, and as readers we are being drawn to them too. In the same way that Howard's sentence about the Situationists drifts free from its tedious context, so Bailey, removed from his tedious context of the megastore is magically transformed into the free-floating immigrants selling CDs on a blanket in the street. Bailey represents labor, capital, and class, Choo and his friend represent an unthreatening form of decontextualized culture and postmodern ethnic color. Interestingly, Choo's positive influence on Levi will be later undermined, and any traces of sympathy that we may have had for these figures is also lost when the Hippolyte painting that Carlene gifts to Kiki (parallel to Mrs. Wilcox gifting Howards End to Margaret) is stolen from the Kippses by Choo.

We first see Carl at a café called "The Bus Stop" where the uneducated hip-hop enthusiast and rapper/poet shows up for the bimonthly

Spoken Word night. Carl puts on an impressive show and is immediately invited by Claire Malcolm (Howard's lover) to become part of the University and join her poetry class: "Are you interested in refining what you have?" she asks (232). Whereas Bast lost his job and slipped quickly into the "abyss," in Smith's rewriting of Forster, Carl is unrealistically promoted from street poet to being in Claire's university level poetry class to being given a job in the archives of Wellington College all within the space of several weeks. Claire feels that she should help this rapper/poet who paradoxically "doesn't have a voice" and that he also needs someone like Zora Belsey (half black / white and middle class) to "speak for him." Zora has become the Helen Schlegel to Carl's Leonard Bast and in the words of Claire Malcolm: "I also think it's a beautiful thing to do for a dispossessed person in this climate" (263).

In Chapter Three we are introduced to the Belsey's "fine middle-class house" built in 1856 with four floors. The original windows, "heavily insured" are kept in a "large safe in the basement" (16). On the staircase leading to Howard's study is a series of framed photos. The one photo that draws the narrator's attention is that of Howard's working-class father, Harold, complete with "flat-cap" which having been discovered in his mother's things after her death, has now been "lifted itself out of its low origins, like Howard himself." Howard's American colleagues see it as a badge of honor: "Many educated upscale Americans of the Belsey's acquaintance claim to admire it. It is considered 'classy', 'mysterious' and redolent in some mystifying way of the 'English character.' " Significantly, Howard "hates it . . . and his father," and his children "do not appreciate it" (18). With the death of Kiki's mother, Carlene, the novel briefly moves to England, since Carlene (an original "Windrush passenger") has English roots via Jamaica. However, in the middle of Carlene's funeral at Willesden Green, Howard walks out because his "subconscious had other ideas" and we are shortly walking among the working-class population of Cricklewood (291):

> The African women in their colorful kenti clothes, the whippet blonde with three phones tucked into the waistband of her tracksuit, the unmistakable Poles and Russians introducing the bone structure of Soviet Realism to an island of chinless, browless potato-faces, the Irish men resting on the gates of housing estates like farmers at a pig fair in Kerry. (292)

Working-class culture, no longer perverse and eccentric as we saw with Bailey is now, like Choo, reduced to a cheerful, colorful ethnic mix. Howard has his roots here: "We scum, we happy scum! From people like these he had come. To people like these he would always belong. It was an ancestry he referred to proudly at Marxist conferences and in print, it was a communion he occasionally felt on the streets of New York and in the urban outskirts of Paris. For the most part however, Howard liked to keep his 'working-class roots' where they flourished best: in his imagination" (Ibid).

Despite what the novel may want us to think about class, or what it might even say openly, the description of Howard's family home speaks volumes. He visits his parents' home and when the door opens a woman is standing there (not his mother) with "a nasty bunch of flowers in her hand" (293). Once inside we see Howard's working-class father in situ:

> He was in his armchair as usual. With the telly on as usual. The room was, as ever, very clean and, in its way, very beautiful. It never changed. It was still frowsty and badly lit, with only one double-glazed window facing the street, but everywhere there was color. Bright and brazen yellow daises on the cushions, a green sofa, and three dining chairs painted pillar-box red. The wallpaper was an elaborate, almost Italianate paisley swirl of pinks and browns, like Neapolitan ice-cream. The carpet was hexagons of orange and brown and, in each hexagon, circles and diamonds had been drawn in black. A three-bar fire, portable, tall, like a little robot, had its metal back painted blue, bright as the Virgin's cloak. (Ibid)

As with Jacky Bast's excessive make up, hair, and jewelry, the working class can be identified and positioned by their relationship to beauty. The ugliness of the scene, its lack of beauty, like the ugly Bailey, places the working class as outside the inner sanctity of the beautiful people: the middle class. Regardless of race, what bothers this novel is the working class, whether it is Bailey, an African-American store worker, or Howard's white working-class father: the narrative voice is equally distant from both. If laughter had been the mechanism of distance and repulsion with Bailey, here with Harold Belsey the working-class subject is contained through pity: "Howard couldn't laugh. It hurt his heart to note the unchanging details. How circumscribed must a life have become when a candy-colored postcard of Mevagissey Harbour, Cornwall, is able to hold its place on the mantelpiece for four years!"[33] Oddly enough, in Zadie Smith's fictive world, psoriasis seems to afflict only the working-class characters on both sides of the Atlantic. We saw that Bailey had it and now "Howard put his hands on Harold's. He felt the little rough patches of psoriasis" (294). Howard worries about slipping back into his old ways as if he had "never gone anywhere or done anything" (295). We are a long way from a four story house built in 1856 with antique windows in a safe in the basement.

As if on cue, Howard knocks a book on the floor that turns out to be "*A Room with a View*. Forster" which Howard "[c]an't stand" (Ibid). His father is not reading the novel, it belongs to his home-help Carol. They sit and watch television and the conversation is stilted and difficult. In a rollicking ventriloquist novel where Smith can supposedly give voice to everyone, she seems unable once again to give her working-class characters anything to say. Finally, Howard tells his father that his marriage with Kiki is probably over. Howard knows that his father could watch four more hours of television before bedtime with his son, but Howard can't do it: he couldn't "do it when he was sixteen and he couldn't do it now" and so "[t]en minutes later he left" (302).

The problem here is that once again class is something that is in the novel but not a living part of the narrative. Like some dangerous supplement, it is both in the novel and yet beyond its reach. It cannot be excluded totally insofar as that would leave the novel open to a self-aware critique that a marginal group was being excluded, but by inviting the working-class subject into the text it is unable to follow through and examine the place of class in the middle-class world that is the novel's real emotional center. So Howard can visit his father, but the narrative cannot grow, nothing can be said here that will contribute to the novel, and the working-class position exists only as a dead-end that Howard and the reader thankfully escapes from. Bailey and Harold's psoriasis help us to keep our distance from these "unhealthy" subjects, and while their shared parallel histories could provide a stimulating link, this is a transatlantic community that the novel seems to have no interest in pursuing.

Monty Kipps complains to Kiki after his wife's death that the one thing liberals love is a fairytale: "I love liberal fairytales! So restful—they put no undue strain upon one's mind" (326–327), an idea which he repeats later: "Kiki, if there's one thing I understand about you liberals, it's how much you like to be told a fairytale" (368). In many ways Kipps has a firm grip on Smith's own narrative: Carl Thomas, an uneducated outsider, with no education and no experience, is soon brought into Wellington College as a "Hip-Hop Archivist" (372). This is similar to Wilcox suddenly employing Bast and bringing him into the family business. However, Forster is honest to admit that such a strategy would be unrealistic and implausible, but in Smith's fluid postmodern economy, all subjects are free to move anywhere, so why shouldn't Carl be magically whisked off into a decent job at the heart of the bourgeois intellectual establishment? Smith points out that "Never in his life had Carl had a job like this one" and one can only imagine what Bailey or LaShonda might say (Ibid). This incredible job arises on page 372 of a 443 page novel, but this fairytale will soon be over. Carl, like Bast, is eternally grateful for this chance and savors the thrill of pretending to be part of the college life "that his mother had always dreamed he would be," but as his co-worker Elisha comments "we're not really a part of this community, are we?" (374). While this liberal fairytale can miraculously be held out to one individual, nothing has really changed on any social level. A counterpoint does exist in the novel in the voice of the French Haitian, Choo: "The same old slavery. Nothing changes. *Fuck* this, man...." However, rather than leaving this radical voice hanging, Smith immediately reels it in again and undermines it with her authorial voice: " 'Nothing changes. *Fuck* this, man,' said Choo, *but it sounded harmless and comic in his accent*" (361–362, my emphasis). In any case, any position voiced by Choo is fully undermined in the novel because Smith has decided that Choo will turn out to be the thief of Carlene Kipps' painting.

The other members of the working class in the novel are treated the same way as Carl: brought in at the start of the novel, touched on momentarily, and then excluded by the end. Toward the final pages Monique is fired by Howard: "Two weeks earlier Howard had let go of Monique, the cleaner, describing her as an expense they could no longer afford" (434). The telling sign is that having left Monique on the margins of the novel for more than 400 pages, Smith has to remind us that Monique is "the cleaner." This strategy of exclusion is parallel to the exclusion of Carl Thomas who has similarly been brought into the text only to be removed. Unlike the repulsive Bailey or Harold, Carl is "handsome" (402) and like the "African queen" Andrea Chapman in McEwan's *Saturday*, once he is working in the library he changes into an idealized happy worker, as opposed to an angry outsider: "Jerome...registered the pleasant change: this open, friendly demeanour, this almost Wellingtonian confidence...Carl prattled on about his library...with an easy egotism" (410). Zora, now relieved of her own liberal, middle-class guilt is happy to see Carl doing well: "Everything's going so well for him right now...he'll be a real addition to Wellington. We need more people like him" (410–411). But despite this easy connection of the prose and the passion, this particular connection of Carl to Wellington will not survive into the last chapters. In *Howards End*, Bast is symbolically crushed by a bookcase, and while Carl works in the library no such obvious fate awaits: instead he just vanishes. Having been given a fairytale job as an archivist of hip-hop, he has an argument with Zora (about sex not politics) and is never heard of again. In *Howards End*, the radical and shocking solution was to have Helen pregnant with Bast's child, but here, in 2007, such a radical solution is beyond the reach of the text, Carl will not be allowed into the middle-class world in any shape or form, and the text ensures that he is fully removed from the denouement.

Jerome was initially in love with Victoria Kipps (a la Helen Schlegel and Paul Wilcox) and then she ends up having sex with Howard and e-mailing him photos of her genitals ("Victoria sent him images of orifices and apertures that were simply *awaiting* him," 380) now it is Carl's turn to have sex with her on the floor of a cloakroom at a party in Wellington. Zora, deeply in love with Carl, confronts him and they argue. She accuses him and Victoria of both being "trash" and he calls her a "fucking bitch" (414). The two African-American girls, far from connecting the prose and the passion have "NOTHING to say to [each other]" although Zora takes one last shot and tells Carl that Victoria is an "airhead" and a "slut" (415–416). In her drunken anger Zora makes it quite clear why this fairytale narrative has to follow Forster in its removal of Carl/Bast: "You go to Wellington for a few months, you hear a little gossip and you think you know what's going on? You think you're a Wellingtonian because they let you file a few records? You don't know a thing about what it takes to belong here" (417). Zora's voice works to undermine the stated desire of the novel which is to somehow include Carl in the middle-class world, but sadly no amount of multiculturalism will change problems of inequality that are due to class. As the novel makes clear, the culture is therefore not excluding Carl because he is African-American, he is excluded because he is working class and "what it takes to belong here" is money. Although the novel has plenty of narrative space for the middle-class Kippses and Belseys, it has very limited space for the Baileys and Harolds, or for the cleaners Monique and Clotilde or Carl or Choo, or for any of the working-class Haitians that live in the shadow of this novel. This explains the large amount of time that that novel spends on affirmative action: the novel wishes to hold out a belief that such things are necessary and vital. Yet the text's narrative clearly exposes that no amount of racial affirmative action will do anything to change the *class* structure of the society. Belsey supports affirmative action out of a liberal idealism, while the conservative Monty Kipps is against it, but for the wrong reasons. Monty has sex with his student Chantelle and Howard has sex with Victoria Kipps: is this meant to offer some kind of political level playing field in which nobody can throw the first stone? While these two sides of the same middle class are hopping into bed with each other, Carl makes it clear that he is aware of his Bast-like role in the lives of the Wellington people. In the same way that Bast became "not a man, but a cause" for the Schlegels,[34] so Carl is made to repeat almost the same lines: "People like me are just toys to people like you . . . I'm just some experiment for you to play with . . . All you people. I don't know why I even got myself caught up with any of you, it can't come to no good anyway."[35] Oddly enough, right after Carl's argument on the street with Zora and he leaves never to be seen again, the novel seems happy to see him removed, as the next chapter opens with images of freshness and rebirth: "The next day was the first day of spring. There had been blossom before today, and the snow had already departed, but it was *this* new morning that broadcast a blue sky to every soul on the East coast . . . ." (419). The sense of newness is also emphasized in the next chapter as it begins with a borrowing from Philip Larkin's poem "The Trees": "A bright spring day. Birdsong. Squirrels . . . *Afresh, afresh, afresh*!" (423, my emphasis). In the same way that the novel seems to be unconsciously cleansing itself of Carl, so Kiki also "did not consciously begin a spring clean" (Ibid).

At this point in the novel, we learn that a painting has been stolen from the Black Studies Department, but despite some speculation that it is one of the cleaners or even Carl, it turns up under Levi's bed, having been stolen by Choo. Levi's feeble "all-property-is-theft" excuse, via Choo, is that the painting was already "stolen" by the Kippses from the Haitian people. Levi and Choo are now exposed as a strange combination of comical/naïve (the middle-class Levi) and menacing (the immigrant Choo). Levi admits that stealing the painting is theft, but then accuses the bourgeoisie of being "vampires" and that his parents paying Monique "four dollars an hour to clean" is also theft (428–429). This argument is soon a moot point as the back of the painting has a note from Carlene, donating the painting to Kiki in addition to the phrase "There is such a shelter in each other" (431). At this moment Kiki rather conveniently collapses in a heap on the floor and the chapter closes.

Inheriting a house that can symbolically "house" the future of England is one thing, and expresses a socially collective desire, but inheriting a painting fails to work as a social response to social problems, and it is no more than a personal solution to personal troubles. The penultimate chapter of the novel has the truth about Kipps and Chantelle and Howard and Victoria's sexual relationships being quickly delivered in two pages. The last chapter has Howard firing Monique, Kiki leaving him, and a brief mention of her plan to sell the painting and give the money to the "Haitian Support Group" (437).

Unlike Bast who lost everything when he lost his job, Howard and Monty keep their jobs. Howard takes a sabbatical, and Monty stays on, symbolically castrated without his "principles." As for Carl:

> He disappeared from Wellington altogether. By the time Zora felt brave enough to ring his cell it was out of order. She enlisted Claire's help in trying to find him; they got his home address from the payment records, but letters sent there received no reply. When Zora dared a visit, Carl's mother said only that he had moved out; she would say no more. (439)

Carl then quickly blends into every other working-class black teenager in town with nothing to distinguish him: "Five months later Zora continued to see Carl's many doppelgangers in the street, day after day—the hoodie, the baggy jeans, the box fresh sneakers, the big black earphones...." (Ibid). Carl has returned to the nameless abyss from whence he came.

The closing image of the novel involves Howard giving a lecture on Rembrandt for a colleague who oddly enough is called Smith. When he arrives Howard is out of breath: "Howard leaned against Smith and was unable to speak." He wants to be sick but Smith assures him that he is "just fine" (441). Inside the lecture hall are various colleagues, friends, old students, and of course his wife, Kiki. He projects the "pahpoint" picture of Rembrandt's "Hendrickje Bathing 1654" and zooming in on the "chalky whites and lively pinks" of her skin "as Smith has explained to him how to do" a moment is drawn out between Howard (the white middle-class professor who hates his father and his own working-class roots) and Kiki (the African-American mother of his middle-class children). What is established between them gently opens up the promise of reconnection through the medium of Art (443). The "only connect" of this novel therefore is one in which the middle-class unite in an academic setting with canonical art as their cement, while Monique is fired, Choo's prosecution is likely (although strangely unmentioned) and Carl abandons a job that in reality he would never have got and returns to the shadows of his class. In Forster's novel the whole outcome of the novel depends on Bast, here in the hip postmodern world of Smith, Carl can be safely removed at the end without causing the edifice to come crumbling down, since, unlike Forster, it was never dependent on him anyway.

If the novel doesn't give Carl the last word we can at least go back to what he said earlier in the novel: "The future's another country, man," said Carl mournfully, and then the punch line seemed to come to him; his face surrendered to a smile. "And I still ain't got a passport" (140). For all of the updated paraphernalia of the novel, for all of its hip and cool engagement with "street" issues and the colorful world of Haiti and slam poetry and e-mail and "pah-point" and the "rollicking satire" that "skewers" all positions, the novel has not moved beyond Forster, and in fact, seems to have slipped back. At one point, early in the novel, Howard is looking at photos of himself and his comment would stand as a satisfactory reading of what has happened to the representation of the working class in the middle-class novel since Forster: "Despite costume changes, the significant features remain largely unchanged by the years" (18).

Will Self

Will Self has recently published *Psychogeography* with Ralph Steadman, and the book jacket describes Self as a literary "*agent provocateur*." Yet while Will Self likes to present himself as the bad boy of English literature, Nick Rennison points out "He is not some class warrior storming the citadel of the literary establishment from the outside but an Oxford-educated, middle-class metropolitan who, despite his protestations to the contrary in interviews, is about as much at the heart of that establishment as you can get, a place he has occupied almost from the start of his career."[36] The first sign that we are in the presence of a middle-class writer, I think, is the way that critics will immediately assert that the author has transcended any kind of sordid limitations like class. For example, Liorah Anne Golomb clearly feels that Self's work springs "from his own experiences but [is] not confined by them" and that he has "transcended trite labels."[37] His firmly established place in the canon of middle-class authors can also be easily assessed if we look at Bradford and Tew. Bradford places him in his chapter on "The New Postmodernists" and immediately puts him in grand company: "born...half a generation younger than Barnes, Amis and McEwan...a combination and exaggeration of the most peculiar characteristics of all three."[38] In Tew, we find Self being discussed in relation to Amis, Ballard, and Nabokov and in both cases Self becomes the writer of postmodern fracture, slippage, and satire. For Tew, Self "capture[s] the shift in gender roles [which] seem tied inextricably to images and conceits of excess and incomprehension."[39] The result is that Self becomes the all-knowing cartographer of the postmodern: "the details of this displaced, almost grotesque reality are alluded to in rapid narrative transit and the helter-skelter image of lives in mutation."[40] In Bradford this mantra is repeated, as we see how Self is "obsessively concerned with the avoidance of predictability, precedent or classification" in which the "conventional polarity between good and evil is disrupted." Bradford even advances the idea that Self goes one step further than Burgess in his "dystopian visions" in that while Burgess creates a "thread of signals via which the reader can trace parallels between what occurs in the novel and the world outside it," Self is "determined to forestall perceptions of causality and notions of plausibility."[41] The result, for Bradford, is a thoroughly disturbing literature that pushes us beyond the borders set down by Amis and McEwan: "it could be reasonably argued that Amis and McEwan were the first to weave into their fiction elements of the inexplicable...but neither allowed this to completely displace what was once called the suspension of disbelief...Self has and continues to do so."[42] The same celebration of Self as a guru of the postmodern city, and his rejection of realism resurfaces in Tew: "In Self the placement of the geographic or spatial provides a psychic-phenomenological grounding and not an expression of a realist paradigm (or ambition)."[43]

Surely these assessments have to be rewritten in light of *The Book of Dave* (2006). In this novel the issues of class, work, father's rights groups, custody battles, unemployment, immigration, and wealth are met head on in a novel that for all of its historical time shifts and linguistic play (only in the chapters set in the future) is fully centered in a realist tradition. How do we square this critical assessment of Self as a master of the postmodern with a novel that examines the frustrations of one white working-class male taxi driver in a recognizably contemporary London? If we focus on the question of class a small clue begins to emerge. Tew had suggested in 2004 that one concern in Self is "the middle-class male who nevertheless exhibits a [feeling of] desperation."[44] In this sense *The Book of Dave* is best examined as a novel that thus expresses a distinctly white middle-class sense of anxiety and desperation when faced with the English working class that in recent years has also become increasingly desperate and anxious. The sense that the working class is expanding, threatening to swamp the middle-class world is also clear from Self's short story "Dave Too" in which a whole society suddenly begins transforming itself into a proliferating population of obnoxious Daves. Interestingly, the reason for this strange condition is never disclosed. As Golomb points out "Self never reveals the cause of this Davism...."[45] The reason it is not revealed is because the horror of "Davism" has obvious ideological roots in class panic.

In "The Burnt-Out Shells of Men," Self reviews Beatrix Campbell's *Goliath: Britain's Dangerous Places* in which she argues that the criminality and violence now gripping the various working-class estates of England is a symptom of what has happened to the male working class in light of the collapse of the manufacturing industries:

> [T]he distinctive face of contemporary criminality and riotous assembly in our society is a male one. On the marginalized estates of modern Britain, devastated by unemployment and economic deprivation, the traditional gender-based social distinctions have been fractured. With young unemployed men thrown back into the physical spaces normally occupied by women, they exorcize their impotence in the form of internecine warfare....[46]

Self responds that "[a]nyone who still wishes to believe that the worst-off in our society are somehow inexorably becoming better off would be well advised" to read the book.[47] Yet rather than responding to these class-based problems with realism, Self's fiction usually moves in the opposite direction, toward the exaggerated grotesque. If questions of class continually threaten to disrupt the smooth surface of *On Beauty*, in *The Book of Dave* Will Self moves away from the grotesque and places the white working-class male at the center of his novel. In essence, Self has taken a regular column from the British satirical magazine *Private Eye* and turned it into a novel. The comical column, "A Cabbie Writes" always follows the same format: a working-class "cab driver" is asked to talk about some topic of cultural or political importance. The results are predictably humorous: "we" educated readers laugh at the idea that an uneducated and usually bigoted cabbie would have anything worth listening to. The ranting monologue usually ends with the clichéd refrain "...string 'em up, it's the only language they understand."[48]

In Self's novel the cabbie, Dave Rudman, is separated from his wife Michelle who has taken their son, Carl, to live with a middle-class television producer called Cal Devenish and Dave soon spirals into depression. In an effort to express himself and be heard in a culture where he is "ex-fucking everything," he writes his angry tirades down in a book that he then buries in Cal's back garden in Hampstead in the hope that his son will find it.[49] After a series of meetings with a psychoanalyst, Dave changes his life, abandons the cab and his anger, leaves London, and moves into the Essex countryside with his new partner, Phyllis. In the course of his transformation, he has written another book that retracts all of his earlier anger. Dave realizes that when he wrote the first book he was "off iz rokkah" and now feels that all "awl we gotta do iz luv eech uvvah."[50] Tragically, this change of heart comes too late as Dave is murdered in Ongar by two Turkish gangsters out to collect an old debt. This leaves the middle-class Carl and his real son, Cal, to close the novel by burying Dave's second book, as a favor to Dave, in their back garden. Alongside this Oedipal narrative is another father search, but this time it is set 500 years in the future. England has been flooded by rising tides and is now a series of little islands. In this future world Dave's first book has been uncovered and treated as a holy text and forms the basis of all social and religious organization in the group of islands known as Ing. So for example, Dave's angry rant about only being allowed to see his son at certain times, in the future has created a society in which the men and the women are divided and the children spend a certain amount of time with their mothers and then with their fathers ("mummytym" and "daddytym" respectively). Since Michelle, Dave's wife had a restraining order against Dave, there is in this future society a "Furbidden Zon," into which no one is allowed entry. Dave's first angry book has thus become the basis of a future religion, Davinity, in which the Knowledge of the Cabbie and all of his utterances are literally taken as gospel, and the London Eye has been replaced with a huge steering wheel. In this future society the father/son search is repeated in the form of Carl Devush, who, having heard that a second book of Dave exists that retracts everything that is in the first, journeys off in search of the second Book of Dave and his real father. In the course of the journey he will travel to Nu Lundun and discover that Symun Devush (who has been living in Ham as the filthy mad exiled Beestlyman) is his real father, and not his step-dad Fred Ridman.

What holds this entire novel together is the most unpostmodern subject one could imagine: a working-class white cab driver with all his homophobia, misogyny, and racism intact. Like Bob Hoskins in Neil Jordan's *Mona Lisa*, he is unable to adapt to the contemporary world and wants to return to an earlier world in which things were simpler. Dave feels that he is surrounded on all sides by bureaucrats, foreigners, empowered women, and homosexuals and he just can't handle it anymore. He joins the support group Father's First out of a desperate desire to get his son back from his ex-wife Michelle.

In British culture, the cabbie is seen as the repository of the worst excesses of working-class Toryism, the right-wing cabbie being the run-of-the-mill stereotype as we can see in "A Cabbie Writes." The cabbie is not figured in British culture as a socialist figure by any means, and here in the novel, far from recording a postmodern fluid subject, Self employs this working-class stereotype on which to hang his satire of the working class. Self's novel serves to position the cabbie as entirely representative of the working class, who are permitted no other voice in the novel. By the end of the novel, the working-class claim to any kind of history will have been jettisoned and the bourgeois Carl and Cal will be its inheritors. The result, I would argue, is a novel that serves to reestablish a solid foundation for a desperate middle class, while returning the working class to a position of silence and exclusion. The satire also serves to ensure that we see how the middle class are not right-wing racists or homophobes: "we" middle-class readers are the norm, we are sensible, and "we" are not extreme, racist, misogynistic, or homophobic: that space is occupied by the working class, by people like "Dave." Like a horrific Marxist nightmare, Self terrifies us with the prospect of a future in which we see the "dictatorship of the proletariat" in which the traditional English working class gives birth, not to healthy socialism, but to a grotesque fundamentalist religion. Having safely absorbed all the negatives that would damage a coherent Blairite version of a classless multicultural Britain, and having linked all of them to the working-class Dave, he can be removed from the novel leaving behind a fully cleansed and firmly established identity for the middle class in the form of the reunited middle-class Devenish family.[51]

Although it could be argued that Self is somehow on Dave's side and that the reader is positioned in the same way, this view is rather hard to sustain. For the novel to "work" it has to be assumed that we are being positioned as a middle-class reader who would be shocked and amused/horrified by Dave's opinions. The novel only functions as a satire if we agree that the idea of anyone treating the words of an ignorant cab driver as a religion is both laughable and horrifying. After all, Self is not a taxi driver, but a middle-class writer, who "in order to research the novel…spent time with a real London cabbie and learnt about the trade."[52] The authorial voice works in such a way as to ensure that we are clearly positioned *with* the narrator/Self and in *opposition* to Dave. The mokni in the novel is reserved for him, for "them," while the Arpee (Received Pronunciation) and the narrator's middle-class voice is for, and with us, the middle-class reader.

Toward the end of the novel, Dave sells his cab and moves out of the city and into the Essex countryside with his new girlfriend Phyllis. Self, like Forster, sees the country and the city in similar terms, and their working-class characters while made to desire it as a space of rural rootedness are never permitted to actually live in it. The working-class protagonist must be preserved in the urban space, not the rural. His new lover, Phyllis, who is middle class but has "fallen through the middle-class safety net" will be allowed to carry on living in Ongar, while Dave will be killed off.[53] For Dave, the city is a place that has used him but offers him no home, but the country is no place for him either. At one point Dave walks from London toward Epping. Helen Brown, interviewing Self in *The Telegraph* focuses on this passage:

> The most beautiful passage in *The Book of Dave* is where the cabbie renounces his Fairway and takes a long walk out of London. The Knowledge "falls out of him." He heads north, past "industrial estates where metal tortured itself and ducked under the echoic stages of elevated roadways." Towards evening, he mounts a hill, passes nettles and brambles and lies back on the crushed grass. "He was disemboweled—he was losing it; and as he lost it, the crushed plastic bottle of his soul expanded with sudden cracks and pops." It's a modern, urban version of Levin's scything moment in *Anna Karenina.* "Yes, you're right," says Self. "I hadn't thought of it like that…but it is very Levinesque. Yeaahhhhh. Good old Levin."[54]

However, this passage is a reminder, not so much of Tolstoy but of Forster's Bast. In *Howards End*, Bast walks out of London trying to escape his social entrapment and walks long into the night and into the countryside. Margaret Schlegel speaks for him: "You tried to get away from the fogs that are stifling us all—away past books and houses to the truth. You were looking for a real home."[55] While this is her middle-class view of what he was looking for, it is telling that in Self, having constructed a working-class protagonist par excellence as the vehicle for his concerns he cannot escape framing him within the limitations of his own ideological framework. In this sense, we can see that it is obvious why such a conservative newspaper as the *Telegraph* would admire this novel seeing as how, as in Forster, the working-class protagonist is predictably made central only to be marginalized, placed on a pedestal only to be mocked, and kept alive for nearly 500 pages only to be brutally murdered in the end. In this novel, Dave is also a working-class protagonist trapped in a middle-class author's novel, and like Bast, is searching for a home: a home that he will be denied. As Dave "wandered aimlessly" out of London, the cabbie, filled with The Knowledge is paradoxically lost: "He found himself by a duck pond that cratered a strip of park...There were hulking nineteenth-century villas to one side, a primary school and an uglification of 1980s flats to the other. He hadn't been making any conscious effort to lose himself—the idea was ridiculous—and yet he had. He didn't know where he was."[56] At this point he bumps into a young woman and he almost asks her for directions:

> A young woman came limping towards him...She had the broken nails and scuffed trainers of poverty...Her dry lips parted and she said "Pliz? Pliz? *She doesn't know where she is...She hasn't got a fucking clue...She looks like she's brought here from Massy-fucking-donia smacked out in a van...Kept locked up in a gaff near here for months getting fucked stupid...Fucked up the cunt—fucked up the Gary...She don't know where she is—she don't even know what city she's in....*"[57]

May be Helen Brown in the *Daily Telegraph* missed this "beautiful" bit, but it is apparent that here on the margins of the novel we see a parallel between the illegal immigrant prostitute/sex slave and Dave himself. Only a few pages earlier, Dave thinks about the streets where he has worked his whole life: "Dave Rudman looked not up at the sky, nor around him at the brutal buildings, but at the ground, at the tarmac upon which his life had been rolled out.... This was the petrified skin he's been feeling all his *prostituted* life...."[58] Dave keeps walking and soon we have the classic kitchen-sink drama moment when the protagonist looks back at his home town, as Dave looks down on London from the heights of Essex:

> Towards evening Dave found himself mounting up a hill. Up he went...Dave turned back to see the city he had lost spreading to the far hills of the south in brick peak after tarmac trough...In the mid distance a river streaked silver and beside it a mighty wheel revolved so slowly.[59]

In the same way that Bast went in search of a home, as Margaret Schlegel said, so Dave the working-class protagonist nearly ninety years later is still looking for a home in the English novel.

Finally released from job and city, he sees the future flood that will wash capitalism and its products into a maelstrom of meaningless garbage: "The city was a nameless conurbation...its plaques and placards, plucked then torn away by a tsunami of meltwater...The great wave came on, thrusting before it a scurf of beakers, stirrers, spigots, tubes, toy soldiers, disposable razors, computer-disc cases, pill bottles...forming salt-bleached reefs which would remain there for centuries."[60] While Dave's prediction will come true in the novel and England will be flooded into an archipelago of smaller Ings, in his present moment he clearly cannot survive in the city and the child that he thought was his biological son has been taken from him. The violent ending allows a modicum of pathos and sympathy for our sad hero but more importantly it prevents the novel from confronting the economic logic that Dave was well aware of. Dave knows that if he stops being a cabbie there is nothing left for him at all: "What would he be if he walked away from it for ever? At my age, with no other training...no qualifications. He saw himself in mid morning on a quiet residential pavement, *a poor, bald fucker delivering leaflets for an Indian takeaway at one-fifty an hour.*"[61] To have ended the novel here would have revealed something very unpalatable about Dave's working-class life, but by being murdered by two evil Turkish thugs, this ideological gap is smoothed over and the blame can be displaced onto a foreign "underclass." This allows us, the middle-class reader, a space to feel sorry for Dave without any middle-class guilt: "we" are not responsible for his fate, nor is it the fault of some economic system that "we" support, quite simply it was "those people."

The reviews of *The Book of Dave* treat its ostensible themes of father/son relationships, environmental concerns, and its satire of religious belief, but these ideas in the novel are really secondary. These are foreground issues, and following Žižek, it is the background of a text that is *ideologically* central. How can we explain this use of a working-class cab driver as the protagonist in an age which has spoken so loudly of the death of class? We need to remind ourselves of Jameson's remark: don't ask what the novel is about, but instead, "How does it work?" M. John Harrison perceptively feels that

> *The Book of Dave* is a novel about trying to come back from the brink of something without quite knowing what it is. Despite his evident articulacy, Dave can't say what's happened to him—he can't lay blame. It wasn't his upbringing, it wasn't the job, it wasn't Michelle, or even, really, the loss of his relationship with his son; it wasn't the depression, or the drugs, or the psychosis, or his book, or even his eventual recovery. Those things, and the indescribably complex feedback relationships between them, serve only to suggest something else, something deeper, some malaise that can only be articulated by a description of its symptoms.[62]

Self likes to talk about the idea of an "umble cabbie" being the perfect person to reconstruct a lost London, a bit like Joyce's comment that if Dublin was lost then we could use *Ulysses* to rebuild it. But whereas Joyce's class is very closely linked to Bloom and of course to his self-portrait, Stephen, Self's *class relationship* to Dave is not simple. Dave is not Self in the way that Joyce was Stephen. Self is not a cabbie, and various publicity stunts of him reading the novel to cabbies from the back seat of a taxi does not make him a member of the working class. As with E. M. Forster and Zadie Smith, the gap between middle-class educated writer and working-class character is one fraught with problems. While Self may feel that we are being led to sympathize with Dave and see the world from his marginalized position, the novel resists such a position, and since the foolish people of the future worship Dave, we are placed above Dave, and above the future Hamsters (inhabitants of Hampstead) who worship the Wheel and put their faith in Davinity. While they stupidly look up to Dave and worship him, the novel implies that we know better, and to do this we have to clearly look down on him. Moreover, Dave's overt homophobia, racism, and misogyny mean that no middle-class reader will get anywhere close to sympathy let alone empathy. So, we have a central working-class character in the novel, but one which has been fully emptied of any value for the middle-class reader (other than as a comic object of ridicule). Ironically, his horridly un-PC views on everything also allows

Self and the reader to express any anger and rage and class frustration about British society without having to admit that it is a position that they would hold, after all, it is not Self saying these terrible things, it is the uneducated working-class Dave. Sadly, the only British readers who might identify with Dave would be members of the racist British Nationalist Party and so, as with McEwan's Baxter in *Saturday* (or Amis's John Self) we are prevented from building any connection to Dave due to his obviously ugly opinions on almost everyone. A quick list of Dave's pet peeves will suffice:

> their food smells fucking awful...dumb fucking paddy...fucking bruvvers, their hoodies pulled down over their mad yellow eyes...the sortuv sideburns those Pakki birds have...Traceys and Sharons without an idea in their heads except Darren's cock and she-said he-said...Fucking lefties...dumb cunts...fucking pikeys...What is this, fucking Delhi!...fucking bitches...fucking nigger sect...spunk-drunk mummies...dodgy wallahs...dumb toffs.[63]

Dave's defensive hate is thus released into the space of the novel but neither Self nor the reader is responsible, this is just Dave's white working-class anger speaking. Using Dave as the mouthpiece, the novel serves to release cultural anxieties that the white middle class is certainly experiencing in contemporary Britain. Large sections of Dave's rants could easily be read by any disgruntled British yob as a true testament of what "real" Brits are feeling right now. So while the novel may set out to expose the ludicrousness of religious fundamentalism through a narrative about fathers and sons, it also carries another level of narrative: one in which frustrated class anxieties can be safely explored and opened up while being simultaneously disavowed.

The future postflood society survives by breeding and eating motos, a kind of genetically engineered pig that speaks like a child with a lisp, as well as using them like horses for transport. In this novel the working-class Dave is also like a sacrificial moto: he is weak and will be killed by the novel, but he is useful, we can ride on him and he assists in providing a framework for the novel, but having taken on board all of the culture's poisonous opinions, he becomes the scapegoat and as such must be punished for expressing such unpalatable views, and so Dave will be killed off before the novel closes.

As in Zadie Smith, Self's novel never seems to locate a position on anything. Insofar as a cabbie, is in Dave's words "ex-fucking everything" the cabbie is a position with no identity as such, he is only defined by what he is not, he is not black, or gay or a woman or an immigrant, and if contemporary discourse has valorized the margins, here is the revenge of the center. The narrative of fathers trying to reunite with sons is also mocked in the novel, not out of some sympathy with an antipatriarchal position, but as a way of blocking any working-class desire. As the Father's First group becomes more radical so tragedy looms large, and one of the members Gary Finch, another "fucking nutter," is broken on the wheel, killed as he falls from the London Eye during a protest.[64] So it would seem that any set of beliefs that would constitute some kind of collective identity for the working class is mocked by the novel, whether it is the mass worship of Dave in the future, or the beliefs of the marginalized father's groups, or even the antiwar protesters in the novel. In fact, anyone who is not Dave or any other marginal groups, these cultural spaces in the novel are not mocked by the narrative voice whereas the narrative undermines Dave's position from start to finish. The novel, as we would expect from satire, has no real position other than to perpetuate its own middle-class ideology which is why the novel seems stuck, shuttling back and forth between two historically parallel worlds. Toward the end of the novel Dave thinks "*The past has become our future and in the future lie all our yesterdays*... Was it a stale aphorism freshly baked, or an ancient pop song dimly recalled? *Dave could not have said*" (465, my emphasis). Since Dave cannot speak, I will suggest that the novel is a stale aphorism in which the present and the future are locked into a deadly repetition, two worlds in which history cannot come alive, and the working-class figure is doomed to be "prostituted" and killed off in this life, and falsely worshipped as divine in the future. Early in the novel Dave tells us how he used to phone Michelle to speak to his young son, Carl:

> "Daddy?"
> "Hiyah Runty, how's it going, mate?"
> "Mummy, issa ghost." (39)

Carl is right, Dave is a ghost. Dave is a thing of the past, yet he stubbornly haunts the present and the future: a residue that the text must continually work to mock, undermine and try to erase.

Even in 522 A.D. (After Dave) when the flood has washed away the last vestiges of capitalism, the divisions of class persist: as Antone Bom grows up he is seen "recoiling from the brutal inequalities of London life; which meant that while the lawyers, the guildsmen and the Inspectorate live a life of opulence and ease, there were beggars starving in the streets of Covent Garden" (298). As he comes into Southwark Street in 524 A.D. we can clearly see Self's vision of contemporary London:

> A veritable river of shit and piss ran down the gutters and the foul cries of the chavs rent the air...it was a shock to discover that the cockneys, when not engaged in abusing each other, were to be seen with their ratty features blotted out by phonics...The toffs had no fear of the hugger-mugger, preceded as they were by fonies, their staffs raised to smite the riffraff, their didduloodoo cries warning that a getter, a Driver or a Lawd was approaching...Antone cast suspicious looks at the denizens of the boozer—a slovenly company of mummies in filthy cloakyfings and tracksuits.[65]

Moreover, the class divisions of the future world mean that the poor have to obey the law while the rich can get around it. As Bom points out

> the truth is that posh mummies and daddies have always shacked up with each other, daddies even as they left the very Shelter itself, going straight to the mummies of their children, children they freely acknowledged as their own...Yet upon whom does this weigh most heavily...I will tell you upon whom, the poor, the cockneys and the peasants, the Taffies and the Scots—even the chavs, who are mere property to be bought and sold, are subject to the rigors of Breakup and Changeover. (373)

Self's disdainful treatment of Dave becomes clearer if we look at Cal Devenish. Cal is a "former writer" (149) who drives past the National Theater while inside, his "fellow bourgeoisie sucked sweets and watched Imogen and Ralph play at queens and kings" (155), he drives a "BMW convertible" (152) and runs a television channel, "Channel Devenish" (150) that makes easy money out of rubbish: "it was a taut balloon of gassy cash. Devenish had developed a series of hit programmes: Tumour Swap, TWOC Rally, Whorecam..." (Ibid). Like Will Self, who is also a regular on English television, the middle-class Cal is also "a panelist on arts review shows and current event forums, a wag and a wit" (Ibid). Living with Dave's ex-wife Michelle in a "Queen Anne house in Hampstead" (148), he is the middle-class figure in the book that we initially see as the nasty stepfather of Dave's son, Carl. It turns out in the middle of the novel that Carl is actually not David's son, and that the middle-class Cal is the biological father. After Dave is killed off, Carl and Cal close the novel, burying Dave's second book in their own garden. So, while the novel is ostensibly focused on the working-class figure of Dave, it is the biological middle-class father and middle-class son who carry the denouement of the novel and who in effect carry the biologically unified middle-class family into the future. In Will Self's political universe it is the middle class who will inherit the earth, and since Cal Devenish and his son generously bury Dave's second book (the retraction) in their Hampstead garden, we can also say that thanks to them, the stupid religion of Davinity will at some future point be dismantled.[66]

One simple way to assess Self's ideology in this novel is to examine his mocking of Dave in relation to his calm authorial omniscient narrator. Writing about James Kelman, Mary McGlynn points out that "Kelman uses disruptions of narrative hierarchy as places to contest our assumptions regarding the limitations of working-class minds, reconfiguring conventional hierarchical distinctions between narrator and character, between educated and uneducated speech, and between written and spoken expression."[67] Clearly, in *The Book of Dave*, this is something that Self is not doing. In fact, the opposite strategy is at work. McGlynn points out that nineteenth-century realist fiction, often "articulates social relations through the construction of a hierarchy of discourses and appears to present history without a narrator while confirming omniscience as the guiding principle of subjectivity."[68] For all of the supposed radicalism of Self's (middle class) narratives, I feel that the overriding narrative framework in *The Book of Dave* has not moved far beyond that bourgeois hierarchy of discourses. Self is not laughing with Dave, but against him, and is thus mocking his Cockney accent rather than using it as a radical critique of middle-class speech. As McGlynn points out, speaking of Faulkner:

> As Ross says, "The mimic always remains in some sense superior to the speech (or gestures) imitated, for he or she possesses mastery of both the originating and the mimicked voice." Additionally, the reader's place in social hierarchies is presumed: he or she must be someone capable of recognizing and understanding both standard and nonstandard language. Ross argues that for Faulkner this means readers who are in the position of well-off whites, able to mimic and understand black and lower-class characters that could not in turn mimic standard English: "Transcribed speech, the product of mimicry, always occupies an inferior position in relation to the diegetic discourse of

> its production. The mimetic voices we hear are always secondary, indulged and condescended to by the reader who shares...the author's power over all the voices."[69]

In *The Book of Dave*, Self uses the narrative voice precisely in this way to firmly establish a norm that Self's class feels is under threat. The novel, far from being Self's usual grotesque narrative of fracture and postmodern slippage, is quite clearly a reassertion of a dominant middle-class subjectivity published at a time when bourgeois ideology is under increasing pressure to reassert itself, and as the middle classes find themselves trapped amid a rising sea of poverty.

The standard greeting in the flooded England of the future is Dave's question to his customers as they climb into his taxi: "Ware2Guv?" Sadly, if we were to ask Will Self and Zadie Smith this same question in terms of where history is headed, the answer that they have given us in their novels is clear: follow the same narrative route that their class has been traveling since the novel was born, with the same dead-end outcomes for the working-class subjects.

Chapter 3

Classless Fictions?: Middle-Class History/ Working-Class Subjects in Martin Amis, Peter Ackroyd, and Hanif Kureishi

Do you still think any of that crap matters, class and so on? It doesn't. It's crap. It's crap.

—*Martin Amis*[1]

Although Amis, Ackroyd, and Kureishi occupy different areas of the literary canon, their work reveals a clear pattern in terms of their political treatment of class and history. This chapter examines how Martin Amis's work is clearly structured to preclude any sympathy for his working-class subjects and that his satire produces a body of texts that preserve and reinforce how we think about class, rather than undermine it. Peter Ackroyd's work has been warmly received by postmodern critics and his work is celebrated for its reworking of history, and yet I feel that once we raise the question of class then Ackroyd's fluid texts take on a rather more troubling aspect as his celebration of "histories" undermines the historical ground upon which to build a dialectical foothold for the working-class subject. The work of Hanif Kureishi has similarly been welcomed for its contribution to the postcolonial debate, but I will explore how Kureishi's class position leaves no space for any collective social agency, and that his other less canonized novels such as *The Black Album* and *The Body* openly reveal the limitations of Kureishi's own class-based ideological limits.

Martin Amis

It is an odd moment in British culture when a tabloid newspaper like the *Daily Express* is covering a disagreement between the literary critic Terry Eagleton and Martin Amis. But this was exactly what happened in September and October 2007 after a media storm broke out, not so much over what Amis had said about Muslims (his comments had been made the year before), but rather over what Eagleton had said about Amis's overlooked comments. Amis's initial remarks had first appeared in the *Guardian* in an essay entitled "The Age of Horrorism" published in September 2006. Nobody really took any notice when this article was originally published until Eagleton, publishing a new edition of *Ideology*, reproduced Amis's remarks in the opening of the revised introduction:

> They're gaining on us demographically at a huge rate. A quarter of humanity now and by 2025 they'll be a third. Italy's down to 1.1 child per woman. We're going to be outnumbered.... There's a definite urge—don't you have it?—to say, "The Muslim community will have to suffer until it gets its house in order." What sort of suffering? Not letting them travel. Deportation—further down the road. Curtailing of freedoms...Discriminatory stuff, until it hurts the whole community and they start getting tough with their children....[2]

Eagleton's reason for quoting Amis was to make the point that this position doesn't come from some "British National Party thug" but is from none other than Martin Amis, "leading luminary of the English metropolitan literary world."[3] Very soon the press "resounded with the Amis-Eagleton row," and yet sadly, as Eagleton points out, the argument was picked up by the press not because there were "vital political issues at stake" but simply because "Amis and I are members of the same school of arts at Manchester University" and that the papers were simply excited at the thought of some "senior common room punch-up."[4] Eagleton does say that a younger Martin Amis would probably not have adopted such a position and that there is in fact a gap between "Amis then and Amis now"[5] suggesting that what has happened in-between is the so-called War Against Terror. The implication being that if a middle-class, educated, self-conscious individual like Amis cannot resist the pull of ideology, how powerful it must sound at the meetings of the British National Party, or for that matter, to average working-class readers of the *Daily Express*, or even liberal readers of the *Guardian*.

This open argument between Eagleton and Amis is highly symptomatic of what has happened to the novel since Thatcher. In July of 2007, Eagleton had already mentioned Amis's remarks on the Muslim community in an earlier essay. In this earlier essay Eagleton was intent on showing how the only political writer that remains today in Britain is Harold Pinter, and even he is little more than a "champagne socialist" at the best of times.[6] Every other single writer has abandoned any sense of a real critique of where we find ourselves: Rushdie, once "a remorseless satirist of the west" is now "cheering on its criminal adventures in Iraq and Afghanistan," David Hare caved in to "Buckingham Palace some years ago," Christopher Hitchens is likely to be remembered not as some "George Orwell *de nos jours*" but as our own Evelyn Waugh since he has "thrown his lot in with the Washington neo-cons," and Martin Amis who is now in favour of strip-searching all Muslims or Pakistanis and is suggesting that "deportation…may be essential further down the road."[7] The result for Eagleton is that we possess a literary terrain in which "scarcely a single major poet or novelist is willing to look beyond such issues to the global capitalism that underlies them. Instead it is assumed that there is a natural link between literature and left-liberalism." What we see here then is the way that a serious gap exists between political criticism and literature, a gap which does not appear as long as we apply pseudoradical postmodern theories. But once we place the contemporary novel under a political microscope, its strength and power as a tool of ideology becomes much more apparent.

Richard Bradford's reading of Amis's work in *The Novel Now* is strictly canonical in its open praise for what Amis is doing, while the same celebration of Amis's skill, insight, deconstructive wit, and flawless ability to explain ourselves to ourselves is echoed from all corners. In the beginning of *The Novel Now,* Bradford says that postwar England has moved to a state in which "class distinctions" became less prominent.[8] Paradoxically, nearly 200 pages later we hear that "Class, with its consequences and peculiarities, is a phenomenon that inheres through all parts of the United Kingdom and Ireland but few would dispute that its germane, divisive elements originated and persist, in England."[9] Given these two opposing positions, it is interesting that at the bottom of the same page Bradford tells us that Amis has "evolved an idiosyncratic brand of *classless* fiction."[10] It is an odd fantasy to think that anyone's fiction could be classless, but I feel that what Amis has done is to rearrange the novel's relationship to class, and like contemporary advertising that has modified itself to appear not to be advertising anything, or has deployed a whole host of ironical positions through which to interpellate us, so too Amis's fiction reveals a modification of the realist form so that it can safely absorb the threat posed by an increasingly large and troubled/troubling working class while simultaneously claiming a high moral ground on which to rest its middle-class laurels.

The traditional and safe way of reading Amis is to see him as a postmodern satirist, or even a postrealist satirist. For example, James Diedrick's essay in *Contemporary British Fiction* (a standard critical text which is used on most university courses on the Contemporary British novel) lays out the standard reading of *Money*:

> *Money: A Suicide Note* (1984) represents a high-water mark in Amis' career, building on the strengths of his earlier novels but far exceeding them in scope, depth of characterization, and organic unity. It also stands as one of the indispensable novels of and about its decade.[11]

Self, the working-class character at the center of this novel has been created by Amis as nothing more than "a prisoner of his own addictions" and this comic spectacle of a character who is "contemptible" "represents a tour de force of satiric representation." Self then becomes the symbol of an "unabashed entrepreneurial greed that characterized Anglo-America in the 1980s."[12]

This is the main way that the novel is read by the critics when they articulate themselves directly, and I think this is probably the way that the novel would be read by the average reader. What is odd is that the protagonist is a *working-class* character who is mocked, exposed, kicked to the ground, and finally stripped of everything. This working-class man is used by Amis to somehow shake a fist at the entrepreneurial greed of a class to which Self never belongs in the first place.[13] It's almost a novelistic version of "Don't give them baths, they'll keep coal in them" as we see that once a working-class figure tries to get into the money game they are just unable to handle it. The ensuing failure of Self to enter into the middle class and play a game that Amis has made him hopeless at, is thus at the root of the novel's "comedy." The implied reader is clearly the educated reader who can laugh at John Self (parallel to the implied reader in Will Self who will laugh at Dave's excesses and ignorance) and here in *Money*, Amis has created John Self as such a cartoonishly dumb character that he cannot even read *Animal Farm* properly.

Criticism has taken this "satire" angle and pushed it to the point where we almost begin to believe that there are no class problems with this novel, and that Amis is somehow always already aware of how he has stacked the deck against John Self, and by some circuitous logic proves that the novel doesn't reinforce class binaries but is actually deconstructing them. Jon Begley is a prime example of this critical bending-over-backward to preserve Amis as a pillar of the canon:

> For some critics, *Money* involves a deliberate effacement of national boundaries, the excesses of Self's "private culture" offering a dystopian representation of a collective postmodern condition or predicament. (Diedrick 75, Edmondson 146). Alternatively, there are critical readings that assert the condition of England as the novel's principal focus...[with Amis] attempting to unmask "the ideological underpinnings of Thatcherism" (Doan 79).[14]

Paradoxically, Self, who is mocked as empty and pathetic now becomes the center of these complex analyses so that Amis has deliberately selected the working-class upstart John Self so as to really undermine and critique, not the working class, but global capitalism: "In addition to Self's decentred inner culture, Amis also signals a broader transition from the sovereign nation-state toward the strategic alignments of late capitalism, the emergence of what Kevin Robins labels 'a new global-local nexus.' "[15] So Amis is no longer just a middle-class writer poking fun at the working class, but a novelistic version of Fredric Jameson who is out to skewer the heart of industrial capitalism: "Self operates as a conduit for Amis's satiric 'amplitude'—the dissection of his 'private culture' illustrating both the national and global repercussions of market deregulation and economic individualism."[16] However, it is clear that while John Self hopes that this new wave of opportunity for the working class will lead to a more level playing field, in the absence of any political framework to bring about an egalitarian society, Self has no political dimension at all and simply hopes that money will bring equality: "You're so democratic: you've got no favorites. You even things out for me and my kind."[17] Of course, the novel will never allow such a thing to come to pass, and by the end Self will be reduced to a tramp, excluded from everything. In this way, Laura Doan's comment that the novel "rightfully" arrests the pretensions of a "working-class *parvenu*"[18] is a little too honest, and it exposes Amis's class position too clearly. Instead, Begley tries to soften the blow: "Contrary to Doan's criticism...Amis's quarrel with the 'forces of democratization'...is premised upon a cultural rather than a social conservatism."[19] In short, the implied argument here seems to be "let us pull back from criticizing the class politics of this novel because Amis is somehow already on your side and is aware of what he is doing, and is working against ideology." Begley even sees Amis as working in the shade of Bakhtin: "Self is a figure of carnivalesque exaggerations, vilifying the normative codes of class and tradition through his modern, transatlantic billingsgate, and embodying the degradation and 'material bodily principle' of grotesque realism."[20] This is far more reassuring than simply assuming, as would most readers, that Amis is out to mock the working class as they begin to appear in the city as Thatcher's deregulations and privatizations open the floodgates on a class that since 1945 had been comfortably putting up money barriers to preserve the exclusivity of its institutions.

Regardless of how we examine them, we are left with some simple and rather straightforward divisions in Amis's novels, which rather than seriously deconstructing anything at all, actually use satire as a way of restoring a sense of cultural balance that were felt to have been lost. Amis has said, "I don't offer alternatives to what I deplore" and of course, he doesn't have to, there is no need or a desire for an alternative; all that is required is a simple return to the bourgeois norm, the status quo.[21] In short, the real target of Amis's satire is his working-class characters, and it is them that we are laughing at, while siding with the very stable positions that the novel provides. Satire is essentially conservative in its desire for a return to a normal center, in this case the center, the norm, being that of the middle-class reader/writer. For all of the theoretical circles that critics may weave around Amis to show that he really is troubling, dangerous, radical, or iconoclastic, in the end we can see that Amis's work serves to offer a clear ideological response to a period in which the working class and levels of poverty have clearly expanded. The working class both expanded upward as they entered into the new money markets of the eighties, and downward, as Thatcherism sows the first seeds of a new underclass. This expansion, as always, is seen as an encroachment and a threat by the middle classes and what emerges in Amis is a body of fiction that, through humor and satire, essentially puts the working class back in their place, offering them up as a category of ridicule and spectacle for the anxious middle-class reader, who can sleep soundly knowing that the philistines, such as Keith Talent in *London Fields* or John Self in *Money* have been safely reduced to a comical heap that need not be treated seriously nor worried about. But as Brecht reminded us "their" laughter is "our" demise. Amis himself has admitted that in the face of "these evils of modern life" the only response is humor: "The comic novelist...all he can do with these evils is laugh them off the stage."[22]

Emma Parker's reading of *Money* in *Martin Amis: Postmodernism and Beyond* provides another example of how criticism goes to great lengths to read Amis as a friend of a Left-liberal agenda. Her thesis is stated as follows:

> Although it is possible to counter the charge that Amis is a masculinist writer by arguing that *Money* offers a critique of masculinity, this essay contends that the novel goes further than highlighting the need to redefine dominant modes of manhood. Offering a queer reading of the text that focuses on the unstable borders of identity and desire, this essay demonstrates that *Money* subverts the ideology of its bigoted protagonist by deconstructing the heteropatriarchal concepts "woman" and "man" and creating what Judith Butler terms "gender trouble."[23]

So, rather than treat the novel as politically troubling, we are in an arena in which Amis is to be rewarded for doing something that postmodern theorists valorize. It also opens up a nice space in which we can separate the nasty working-class Self from the hip all-knowing author, Martin Amis. The novel itself does not subscribe to anything as dull as an ideological "position" that can be examined, and the novelist is seen to be in step with the critics. All that is left is then to show how, in this case, the novel is deconstructing "heteropatriarchal" codes along lines that would now be acceptable by queer theorists such as Judith Butler. The novel is thus shielded from any serious criticism, and in fact what we are reading is no longer "criticism" but literary praising, with Parker giving Amis the theoretical stamp of approval in his fictional passport. Thus *Money* becomes not a troubling class-bound novel, whose treatment of the working-class protagonist is a real problem, but rather "a rich, subtle, and ambitious novel, [which] challenges male hegemony with more than a critique of masculinity that reifies patriarchal structures. By destabilizing the binary categories of gender and sexuality, the novel privileges a queer perspective" (61). Moreover, "*Money* consistently presents gender as unfixed and fluid, [revealing] the novel's feminist sympathies..." (Ibid). By the end of this essay, we are ready for a conclusion that raises Amis to the level of a fictional/theoretical superhero: "Amis rejects the notion of a singular and secure gender identity...[and] suggests the possibility—or indeed the necessity—of transcending gender altogether" (68). John Self is apparently taken to this theoretical nirvana when Parker decides that toward the end of the novel, since this working-class narrator with "limit[ed]...awareness" does grow toward an understanding of his own "queer-ness" he can now be allowed to begin to "transcend binary categorization" (59, 63, 68). The conclusion of the essay thus praises Amis in that he "anticipates the emergence of queer theory in the early 1990s" and not only that, he goes one step further because "unlike queer theory [Amis] does not overlook that formations of gender and sexuality are shaped by capitalism" and thus *Money* is not only a "powerful critique of capitalism" but is also "an equally powerful and previously unacknowledged critique of heteropatriarchy" (69).

So, first there is this desire to praise the novel for its stellar achievements, and second, which obviously emerges from the first, there is a desire to articulate a blindness to those ideological aspects of the novel that are quite openly troubling from a class perspective. This kind of reading also reveals how easy it is for the novel to be absorbed by postmodern theory from Derrida to Butler and beyond. Another consideration is that this kind of criticism, while mellifluous to the academic conference audience is surely not the way the novel would be read by the average reading public. Are we to assume that the average reader of *Money* would feel that the novel has a queer/feminist politics at its core, and that in the end, having been beaten up and reduced to a tramp, John Self is now ready to "transcend binary categorization"?

If we choose instead an essay on the economics of *Money,* we are confronted with the same thing but in a different costume, and rather than anticipating queer theory, we will now be shown how Amis has gone beyond Marx in his understanding of contemporary capitalism, while the novel will reveal to us an understanding of money and culture that we would be blind to if it were not for Amis's text. Tamas Benyei's thesis is as follows:

> It is in the interstices of this paradoxical circulation, the folds and vents of figurative capital, that my reading of the novel resides. Instead of reiterating the critical clichés concerning the homologies between money and language, I am interested in the uniqueness of this text's "excessive self-reflexiveness" (Keulks, 177), the ways the verbal universe of this "Sado-Monetarist" (Brantlinger, 208) novel performs the feat of self-enfolding. Rather than simply observe the way *Money* conceives "the correspondence between the mode of economic exchange and the mode of signifying exchange" (Goux, 96), I will discuss the role of monetary metaphors in the novel's textual strategies or textual "economy." I am

> therefore concerned with the homologies, rifts, and spillings between the textual and the rhetorical, the monetary and the economic, the cultural and the psychological levels or orders of the book. (37)

Once again we are in the postmodern realm of the fluid, the blurred and the fuzzy. We are in a novel where we see only a "collapsing of disparate levels" (Ibid) but instead of it being a collapsing of man/woman into a transcendent queer-ness now we are in a novel in which money and allegory ride each other guided by Amis's insights and knowledge: of course, Self is not included in this knowledge, he remains the ground on which this knowledge is reared. While the text can read (and deconstruct) anything, Self is unable to read successfully. As Benyei points out "Self fails to perceive the allegorical world of *Animal Farm* so too does he fail to read his own world" (38). His ignorance thus opens the door for *our* insights: "he sees things in terms of price and value. His inability to decipher—or even notice—allegory therefore parallels his inability to form relationships that are not based on economic exchange" (Ibid). Rather than moving this analysis toward Marx, and what it might mean to have a working-class character whose "inability to recognize" anything and whose "ignorance" (47) is at the heart of the novel's vindictive humor, we move predictably away from such questions and toward the safer "textual" terrain of Derrida and Barthes:

> The textual economy of *Money* therefore resembles money: surplus resides in circularity, doubling, repetition, the difference with the same. This production can act as a register of pleasure, as Derrida suggests, explaining how metaphor yields a "dividend of pleasure." ("White" 239) Roland Barthes concurs, writing that a word "can be erotic on two opposing conditions, both excessive"... In *Money* words are eroticized in both of these ways, creating an excess that defies the logic of economic transactions. (Ibid)

The result is that we are left with a novel that reveals to the reader that "[t]hrough Self, consumerist society is portrayed as a demonic, mass-produced version of the 'non-economic' significance of waste...." (48–49) and that "John Self [is] the exemplar of consumer culture, *cretinization*, and so on...and we are left in the end, with a sense of his excessive, inadmissible life" (52–53, my emphasis). Sadly, for all of its theoretical decoration we are back where even the most cursory reading of the novel would leave you: that Martin Amis portrays John Self as a cretin.

Although these readings are no doubt productive on some level, I feel that they move readers away from the novel rather than into it. The theoretical frameworks seem to take over, and in their eagerness to speak favorably of Amis, they succeed in silencing any other way of reading his work. In all of these examples, Amis is treated as a revered author who the critics stand in awe of, or they aim to show that Amis is quite aware of the intricate theoretical work they subscribe to and that his novels deploy a barrage of strategies that serve to undermine, dislocate, rewrite, and expose the obscene machinations of power and ideology. But why should we automatically assume that Amis's texts are operating in this way? If, as postmodernism claims, we should be listening to the margins, then the marginalized silenced voice in all of this Amis's criticism is the voice that would dare to say that his work is thoroughly ideological in the most obvious of ways and that far from deconstructing the frameworks of heteropatriarchy, or capitalism, or masculinity let us propose that his texts may actually reinforce ideological frameworks. Why is this position so hard to articulate? Why is such an option not on the academic menu?

Philip Tew has an essay on class in *Martin Amis: Postmodern and Beyond*, and we would hope that perhaps it could be an occasion for a foray into actually critiquing Amis. Tew moves closer to the kinds of critical questions we need to ask, pointing out that what we have in *Money* and *London Fields* are novels written by a thoroughly "middle-class writer,"[24] but beyond that he seems to pull his punches. Tew, offering a critique of Anne-Laure Fortin-Tournes's suggestion that *London Fields* is an "inversion of hierarchies and traditional humanist values" wonders, rightly I think, "whether such parodies of the working-class or proletarian male found in these novels can be sufficiently ironic to be reduced to generic, textual, or postmodern matters, especially when articulated from positions of cultural authority, whether represented by the novel form itself or from Amis's own self-evident class-specific position."[25] His thesis states that he "will dissect Amis's view of urban working-class masculinity and in doing so interrogate the conflicted and perhaps undermining position of the author in class terms."[26] Hopefully what will emerge will be a reading in which Amis's "class prejudices" will be seen as an "ideological viewpoint."[27] Tew begins by criticizing Lea and Schoene's reading of how Amis deconstructs masculinity pointing out that their analysis "remains profoundly universalistic and uncritical of the class blindness that haunts contemporary British fiction and academic exegesis."[28] I would agree with Tew that the satire and comedy in Amis do not serve to cleverly deconstruct power but are deployed in its service. As Knights points out regarding *London Fields* (and I would see it as being at the heart of *Money* too), the novel articulates "collective fears, haunting the moment of writing...the degradation of the city, the emergence of an alienated and violent underclass."[29]

Amis is often celebrated by critics for his subtle use of satire but the satire always seems directed at the working-class characters like Self and Talent. While the working classes are satirized for their addiction to pornography, or drink or money or violence, these criticisms do not extend to the authorial voices in the novels. I would argue therefore that Amis's satire functions through reestablishing and reinforcing a class system that is felt to be under threat from below. As Tew points out, "all these comic devices serve to evoke an authorial presence lurking in the text like some pantomime monster. They reestablish a privileged position based on authorial tradition and the finely calibrated nuances of the English class system."[30]

Tew's approach is surely a lot closer to how Amis's novels are consumed in situ. As he points out, "however pluralistic the novel becomes" it really doesn't matter because in the last instance "the concerns of the working-class characters seem narrow, their analysis of life cynical and blinkered."[31] In fact, as Tew points out, this is how many critics also see someone like Self. He is described as an "upstart" (Eric Korn), a "guttersnipe" (Karl Miller) and "the epitome of the racist, sexist homophobe" (Laura Doan), and a "*parvenu par excellence*."[32] Keith Talent fares no better, since he is seen as a "wife beater, rapist" (Penny Smith), a "working-class yob" (Brian Finney) and for Peter Stokes, he is simply an "overgrown Dickensian street urchin."[33] In an interview with John Haffenden, Amis makes it clear what he thinks of his "stupid narrator" (8) John Self: "I also mean to have him be stupefied by having watched too much television—his life is without sustenance of any kind—and that is why he is so fooled by everyone, he never knows what is going on. He has this lazy non-effort response that is wished on you by television—and by reading a shitty newspaper."[34] The result is that while these working-class characters are at the center of these novels, they are also relegated to the margins by the "superior, ironizing voice" of the author: "Both characters are apparently central and yet peripheral, relegated into parody and cliché by the demands of the text."[35] I think that most readers will readily admit that Self is simply made fun of by the novel, and by the end he is punished for his overreaching by being reduced to nothing. In essence he is punished for thinking that he could escape the parameters of his class. As Tew points out "The problem remains that the parody called Self is Amis's creation, his bauble, his toy."[36] In this way, the satire of Self doesn't spread out into Amis's own class, but remains quite simply "a vision of the unknowable other especially in class terms that rests upon the intellectual power of the middle-class writer."[37]

In *Money*, Self started out working class, tried to access a different world of money and power and failed miserably, and is reduced to a tramp by the end of the novel. As a political novel then, we find ourselves confronted with a very sad state of affairs. Even in *1984*, Orwell's Winston Smith felt that some hope lay in the proles if it wasn't for their love of drink, sex, and the lottery, and in this novel, published in 1984, Amis has finally abandoned even Orwell's slim hope. It is therefore not surprising, given Amis's own middle-class position, that he would say the following: "John Self in *Money* ends up as a tramp, and yet I feel that it's my first happy ending. I would hate like anything to be a tramp, but it felt right for him . . . he has no culture and has never read anything . . . He does end up dead in a way—outside the novel, outside money and *Money*, in endless and ordinary life . . . but he has no informing ideology of the way he lives."[38] The way the novel ends is a "happy ending" for the middle-class author, because the upstart has been returned from whence he came, like an alien that came out of nowhere, threatened to dismantle all that "we" hold near and dear, and then is safely jettisoned into outer space, kicked to the curb and into the arms of his working-class girlfriend, Georgina. In the same way that Baxter's violent nature is due to his "genes" in McEwan's *Saturday,* so the ending of *Money* can be interpreted as Self's fault, rather than that of class: as Tew points out, Amis has written it so that "Self reverts to type."[39]

If we fast forward to 1996, we see how nothing has changed in Amis's fiction during the twelve years since *Money* was published. In the end of *Money*, Self had told us that he gets a job from Fat Vince, minding an ice cream van in Hyde Park, and Fat Vince tells him that he might "have a future in the bouncing business."[40] Self thus returns in the short story "State of England" (1996) in the guise of Big Mal (the working classes are such *un grand mal*!) whose writing "left much to be desired, to put it mildly. Not what you'd call overly clever on the reading, neither" and who is "five feet nine in all directions" and makes "a pretty good living from his fists" as a night club bouncer.[41]

The narrator points out how Big Mal, with his "crinkly linen suit" and his cell phone, is perhaps finally free of class:

> ...all that prejudice against people such as himself was gone now. Or so they said. And maybe they were partly right. Mal could go into virtually any restaurant he liked and sit there surrounded by all these types squawking and honking away, and pick up a tab as dear as an air ticket. He could go to this or that place. And yet nobody could guarantee that he would *feel okay* in this or that place. Nobody could guarantee that, ever.[42]

So, far from living in a classless society, Big Mal is still held firmly in place by class. Paradoxically it is class, more than a smack in the gob, that has the power to make Big Mal squirm: the man "who grunted with a kind of assent when he saw a swung fist coming for his mouth, could nonetheless be laid out by the sight of a cocked pinkie. A! Always it was with him, every hour, like an illness, like a haunting."[43] Despite this, Big Mal lives in a thoroughly globalized culture where prejudice is supposed to be a thing of the past:

> So class and race and gender were supposedly gone (and other things were supposedly going, like age and beauty and even education): all the really automatic ways people had of telling who was better or worse—they were gone. Right-thinkers everywhere claiming that they were clean of prejudice, that in them the inherited formulations had at last been purged. This they had decided. But for those on the pointed end of the operation—the ignorant, say, or the ugly—it wasn't just a decision. Some of them had no new clothes. Some of them were still dressed in the uniform of their deficiencies. Some were still wearing the same old shit. Some would never be admitted...Now that prejudice was gone everyone could relax and concentrate on money. Which was fine if you had some.[44]

Big Mal, as the plot makes clear, has no money. A supposedly lucrative trip to America soon falls apart and he ends up doing some serious dumpster diving until his ex-wife gets him a ticket back to England, where he engages in a failed car-clamping business scheme in London with his pal, Fat Lol. This business venture comes to a halt when they get beaten up by a group of irate middle-class "operagoers" whose cars they have clamped.[45] It is this beating from a middle-class crowd the night before, which now finds him seriously weakened with a painful throbbing scar on his face as the story opens. Big Mal has come for his son's sports day and the fathers are lined up to run in a father's race. Big Mal, hampered by his injury and the bottle of whiskey he consumed the night before, doesn't stand a chance:

> It was the gunshot that made the herd stampede. Instantly Mal felt about nineteen things go at once. All the links and joins—hip, knee, ankle, spine—plus an urgent liquefaction on the side of the face. After five stumbling bounds the pain barrier was on him and wouldn't get out of the way. But the big man raced on, as you've got to do.[46]

So, throughout Amis's fiction the working class (fat and stupid as always) are always running, desperate to keep up, while the narrative voice and the reader can stand idly at a safe distance laughing at this comical display of working-class powerlessness from a class that always seems to be on its last legs.

Peter Ackroyd CBE

When it comes to recent literary criticism and literature, it would seem that representations of "history" have burgeoned, so that while there has been an attempt to make class impotent as a viable category of public discourse it seems to have been replaced, at the level of the novel, by a surplus of discourses about history. While this seems hopeful, and one would assume that we would see class being examined as a result, there is an absence of class amidst all of this "history." Partly, as David Cannadine points out, this is all due to the fashionable "linguistic turn" in which postmodern lenses can see language but not labor, and in which the real seems to have magically evaporated:

> [M]any historians no longer regard class as the study of the vexed relations between land, capital, and labor and of the political conflicts arising out of them. Instead, they see class as the study of the language that people used...Classes never actually existed as recognizable historical phenomena, still less as the prime motor of historical change. They were nothing more than rhetorical constructions....[47]

This is rather convenient and it is not surprising that bourgeois culture has sought to popularize this idea. Literary criticism has responded to this linguistic turn by turning to history, as if giving itself some kind of legitimate grounding, only to then turn around and dismantle that grounding in the name of postmodern freedom from oppressive grand narratives. As Del Ivan Janik makes clear, there seems to be "no end of history" when we look at the contemporary novel despite Baudrillard and Fukuyama's post-Hegelian assertion that history had come to an end.[48] In fact, this presence/absence of history is part of the same phenomenon: as history is moved out of the union meeting and into literary journals, so with the death of history comes the birth of endless textual "histories." So while "the past as a referent has been effaced" according to David Bennett, the shelves are full of novels where "the concept of history [is] alive and well."[49] Looking at a range of novelists, Janik suggests that these works "in their various ways…insist upon and demonstrate the validity, necessity, and difficulty of acknowledging, confronting and dealing with the past."[50] However, what I am concerned with is how the contemporary novel seems to be flooded with history while leaving the issue of class high and dry.

The easiest way into this problem is through the work of Peter Ackroyd. Coming from an openly theoretical perspective, Ackroyd's work is a site in which history is everywhere present, and yet where ideological tensions that emerge from that history have clearly been erased. Like Nietzsche's coins that remain in circulation long after the faces on them have worn off, history is Ackroyd's subject but *sans* ideological conflicts, or the question of class. In many ways Ackroyd's work clearly illustrates the ways in which his Yale school brand of deconstruction deals with class: we are expected to keep moving among the "signifiers" of history, while never getting to the "signified" of class. It would seem that it is "play" we are interested in, not work.

A clear example of how Ackroyd is produced by criticism can be seen in the way that he is read by David Leon Higdon. Higdon points out that Ackroyd doesn't see himself as a historical novelist or as a postmodernist but instead sees himself as part of the " 'English music' and Cockney visionary traditions."[51] Far from the working-class communities of the "Cockney" East End, Ackroyd returns from Yale University and publishes his "Notes for a New Culture" in which he openly celebrates the work being done by Derrida and Lacan while castigating the English for their addiction to the "related values of humanism and subjectivity."[52] Ackroyd soon after comes to be seen by critics as the practitioner of Hutcheon's "historiographic metafiction," a label which is attached to novels that are "both intensively self-reflexive and yet paradoxically also lay claim to historical events and personages."[53] As Higdon points out, Ackroyd clearly remarked, in a review of Timothy Mo, that "historical fiction" today is marked by "its disavowal both of conventional realism and self-conscious experimentalism."[54] The result is that Higdon applies no critical pressure on Ackroyd but instead operates as if the novels naturally speak for themselves. So *The Great Fire of London, The Last Testament of Oscar Wilde, Hawksmoor,* and *Chatterton* are all admiringly examined for the skill and artistry with which the author weaves his complex and subtle narratives. For example, discussing *Chatterton,* although it could be any one of Ackroyd's novels:

> In an allegorical moment, Merk attempts to strip the forged Chatterton portrait of its additions, only to discover an ever-receding original, but the layers begin to interact and slough away, collapsing the search for the original, truly an image of Derridean *differance.*[55]

Brian Finney draws out the same line:

> Ackroyd's repeated use of intertextuality in *Chatterton* constitutes the literary corollary to Derrida's theory of difference and the "trace." [Ackroyd's writing] offers a world of pure signifiers disconnected from any claim to absolute meaning. Writing, Ackroyd explained...has excised the last vestiges of meaning, since its form is now that of 'la signifiant de la signifiant' [the signifier of the signifier]...The written trace then is the original absence, an effect without a cause.[56]

However, this position leaves me with a strange sense of unease, since Ackroyd's texts are simply being celebrated and not critiqued, and I cannot resist the feeling that class or simply the ideological tensions that class inevitably produces have been removed along with those "last vestiges of meaning" and that we are now safely ensconced in a textual world where "histories" can be consumed without the troubling difficulties that history brings with it. Paradoxically, ideology always leaves a trace of class difference, but in Ackroyd all traces of class difference have been absorbed back into the textual play of *differance.*

Realism as a vehicle has clearly been dismantled in Ackroyd so that we find ourselves with a form of textually enforced pluralism in which past and present can mingle, overlap, and reappear, but no space is created for any grounding in the real that might throw this play into disarray. Laura Colombino traces this fluid treatment of the city to the (re)adoption of Situationist strategies in the 1980s:

> This idea was resumed from the early 1980s when many writers, artists, and critics tried to counteract "the capitalization of culture and

> privatization of society under Reagan, Thatcher, Kohl, and company—even as these transformations made such intervention more difficult"—precisely by the retrieval of situationist strategies.[57]

The result was "the recognition in the cityscape of a 'potential for playfulness' and an extension of bodily 'rhythms.' For many British writers following this tradition, London turned into a palimpsest bearing traces of the subject's corporality and creativity."[58] The other possibility, which we also see deployed in Ackroyd, is how the "enrichment of given meanings implied the conjuring up of memories, hidden presences, and past lives concealed in the urban text... (as in Ackroyd's *London: The Biography*)."[59]

The urban space, the home of the working classes, thus becomes a palimpsest of ungrounding in the hands of Ackroyd and thus the novels free themselves from the restrictions of realism and evaporate into the purely formal and aesthetic realms of linguistic and textual play. As Finney remarks: "Imaginary closure is achieved by purely imaginary means, means that defy any attempt to read the novel in a mode of realism. The ending [of *Chatterton*] celebrates the triumph of art and the autonomy of the literary work *over the contingencies of life and their historical representatives*."[60] Why then is this a triumph? To claim that we have arrived at a point where our separation from history is a "triumph" surely exposes the sad paradox at the heart of this celebration of Ackroyd's "historiographic metafiction." In drawing on Derrida and Lacan, Ackroyd has succeeded in providing the bourgeoisie with the ideological novel par excellence whereby the reader can be effectively insulated from the contradictions that history produces. The text is hence inoculated from any traces of realism that might dismantle the hermetic illusion of self-sufficiency, and history can be elaborately presented and layered with no anxiety that something unpleasant will show up to spoil the flaneur's slippery fun.

Moreover, this appearance of pluralism is clearly based on the firm exclusion of certain elements and this becomes clear in an interview when Ackroyd was asked why there are no women in his "English tradition" such as the "visionary" Virginia Woolf.[61] Ackroyd claims that while Woolf's *Orlando* would be a good example, he apologizes for the absence of such a writer, claiming that as a man he cannot write about women: "You see, I am always writing about myself, as I said to you, and I can't write about myself as a female."[62] But the response about his anxieties over Woolf's gender is a distraction. The buried anxiety here is that the disturbing presence of Woolf's obvious middle-class position, and not her gender, would make it impossible to see her as part of a smooth undifferentiated "Cockney tradition." These absences make it clear that Ackroyd's tradition is not all-encompassing, nor is it open and plural but is based on a particular ideological ground. A ground that is clearly that of the middle-class author, despite Ackroyd impressing on us that "[he] was brought up in a working-class area and lived in a council house."[63]

Tamas Benyei follows Wolfreys and Gibson in establishing that Ackroyd is "radically anti-referential and anti-mimetic" and agrees with Richard Todd that Ackroyd has a "gift for historical ventriloquy."[64] Benyei repeats the critical mantra that Ackroyd's work is one in which "the origin is not a single point but manifold . . . constantly being created by the very act of retrospection and remembering." A novel like *English Music* for example, is "pervaded by a constant vacillation between tradition as a quasi-mystical essence or centre and tradition as archive, a textual field of dissemination where the subject appears as a product or effect of language." *Hawksmoor* is similarly "pervaded by a fundamental ambiguity that is encapsulated in Derrida's insight, according to which it is impossible to divide 'spirit' from 'ghost' . . . ."[65] The novel thus becomes a place where

> the self is depicted as the repetition of past selves . . . and the novel indeed can be seen as a fabric of text, made up not of characters and events, but of the recurrence of innumerable scraps of language, although not in a way that the reader could systematize . . . there is no speaking subject behind these scraps . . . Detective Hawksmoor is made up of intertextual allusions and bits of preceding chapters.[66]

The result is a "postmodern novel that flaunts the textuality of its world" in which we have to stand by and watch the "annihilation of the subject on the ordinary plane, and the dissolution of the subject into the endless sea of textuality."[67] Moreover, neatly closing the gap between theory and practice (as we saw with Martin Amis) Ackroyd has written, in *Hawksmoor*, a novel in which "the mystical conception of the subject finds its unlikely echoes in post-structuralist theory . . . and the postmodern notion of disseminating intertextuality."[68] This is, I feel, the standard way of reading Ackroyd, and to be fair, this is not such much a critical posture as simply a careful retelling of what we actually find in the novel. The average reader who finishes *Hawksmoor* is quite aware that Detective Hawksmoor is on some level Dyer, and has no trouble in understanding, as they close the novel, that history is a spiral that repeats and overlaps and recycles itself. On one level these "critical" assessments of Ackroyd, from Wolfreys to Benyei are not so much a radical theoretical practice, as simply a theoretical echo of the novels' concerns. This closed loop of novel and theory also creates a text that is seemingly fenced off from the real and becomes critically unassailable. The fluidity of the postmodern novel is thus simultaneously its badge of honor and its protective armor. As Jameson points out: "As an ideology which is also a reality, the 'postmodern' cannot be disproved insofar as its fundamental feature is the radical separation of all levels and voices whose recombination in their totality could alone disprove it."[69]

Alex Link's reading of Ackroyd's *Hawksmoor* reveals how the complicity between postmodern fiction and postmodern theory produces rather thin results. Link establishes that there is a tendency to read *Hawksmoor* as a novel about "undecidability" and points out how Jeremy Gibson and Julian Wolfreys are wary of attempting "any kind of thematic reading" of the novel and how "Susana Onega and Roger Salomon are in agreement that the novel is an unmitigated rejection of Enlightenment reason."[70] This, he feels, is too easy, and instead he aims to show how Ackroyd is using Dyer and Wren and Hawksmoor to raise not a simple question of postmodern undecidability and slippage between past and present, but that *Hawksmoor* is a text which reveals that history is alive and kicking and, like Hawksmoor's churches, stand as uncanny reminders in the present of a past that is still with us, and challenging us. However, despite Link's promising desire to move beyond the regular postmodern reading of Ackroyd, his work ends up reproducing another variation of postmodern theory and its disavowal of anything remotely connected to some form of dialectical historical change. Link argues that "...working in complicity, both Dyer and Wren produce Lefebvrean abstract spatialities to repress, in processes of abjection, excess in the form of the feminine, the popular, the poor, the body, and the corpse."[71] These repressive abstract spaces are then transformed once we rediscover them in the twentieth century: "Over time, however, Dyer's churches become sites of potential opposition as they, too, become repressed sites in the cityscape and, unhinged from any coherent system of order, come to function in twentieth-century London as uncanny Lefebvrean absolute spaces."[72] The difference is that while the Lefebvrean abstract spatialities are repressive, the absolute space, predictably valorized by the postmodern theorist, is one whereby the space exists somehow beyond capital and is somehow magically free to release a multiplicity of voices that then interrogate the oppressive abstract spatialities:

> Henri Lefebvre's distinction between absolute and abstract spatiality is entirely salient to an understanding of Hawksmoor's spatial politics. Absolute space, Lefebvre explains, is made up of sanctified or consecrated "fragments of nature" existing *outside of capitalist relations* and governed by the logic of natural processes. (48) Abstract space is the product of a homogenizing power. It is the institutional ordering, or synthesis, of heterogeneous spaces, largely through capitalist relations, which simultaneously forecloses on history and nature, making them mediated "nostalgia" and "regret" respectively. (49–51) Abstract space is space whose political inscription tends to be naturalized through the discursive mechanisms of power.[73]

What is emerging here is a comforting picture of Ackroyd as the liberator of history, an author who is putting history into practice, and through the form of the novel is making visible the oppressive abstract spaces that limit us, providing us with a key to the real by showing us the living absolute spaces that, since they exist "outside of capitalist relations," can thereby set us free as plurality and difference flood in. Link says that the oppressive abstract space is maintained through the " 'illusion of natural simplicity' or 'opacity,' the 'realistic' illusion which lifts the object in question—a space, a monster, a Gothic scene—out of reach by declaring it monadic, natural, monolithic, and impervious to analysis."[74]

However, while this analysis may be appropriate for architecture, the analogy to fiction is misleading. Bradford suggests, as in Benyei, that Ackroyd's work creates "a spiral of questions: the past and the present begin to become unnervingly similar and our notion of the present as a secure and by implication, superior perspective is undermined."[75] This sense that the reader is "undermined" in trying to establish some historical footing makes Ackroyd's work not so much a Lefebvrean absolute space, the exact opposite: it is Ackroyd's novels that are Lefebvrean *abstract* spaces that are "impervious to analysis," and in a typically postmodern sleight of hand, become a form of empty realism, or what Jameson terms a "pseudoexperience"[76] of history which, to rewrite Link's earlier quote "lifts the object in question—[Ackroyd's novel]—out of reach by declaring it monadic, natural, monolithic and impervious to analysis."[77]

Link treats these absolute spaces as the return of the repressed, that ghostlike, haunt and critique the present:

> [they] reemerge as uncanny, counterrational spaces. Thus *Hawksmoor* offers an interesting sophistication of Lefebvre's sense of absolute spatialities by distinguishing the novel's eighteenth-century churches, which are instruments of a systematic disorder, from the same churches in the twentieth century, where they emerge as a return of the repressed that ruptures the urban fabric.[78]

But it is clear that what is repressed by postmodern theory is the grand narratives, as the monad comes to replace Hegel. Link claims that the novel shows "the ability of popular voices to open up and to take advantage of the disjunctions in urban spatiality generated by competing discourses of power... the transformation of the churches into uncanny, absolute spaces... offers the churches as sites *relatively free from capitalist relations*, opening them to alternate, local counterknowledges."[79] But where are these popular voices in the novel itself? And what are we to make of "popular voices" that are simultaneously protesting against the oppressive "capitalist abstract spatialities" and yet somehow are already magically "free from capitalist relations"?

Having suggested that we can move beyond a simple postmodern reading of Ackroyd, Link ends up reaffirming and rehearsing the usual framework:

> *Hawksmoor* suggests at least the following three things: first, that the organization of urban spaces is driven by inherently masculinist processes of abjection; second, that the unruly play of the popular opens urban spaces through the grotesque, foregrounding the uncanny materiality of London's monumental signifiers and raising the uneasy possibility that historical progress is an illusion; and third, that the complexity of urban codes opens a space for a multiplicity of possible urban histories that are at once textual constructs and political necessities.[80]

So here we see the same happy ending that postmodern theory is repeatedly drawn to: the monolithic grand narrative of the masculine is oppressive, the diversity and plurality of popular voices opens up the urban space resulting in the truth that historical progress is just an "illusion," and that finally the complexity of the urban opens up a multiplicity of *histories* to replace the "abstract capitalist spatiality" of some nasty monolithic history.

But paradoxically, while this is something that postmodern criticism may wish to say about Ackroyd, his own comments on these matters show that he is far from concerned with dismantling grand narratives, and in fact is openly celebratory not of the ludic and the undecidable, but is firmly rooted in a religious *grand recit:* Catholicism. While asserting that he is not a "practicing Catholic," his early education by "Benedictine monks in Ealing" did leave a mark on him, which emerges in "other forms" and, as he says, "if you are formed in a Catholic education, you imbibe a sense of the sacred which never actually leaves you."[81] He then goes on to distance himself from the much lauded *Notes for a New Culture*, dismissing it as a work that came out of the "impatience of youth."[82] In contrast what he stresses is the "latent Catholicism of the English race": "England has been Catholic for 1,500 years and has only been Protestant for 400, and I am very interested to rediscover the Catholic roots of English culture…."[83] He places himself at this juncture in opposition to the group of what he sees as Protestant writers who have emerged from programs such as the writing program at "East Anglia University" (which would include Bradbury, McEwan, Ishiguro, and Tremain) claiming that it is a "very secular Protestant consciousness which comes across, [from the program] which I don't find appetizing at all."[84] What they lack, he feels, is a "sense of transcendence."[85] Seeing himself as opposed to "atheists, like Fowles," his desire to play with history and time is being driven more by Christ, than Derrida: "I was thinking about people who ask me why I play with time and history. Well I suppose it is a Catholic consciousness trying to formulate faith in a different way. Trying to give the sense of the sacred some new dimension. But what this is I don't know."[86] In the light of these comments it is now clear why the *church* as an institution (and not just architecture) is at the center of *Hawksmoor*: "You could not have Prayed last night, *said I*, as the Observations recommended. No, *he replied,* and I have lost my compass as a Penance for it."[87]

This religious side of Ackroyd seems to be a rather hidden arena of Ackroyd criticism, and understandably so, as his Catholic faith is surely embarrassing to liberal intellectuals and critics who would want to see Ackroyd as the poster child for postmodern fiction and plurality, and not as a Christian writer who is quite happily holding on to the grand narrative of religion. The way that this embarrassment has been dealt with is by avoiding mentioning religion directly in critical discussions of Ackroyd, and instead to phrase it as a concern with "cosmic myth" and "storytelling" that can cross, mix, and unite historical periods into a unified (but somehow plural) framework that is, and yet is not, a grand narrative. So for example, in Dominic Head, Ackroyd's religious rough edges are neatly swept under the poststructuralist carpet:

> The "frame of origin", of course, is quite other than a moment of origin. Rather, the novel [*First Light*] is projecting a Whitmanesque order of cosmic communion in which all matter is conjoined in a process of continual recycling. In this sense the reflections of the recuperating Damian Fall, which conclude the book, carry a summative authority: "why is it that we think of a circular motion as the most perfect? Is it because it has no beginning and no end?" he wonders. (328) The succour that this cosmic philosophy is shown to offer does not entirely overshadow a sense of personal history. It is partly in tune with the evocation of the past as a determining feature of the present, and with the suggestion of a kind of constructed "race memory" as a framework for continuity.[88]

A race memory for the "English" it may be, but one rooted in Catholicism? What about a "class memory"? On what "cosmic" grounding could that be located? This same desire to see in Ackroyd a strange mixture of Derrida and the "cosmic" is also found in Tamas Benyei: "the mystical conception of the subject [in Ackroyd] finds its unlikely echoes in poststructuralist theory, and the quasi-mystical notion of a spiritual tradition merges with the postmodern notion of disseminating intertextuality."[89]

Fredric Jameson has noted the contemporary tendency to create "historical" novels, and that while modernism was concerned with time (as in Proust, Joyce, and Woolf), the postmodern has gone in the opposite direction and claimed "space" as its territory: thus we have witnessed an explosion of "wild imaginary genealogies and novels that shuffle historical figures and names like so many cards from a finite deck." This is all part and parcel of the discovery by postmodern historians that "all is fiction...and that there can never be a correct version, the end of master narratives...along with the recovery of alternate histories in the past...."[90] What we see in novelists like Ackroyd is what Jameson refers to as "a semblance of historical verisimilitude [which] is vibrated into multiple alternate patterns...which offer postmodern writers the most remarkable and untrammeled movement of invention [and thereby] convey the feel of the real past better than any of the 'facts' themselves."[91] Moreover, Jameson feels that because these novels chime in nicely with postmodern theories, "[s]uch fabulations—[are] not unexpectedly cheered on by a whole generation of ideologues complacently but with relish announcing the death of the referent, if not the end of history itself...."[92] The result is that we can experience history, or a simulacrum of it, without having to bang our heads against the messy problems thrown up by history, or as Jameson puts it: "The new free play with the past...—the delirious nonstop monologue of its postmodern revision into so many in-group narratives—is obviously equally allergic to the priorities and commitments, let alone the responsibilities, of the variously tediously committed kinds of partisan history."[93]

However, Jameson feels that such fictions can also be seen in another light, which is to say that the desire to unleash a Pandora's box of histories is merely a symptom of a historical period that finds itself suffering from historical blockages that cannot be satisfied in the real, and that as a result have been forced back into the space of fiction. Brian Finney has pointed out that "Ackroyd's attitude to the past is paradoxical: he has, he has said, both 'a reverence for...the past' and a continual need to 'reinvent it, recreate it, almost destroy it, by making up stuff.'"[94] We can now see that rather than reading Ackroyd's fabulations as simply exercises in postmodern play, we can read them as symptoms of a postmodern malaise and a buried, or misdirected, utopian desire. Quite simply, in the words of Jameson "the making up of unreal history is a substitute for the making of the real kind."[95] The historical desire for praxis has been repressed by the current postmodern love of the spatial textual surface, and in their love of fabulation, such postmodern novelists inadvertently reveal an urge to bring history to life. For Jameson then, this fashion for "unreal history"

> mimetically expresses the attempt to recover that power and praxis by way of the past and what must be called fancy rather than imagination. Fabulation...is no doubt the symptom of social and historical impotence, of the blocking of possibilities that leaves little option but the imaginary...agency here steps out of the historical record itself into the process of devising it...Narrative invention here thus by way of its very implausibility becomes the figure of a larger possibility of praxis, its compensation but also its affirmation in the form of projection and mimetic reenactment.[96]

At the end of his interview with Susan Onega, Ackroyd tells her that he is working on a new novel "set in the future, which should be a

Catholic England in 300 years hence."[97] Sadly then, Ackroyd's textual politics are symptomatic of the current blockages to historical thinking, revealing that Ackroyd's "Cockney visionary tradition" can only see as far as a future centered on what is surely, as James Joyce made clear, one of the most debilitating of all grand narratives: Catholicism.

Terry Eagleton has also pointed to these ideological problems in Ackroyd's work. In his review of *Albion,* Eagleton makes it clear that the problem with Ackroyd's version of English history is that it is "in typical postmodernist style, history as political invention" and that the retreat into aesthetics (which Finney saw as a "triumph") is in fact a denial of the very history that Ackroyd claims he is excavating:

> The English imagination, Ackroyd writes, "takes the form of a ring or a circle. It is endless because it has no beginning and no end. . . ." The verbal infelicity of a circle being endless because it has no end betrays the shoddy sentimentalism of the thought. Like all nationalist mythology, *Albion,* needs violently to erase actual history from the nation's narcissistic self-imaging.[98]

We are left then with a novelist, celebrated by the canon whose work leaves us not with a history to work from, but a chimera and a simulacrum of history, and with no ground on which to build even the most tentative subject position.

Hanif Kureishi CBE

John Kirk has made it clear that Hanif Kureishi "could not be described by any stretch of the imagination as a working-class writer," yet literary critics insist that his work is somehow vital in helping us to see through ideology.[99] Dominic Head reveals how easily class can slip between critical fingers when he suggests that *The Buddha of Suburbia* reveals a protagonist who is representative not of a particular lower middle-class background, but broadens this to make Kureishi appear as the representative of "a *culture* in transition," with Karim as the embodiment of "suburban multicultural identity."[100] Such comments result in the evaporation of class identities. Steven Connor has suggested that Kureishi has an ambivalent relationship to the typical novel of "class mobility" as exemplified in the novels of Braine, Sillitoe, and Drabble in that his texts have a tendency both to "signal and decline" an allegiance to this tradition. The ambivalence comes from the fact that Kureishi's desire to "celebrate hybridity" cannot be incorporated into the form of these class-based novels.[101] Kureishi has even announced that his influences are much more middle class than he would like to admit: "Looking back on the novel—though I might not like to admit it—I was influenced more by books like *Lucky Jim* and early Evelyn Waugh...." The result is that *The Buddha of Suburbia* essentially abandons any central focus on class for the bourgeois tradition of the bildungsroman, albeit one updated to include a multicultural protagonist and, in Head's words, an "essentially transitional world-view."[102] Valid and viable working-class participants in his texts are conspicuously absent. As John Kirk points out, in *My Beautiful Launderette* the bedridden, alcoholic figure Old Papa becomes the impotent figure of the Old Left: "The 'death' of socialism is thus echoed in Papa's lament that 'the working-class are such a disappointment to me.'"[103] This same middle-class distance from the working class shows up in *The Buddha of Suburbia* in the form of the Communist organizer, Terry, that Karim meets at Pyke's theater. Terry throws scorn on Pyke's world: for him it's just "a lot of reformist and flatulent 'left wing' politics! Its plump actors pretending to be working-class, when their fathers are neuro-surgeons...."[104] However, this radical position is undermined in the novel, as Karim tries to seduce Terry to see if his "politics" would stretch as far as hopping in to bed with him. The same rejection of any extremes is also dismissed in the novel through the use of Charlie. Charlie's middle-class background immediately qualifies him for hero worship in the opening chapters, but his drug addiction and sexual excesses mean that the novel soon undermines his middle-class decadence.

This novel is often treated, via some combination of Stuart Hall, Homi Bhabha, and Judith Butler's theories, as revealing how the issue of "performance" is at the heart of any successful postcolonial strategy. For example, Anthony Ilona tells us that in *The Buddha of Suburbia* "different identities are not only celebrated here but performed on a huge scale."[105] Yet the novel makes clear that these different identities are not "celebrated" at all but are being rejected as artificial and empty. By the end of the novel, Karim has rejected everything else in favor of what he feels is the only thing that was "worth doing": being a writer.[106] Rather than making him into some kind of fluid postcolonial self built out of a performance, Karim says of his writing: "I felt more solid myself, and not as if my mind were just a kind of cinema...."[107] By the end of the novel, in true Proustian fashion he has become the author who will write the book we have just finished.

Karim does not desire some fluid hybrid self at all, in fact what he wants is the solid identity that being an author provides, which also includes distancing himself from those around him. Interestingly, the only other thing that is not mocked as fake in the book is Jamila's political engagement with feminism: her sense of political commitment, which Karim cannot share, means that she too can "live a useful life in white England."[108] However, the author Karim, who misses all the political demonstrations, finally undermines her political identity by calling her a "supercilious bitch" (216).

Anthony Ilona's work sums up the standard way of reading Kureishi's oeuvre.[109] Ilona begins with two excerpts from George Orwell's essay "The Lion and the Unicorn: Socialism and the English Genius" that focus on his comments regarding nation/nationality. Ilona, while skipping over the socialism part of Orwell's essay (to which we shall return later), presents Orwell as the ogre of British letters whose horrid views of England must be dismissed if we are to make room for what Kureishi terms a "new way of being British."[110] Ilona sets Orwell up as offering a rather reductive model of Englishness in which only two modes are possible: Ilona feels that Orwell offers one model of England that is "essential" ("suet-puddings" and "red pillar-boxes" that enter your soul) while the other is "relational" whereby Englishness is denoted only through contact with those who are not English (the Englishman encountering the "European").[111] Rather than exploring how these ideas are linked to Orwell's main discussion of socialism and the struggle against Fascism, Ilona dismisses Orwell's positions since for him "both observations are burdened with fallacious notions of interaction and diversity."[112] The problem, Ilona feels, is that Orwell's ideas of the nation relies on a "mass conception of unilateral sameness within a group or community of individuals," which for a card-carrying postmodernist like Ilona smacks of a nasty degree of positivism, and a lack of fluidity. Ilona feels that Orwell therefore "fails" due to a reliance on "timeless" cultural traditions and "rigid principles of social classification." The result is that Orwell's thinking is apparently held back by his lack of postmodern hipness: "Thus, the development of a genuinely interactive vision of British national identity... is here retarded by a fixation with the need to legitimate an internal oneness in the mass-conception of 'Britishness.' "[113] Unlike the fluid flexibility that Kureishi will supposedly be articulating, Orwell is thus seen to be trapped by his own "totalizing delusion." In opposition to this essentialism, we are presented with the stock-in-trade reading of Kureishi who offers us a "mutable concept of nationalism" that can "recognize internal diversity" and is in "direct contrast to essentialist notions of British national identity," and provides us with a "new way of being British" (Kureishi's phrase) that is a "less insular and more flexible approach towards notions of diversity...."[114] However, as much as Ilona would like to see Kureishi lining up *against* Orwell, if we read "The Rainbow Sign" we see that Kureishi actually agrees with Orwell over the question of essentialism: "It is strange to realize...how British you are, the extent to which, as Orwell says: 'the suet puddings and the red pillar boxes have entered into your soul.' It isn't *that* that you wanted to find out. But it is part of what you do find out...."[115]

In the struggle between Orwell and Kureishi, Ilona feels that the winner is obviously Kureishi whose fiction is not retarded by the ogre of essentialism. Kureishi therefore "purposefully restages and circumscribes the contradictory motion in nationalist discourse between positivist assertion (essentialism) and negative reinforcement (relationalism) in his work."[116] Moreover, not only the essentialism of Englishness, but also the essentialism of Islam has to be condemned if this fluid diverse bourgeois self is to be victorious. Ilona looks at Kureishi's essay "The Rainbow Sign" in which Kureishi makes it clear that the rise of Islam in Pakistan in the 1970s is also a nonviable position as it also, like Orwell's socialism, slips into a " 'return to ignorance' and essentialism...for its reliance on 'revelation' and 'scripture' rather than reason" (97). So, like Karim distancing himself from Terry and Charlie, Kureishi is distancing himself from both ideological positions in that conventional Englishness and Islam, according to Ilona, suffer from "an irrational principle of intolerance towards human diversity and mixture" (98).

Drawing on Rushdie's idea in *Imaginary Homelands* that we must accept the "provisional nature of all truths, all certainties," we are now in a position to release the ideal postmodern bourgeois subject that Kureishi has been building in his fiction (Ibid). The usual terms are scattered for our delight: "continual relocation...oscillatory...provisional veracity...caught between two worlds...fragmented memories" (Ibid). Like Rushdie, Kureishi offers us a self that avoids the "discursive shackles of nationalism with its contradictory doctrine of *e pluribus unum*" and which also "undermines bounded notions of identity and nation" that displaces "the idea of inward homogeneity and stability and timelessness" (99). This self thus offers a "viable, more flexible alternative" and a way out of the "Orwellian predicament." The outcome is a "revitalized and broader self-definition"

(102–103). Of course, while critics have seen this as a sign of a "culture in transition" as Head said, all we are really seeing is a revitalization of the bourgeois self, and the self-examination of a bourgeois culture in transition.

Kureishi is often read as offering the reader a celebration of heterogeneity and difference. But what does this reading represent, and despite its seeming all-inclusiveness, what is it excluding? Ilona's postmodern multicultural reading of Kureishi creates a model in which Orwell's Englishness and by implication his socialism are bracketed off with Islamic fundamentalists on the one hand and then following a strict binarism, the fluid postmodern "viable" performative self is offered as the way out of the cul-de-sac of "Islamosocialism." There are obviously glaring concerns here. The first concerns the way that both Orwell's socialism and Islamic fundamentalism are seen as threats to the fluid bourgeois subject that global capitalism requires. While they may be a seamless threat as far as bourgeois ideology is concerned they are surely not to be conflated. From the point of view of the Left, Islam, like Christianity, is surely a block to proletarian consciousness and shares virtually no values in common. Yet for bourgeois ideology, it becomes a very convenient (and economical) historical moment in which one enemy can be used to take out another. So while Orwell saw the need for a thoroughly unified Socialist England to keep England from being swamped by Fascism, in a post-grand narrative world, Islam/Fascism/Socialism are now all grouped together as rigid "totalizing delusions" that can be successfully countered by the development of a microlevel of identity politics in which isolated, fragmented selves, produce a nomadic nation without roots or structure thus preventing Islamist fundamentalism or indeed, socialism from ever taking root. Eagleton has reminded us, however, that the fluid postmodern self only works as long as the culture stays the same, but if Fascism should return in the future this "flexible, fragmented" self will be unable to present any form of resistance. For Eagleton, in the face of a resurgence of Fascism, postmodernism's "distaste for ideas of solidarity and disciplined organization, its lack of any adequate theory of political agency: all these would tell heavily against it."[117]

While *The Buddha of Suburbia* has become a canonical text in academic circles, Kureishi's *The Black Album* has drawn much less critical attention and *The Body* even less. The reason, I think, is that these novels expose something that *The Buddha of Suburbia* keeps in the margins. In *The Buddha of Suburbia* (essentially a comedy),

Karim Amir floats along adopting and then rejecting one false self after another until he arrives at "himself" and becomes a writer. The novel is thus easily absorbed into the Western tradition of the bildungsroman and can be read to reflect, as we have seen with Ilona, as a simple moment of transition to a new Britain. But in *The Black Album* the protagonist Shahid finds himself seriously torn between contesting ideological positions and in the end these other positions are not resolved by the introduction of any kind of fluid self, but are simply rejected outright, and in their place he turns to his inner life and love affair with his white literature professor Deedee Osgood. As with Ilona's reading of Orwell, this novel duplicates the bourgeois assumption that what must be rejected outright are both the Left as well as the new Right of Islamic fundamentalism, leaving Shahid with only his love affair with Deedee as a marker of his new viable self. However, this is not so much a resolution of cultural contradictions as a retreat and a withdrawal from the public sphere and the problems that it poses, and the novel thereby reveals that this flexible self, when confronted with the political, can only withdraw. Shahid, and the novel itself, cannot cope with these ideological contradictions and so shuts them down by moving Shahid into the personal, private space of the body and sexual desire.

Symbolically renting a room in a large house next to the fundamentalist poet Riaz, the student Shahid is pulled into the Pakistani community at his college and its engagement with Islamic fundamentalism. A barely disguised Salman Rushdie affair becomes a catalyst for a student protest and Shahid is reluctantly drawn into a rather ugly college demonstration at which a copy of "the book" is burnt. Shahid cannot fully go along with this rigid belief system and partly out of his love for Deedee betrays the group and his racial community:

> He felt ashamed. He was someone who couldn't join in...Looking across the crowd at Chad's expression, he was glad of that. He never wanted his face to show such ecstatic rigidity! The stupidity of the demonstration appalled him. How narrow they were, how unintelligent, how...embarrassing it all was![118]

He also gets into trouble with them because while typing up Riaz's Islamic poetry, he has been changing some of the lines and is criticized for being a "double agent" (246). Although the Islamic position has been eliminated as a space of extremism and intolerance, so the novel also serves up a dismal example of what the text sees as another risky (and failed) "totalizing delusion": socialism. While this is implicit in *The Buddha of Suburbia*, here in *The Black Album* it is laid out for all to see. Shahid is having an affair with Deedee Osgood while she is still living with her husband Dr. Brownlow, another professor from Shahid's college. Brownlow is fully aware that Deedee is sleeping with her young student but is presented as a weak and impotent figure of the Left (like Old Papa in *My Beautiful Laundrette*) who has given up caring. Having been a lackluster figure throughout the novel, he gets involved in the student book burning protest, and so we can safely dismiss him as a holder of any viable self, since his socialism has now merged with Islamic extremism. Brownlow is a Marxist, and he becomes the only comic figure in this otherwise rather serious novel, and while his past may have been politically committed, his present has returned as farce. His bookshelf tells us all we need to know: "There were books on China and the Soviet Union...books on Marcuse, Miliband, Deutscher, Sartre, Benjamin, E. P. Thompson...books on Marxism and history, Marxism and freedom, Marxism and democracy...." (249).

Toward the end of the novel Shahid and Brownlow meet each other at Deedee's house, and Brownlow has been made "redundant" for participating in the book burning student protest (250). Shahid tells Brownlow that he is "just a weak bastard." Brownlow responds:

> you i-idiot, everything I believed in has turned into shit. There we were, right up to the end of the seventies, arguing about society after the r-revolution, the nature of the dialectic, the meaning of history. And all the while, we debated in our journals, it was being taken from us. The British people didn't want e-education, housing, the a-arts, justice, equality...they're a bunch of fucking greedy, myopic c-cunts.
>
> "The working-class?"
>
> "Yes!"
>
> "A bunch of cunts"
>
> "Yes"...he was sobbing. "I can't say they've betrayed us—though I think it, I do! It's not true, not true! They've b-b-betrayed themselves!...C-c-cut my throat. Please...no direction home! [he was] gibbering like Gogol's madman awaiting the straitjacket...." (254–255)

Dr. Brownlow starts rummaging through his possessions searching for his copy of "Let it Be" so that he can listen to "Hey Jude": "Shahid turned and trotted forward a few steps, as if he were about to take a penalty. He aimed and gave Brownlow a ferocious kick up the arse. Brownlow sprang forward like a diver and sprawled over the books, his head terminating in an empty cardboard box. Thus enclosed, he lay groaning, 'But it says everything...everything!' He made no effort to move" (256).

When Deedee and Shahid return to the house, which is no longer really safe since Riaz and his fundamentalist friends are out to make Deedee pay for calling the police on them during the book burning, Shahid is happy that "[a]t least Brownlow's fucked off for good" (273). Deedee and Shahid think they are safe for the moment, but Strapper, Shahid's white underclass drug dealer shows up. While they have been on generally good terms throughout the novel, Strapper betrays Deedee and Shahid. Once he has been let inside the house by Shahid, he then surreptitiously opens the door and lets in Riaz, Sadiq, and Chad who are after Shahid for betraying them. Strapper, who decides that he is angry with people like Deedee for having a nice big house ("middle class and poncy") sets fire to the curtains: "It's going up, it's going up! Fuck everything! Fuck you all!" Shahid's brother Chili, rather worse for wear due to an out of control cocaine habit, steps in and threatens Riaz: " 'Fuck off,' he ordered the others. 'Leave my brother, otherwise this brother gets his gullet split' " (275–279). Deedee has extinguished the fire, and the angry Islamists flee into the night. United by drugs not race, Chili and Strapper go off together to score cocaine, conveniently leaving Deedee alone with Shahid. Having reestablished peace in the house they go to bed, and the next day they decide to "go away" (285). While making coffee, Shahid reflects on the events of the past few weeks:

> How could anyone confine themselves to one system or creed? Why should they feel they had to? There was no fixed self, surely our several selves melted and mutated daily? There had to be innumerable ways of being in the world. He would spread himself out, in his work and in love, following his curiosity. (Ibid)

There is no need for any theory to explain what is happening here. Shahid is simply restating a theoretical truism of postmodern/postcolonial theory as we have seen in Ilona and others. However, a fluid self, as Eagleton points out, is not a challenge to the bourgeois self, it is the bourgeois self and is just the kind of self that multinational capital desires: to paraphrase and rewrite Shahid: "There are no fixed markets, why should capitalism limit itself to one market or one country. Capitalism must spread itself out...Following its profits."

Earlier in the novel Shahid had said that "he would embrace uncertainty" and this becomes the credo of the novel's resolution

(238). Yet this denouement has been worked through in rather stark ways. There are clear areas of the novel that Shahid shuttles between and when the undesirable areas have been exposed as limiting he simply rejects them. So Brownlow and his socialism can be easily mocked and kicked up the arse, Chili's love of money, business, and fast cars can be dismissed as it slips into cocaine abuse, Strapper and the white underclass are not a viable community either, and the extremism of Riaz and the fundamentalists is clearly rejected. All that is left is the small corner of Shahid's own private life and his relationship with his white middle-aged college professor. All collective action (the Left and the Right having been blurred with Brownlow and Riaz) has been dismissed and all that remains is the bourgeois inner life and the fluid self of pleasure and personal desire. To close this novel with a happy ending the couple simply "go away" from London and its racial and class tensions: "they left..." on the train to some unspecified seaside resort where they will "spend the weekend in the cheap bed-and-breakfasts of a seaside town, walking on the wet beach, lying wrapped up like pensioners in deck chairs on the pier...." (285–286). As the train leaves Victoria, Deedee pulls out a bottle of wine and they toast their victory over the oppressive forces that tried to fence them in: "He looked out of the window; the air seemed to be clearer.... They looked across at one another as if to say, what new adventure is this? 'Until it stops being fun' she said. 'Until then' he said."[119]

It is clear that the fluid self that is being celebrated here is not really at all social, but is in fact antisocial. This new self that somehow represents a "culture in transition" is simply the reshaping of a bourgeois self and the redrawing of its boundaries. It is powerless to resolve any social tensions and can only slither around them as it mutates and polymorphously engages in its endless play of differences. This fluid self, so celebrated by postmodern and postcolonial theory is not a challenge to capitalist ideology but actually shows us that ideology at work. As Eagleton makes clear "[c]apitalism is naturally anti-foundational, melting all that is solid into air [and] [a]nti-foundationalism reflects a hedonist, pluralist, open-ended culture...which can also yield real market benefits."[120] The paradox here is clear, as Eagleton makes explicit: "[a] pluralist culture must in any case be exclusivist, since it must shut out the enemies of pluralism,"[121] and while Shahid may feel that he is finally "free" by the end of his experiences, and that he will now live in "uncertainty," we should not forget, as Eagleton reminds us, that "[i]dentity politics is one of the most uselessly amorphous of all political categories."[122]

Raymond Williams has also suggested that a common culture cannot be built on such a thin thread and that it could only be laid out, as Eagleton says

> by politically securing what he rather evasively calls the "means of community", by which he means, in effect, socialist institutions. And this certainly involves common belief, commitment and practice. Only through a fully participatory democracy, including one which regulated material production, could the channels of access be fully opened to give vent to this cultural diversity. To establish genuine cultural pluralism, in brief, requires concerted socialist action. It is precisely this that contemporary culturalism fails to see. William's position would no doubt seem to it quaintly residual, not to say positively archaic; the problem in fact is that we have yet to catch up with it.[123]

By way of a coda, I would like to consider why it is that Kureishi's novel *The Body* has failed to make it into the current theoretical/critical canon.[124] What is it about this novel that leaves critics somewhat silent, while *The Buddha of Suburbia* produces no end of criticism? In *The Body*, the openly middle-class protagonist, suitably named Adam, is a writer in his "mid-sixties."[125] Like the canonized Kureishi, Adam is also famous. Early in the novel he bumps into a student at a party who tells him "We're doing you. You're on the syllabus" (6). This middle-class milieu is also reinforced as we hear how his wife Margot is a "counselor, training now to be a therapist" while their children, having left home, are training to be "a doctor" and a "film editor" (2). Tired of his middle-class life and his tired body, he gets involved in a medical procedure that enables him to switch his brain (and thus his mind) into a younger body. He tells his wife and family that he is going on holiday, and pays for a "short-term body rental" (23). It is also clear in the novel that such a procedure is only available to the rich, since there are "people who would never be able to afford new bodies or even to feed adequately the one they already had" (128). He wakes up in his new body and is happy to be "a new combination. Anyway, hybrids were hip" (44). Adam, who now calls himself Leo, decides that the "identity theorists are going to be busy worrying about this one" and is happy to be "beyond good and evil" (44–45). The self that he has chosen is "neither white nor dark but lightly toasted, with a fine, thick penis and heavy balls. [He] would at last have the body of an Italian footballer" (27–28). He ends up traveling to the Greek Islands and after becoming a kind of gigolo/massage therapist for a group of "middle-aged, middle-class" (73) women at a spa, becomes bored with this empty, free-floating existence and decides that he wants to go back home to his old body. The rejection of the postmodern aesthetic of the fluid self is made clear when Leo is talking to Matte who works for the medical company behind the procedure. Matte is excited about the future: "Soon everyone'll be talking 'bout this. There'll be a new class, an elite, a superclass of superbodies... Bingo! What do you want to be today!" Leo is not so sure: "If the idea of death itself is dying, all the meanings... have changed. We seem to have replaced ethics with aesthetics." To which Matte replies: "Bring on the new meanings! You're a conservative, then." Leo's reply is telling: "I didn't think so...." (114).

Leo realizes that he cannot stay on the Greek Islands forever, like Odysseus captured by Circe and made into an immortal, and so, like Odysseus, he decides that he wants to go "home" to his old body and his middle-class life:

> I'm not sure why, but I returned to the part of London I knew. I felt safer... it had been a mistake to "hire" a body for six months... I missed my old life... I was in limbo, a waiting room in which there was no reality but plenty of anxiety... I missed me. (127–135)

Tragically, his original body has been destroyed, and rather than being captured by the clinic he runs off into the night. The novel ends with the protagonist cut off from his middle-class life and cut off from his old self: "I was a stranger on earth, a nobody with nothing, belonging nowhere, a body alone, condemned to begin again, in the nightmare of eternal life" (149). Therefore, the reason why this novel is marginalized by the critical canon is that this conclusion does two embarrassing things. First, it functions as an open critique of the supposed jouissance of the postmodern self that Ilona described above as a "continual relocation... oscillatory... provisional veracity... caught between two worlds... fragmented memories." Here, in Kureishi, such a position is exposed as simply being "condemned" to a living "nightmare." Being cut loose from history and his class-based identity does not provide postmodern play and freedom for Leo/Adam, only horror. Second, this conclusion is embarrassing to the parameters of postmodern liberal criticism that always desires to appear "classless" since Leo's final desire is for the stability, comfort, and safety of the grand narrative of his white middle-class life and a desire to return to the lost Elysium of bourgeois culture and society.

Chapter 4

We're All Bourgeois Now: Realism and Class in Alan Hollinghurst, Graham Swift, and Jonathan Coe

In this climate of Aesopian languages it is absolutely essential to reiterate that most things are a matter of class.

—*Aijaz Ahmad*[1]

While "realism" has been accepted as the depository of the real, the true, and in many cases, seen as the home of class issues, this chapter explores the ways in which middle-class novelists such as Hollinghurst, Swift, and Coe have used realism as a double-edged sword that while appearing to offer a critique of ideology and class power, paradoxically offer us narratives in which class tensions are simultaneously raised and removed.

In *Modern British Fiction 1950–2000*, Dominic Head has a chapter on "Class and Social Change" that is symptomatic of how the academy chooses to speak about literature and class. Contrary to the statistics which make it clear that class divisions, inequality, and poverty in Britain are still structurally present, Head repeats the purely ideological assumption that class is no longer very important because "[t]he broad trend since [the 1950s] has been towards greater prosperity for working people, a process that undermines the economic basis of class affiliation."[2] While Head does cite Arthur Marwick's data that reveals how class has "remained constant," he goes on to give greater credence not to the sociological facts but focuses instead on the "*common perception* that the codes and offices of a ruling class are being steadily dismantled, and this implies a dynamic of social leveling. . . ."[3] Significantly, Head feels that "Narrative fiction has played its part in this changing perception. . . ."[4] So, narrative fiction has fulfilled its ideological function by contributing to a "common perception" that class is "dissolving" and that the ruling class is being "dismantled" even if in reality it is not. Head's chapter on class is also interesting for what it leaves out as much as for what it includes. While the focus on class is admirable, he moves away from the contemporary mainstream middle-class canonical authors, and shines his light on the overtly "class based" authors of the 1950s and 60s. Having covered the gentle criticisms of the English class system by Kingsley Amis, he then spends much of the chapter on John Wain, John Osborne, John Braine, David Storey, Allan Sillitoe, Barry Hines, Sid Chaplin, and Raymond Williams. I feel that the unconscious assumption is that if we are to consider "class" in the novel then we should be looking at the "working-class" novel, thereby reinforcing the idea that *this* kind of novel is about class, while other novels are about larger "human" issues. Half of the chapter focuses on the problems of the working-class novel, while the remainder deals with what Head calls "The Waning of Class-Consciousness" since the end of the 1960s and also with the "Rise of the Underclass."[5] Here too we continue to focus on "working-class" authors, so in addition to James Kelman and the early working-class novels of Pat Barker, he turns to the working-class realist novels of Livy Michael whose "gritty" council estate novels offer us documentary-style proof of poverty in Britain. Toward the end of the chapter we do get to consider the role of the middle-class author in all of this, but instead of staying with the present historical moment Head again moves back to the safety of the 1950s by looking at the narrow middle-class worlds of Angus Wilson and Barbara Pym. Only in the final section of the chapter, "The Role of the Intellectual," do we arrive at a place where (for two pages out of thirty) we can finally discuss the contemporary middle-class author and class. The section opens with a discussion of the middle-class author Penelope Lively whose novels, Head feels (in line with postmodern theory) undermine the reality of class differences: "In *Spiderweb* (1998) Lively shows us, implicitly, that traditional notions of class have become irrelevant, and (through Stella) that the professional intellectual class is without power or discernible function in the melting-pot that has resulted."[6] So in the discussion of our own moment, the class tensions of the 1950s and

60s have magically evaporated, as we see only a "new structure" that mirrors a new "global development." The problem for the novelist (of any class, we assume) is that older "internal systems of class differentiation [are] rapidly overtaken by an international economy that renders the national social explanations obsolete."[7]

So we are back to the thoroughly ideological framework, which asserts that traditional models of class are invalid and that we need to stop going on about old ideas like class and look at "new ways of being British" as Kureishi had said. Yet Head points out that these changes in Britain have also produced formal problems for the novelist: "This new global context necessarily demands new novelistic forms and even [Raymond] Williams, despite his earlier intentions, demonstrated his understanding that realism could not meet the requirements of the end of the twentieth century."[8] This chapter explores the relationship between realism and class in this supposedly "new" economic environment. Head is suggesting that economic changes come along and the novel then somehow has to react to those changes and find a way of representing this "new structure" and/or to find new (middle class) ways of representing them. If, as Head says, realism is a form that belongs to a preglobalized culture and economy, how do we then explain its persistence in our current moment? The answer is clear: it persists because as a genre and a form the realist novel is the main pillar of the institution of literature, and having fought off the foreign detours of modernism, magical realism and experimentalism, it can now safely continue to function as a conduit for middle-class ideology. In any case, thinking of the struggle as a struggle between different styles and genres only serves to distract us from the question of class. Is a middle-class modernist somehow more political than a middle-class magical realist novel or a middle-class experimental novel? We are stuck in a false debate: it is not the genre or the form that should be at issue but the class foundations of the author as well as the ways in which the novels "manage" the issue of class.

In *Marxism and Literature,* Raymond Williams points out that even at the best of times Marxist literary criticism has gone along with the received notions of "literature": "It is significant that 'Marxist criticism' and 'Marxist literary studies' have been most successful, in ordinary terms, when they have worked within the received category of 'literature' which they may have extended or even revalued, but never radically questioned or opposed."[9] In this sense then how can we begin to oppose "literature"? Let us begin with the author function.

Raymond Williams sees the Author of "Literature" as emerging from their particular milieu, and in his words the author is:

> a characteristic form of bourgeois thought. No man is author of himself, in the absolute sense which these descriptions imply. As a physical individual he is of course specific, though within a determining genetic inheritance. As a social individual he is also specific, but within the social forms of his time and place...[so that even the] "contents of consciousness are socially produced."[10]

With this in mind let us look the work of three contemporary British middle-class authors who have all written work that either directly deals with British politics, as in the case of Alan Hollinghurst in *The Line of Beauty* and Jonathan Coe in *The Rotter's Club* and *The Closed Circle*, or, as in the case of Graham Swift's *Last Orders*, where the focus is a detailed examination of the lives of the postwar (white) British working class.

Alan Hollinghurst

Alan Hollinghurst is clearly at the heart of the British literary establishment. Educated at Magdalen College, Oxford, he then taught at Oxford until 1981, after which he became deputy editor of the *Times Literary Supplement* where he worked until becoming a full-time author. He was named as one of Granta's "Best Young British Novelists" in 1993 and was awarded the Booker Prize in 2004. When Alan Hollinghurst won the Booker Prize for *The Line of Beauty*, there was the predictable outrage from the conservative media that an openly homosexual novel was being rewarded a major literary prize: "Gay Book Wins Booker" cried the *Sun*, while the *Daily Express* headline was "Booker Won by Gay Sex."[11]

Kaye Mitchell in *British Fiction Today* takes this open aversion to Hollinghurst as a sign that he is a confrontational writer who is challenging mainstream culture with his "in-your-face" realism and no holds barred treatment of homosexuality. For Mitchell, following Eve Sedgwick, Hollinghurst's work manifests in subject and form "a queer narrative...one which fails to signify in any stable or 'monolithic' way."[12] In short, she feels that such narratives are troubling and are engaged in "transgression" and are openly out to upset "heteronarrative" norms of "intelligibility and signification."[13] In the same way that Hollinghurst is figured as a subversive outsider of the literary establishment, so Nick in *The Line of Beauty* is also figured by Hollinghurst himself, and Mitchell, as an outsider (he is after all called Nick *Guest* for a reason). So for Mitchell we see Nick through the lens of his own "self-definition" as

> ...aesthete, observer, outsider; he is one who looks, implying a kind of distance, judgement, perspective; this lends him a certain authority and status but also reflects his lack of real belonging in this world of his wealthy friends.[14]

Fredric Jameson in *The Political Unconscious* says of Gissing that his problem, like Dickens, is the problem of the "'objective treason' of intellectuals perpetually suspended between two social worlds and two sets of class values and obligations...."[15] All of the authors that we are examining in this book are positioned in this way. For Jameson, the positionality of the middle-class author condemns them to a "peculiarly social form of Hegelian Unhappy Consciousness which [forbids] any successful and definitive class identification."[16] This problem can be clearly seen in the case of Nick Guest/Alan Hollinghurst. Mitchell feels that Nick's homosexuality in the beginning of the novel is somehow not quite real, and that his lack of real experience makes his gayness something of an aesthetic, or theoretical category: it is "ideal and imagined, rather than concrete and lived."[17] Now, what is crucial here for my analysis is that while his *desire* is focused on his straight, upper-class friend from Oxford, Toby (who belongs, to an "upper middle-class family," as Hollinghurst has said, as opposed to Nick's lower-middle-class background), his actual sexuality only manifests itself, and becomes "real," through the black working-class character, Leo.[18] So while his gay identity is not real, Mitchell tells us that "It is sex, then (the encounter with Leo in Kensington Park Gardens), which marks his entry into such an identity...."[19]

What intrigues me about this analysis is that while Mitchell goes to great lengths to situate the politics of gay narratives and gay fiction, the fact of Leo's class position is never mentioned. Mitchell wants us to remember that the act of cruising makes the gay man "a collector of sexual experience and, in a more crudely capitalist way, of men" and that "the 'beautiful things' that Nick loves cannot be divorced from their economic value," and moreover, she reminds us that "gay male sex is increasingly and obviously linked to capitalism...." She also quotes Tim Edwards to bring home the point that "the sexual pick-up system is deeply set in a series of modern developments, including capitalism...The homosexual pick-up machine is, in fact...a reflection of the internalisation of industrial, capitalist values of efficiency and productivity" (45–47). However, while there are these attempts to give a materialist reading to homosexuality the fact that Leo is working class is avoided, and in her entire essay, which centers around *The Line of Beauty*, Leo's *only* mention comes in the one reference (placed in parenthesis by Mitchell) cited earlier. I will return to Leo's class position and his race in a moment, but firstly let us see where Mitchell takes her analysis.

Mitchell feels that the public sex in the novels of Hollinghurst is then to be "interpreted as liberationary—a refusal to accept the suppression and containment (domestication) of homosexuality, a defiant 'queering' of the public realm, a defiance of public norms of decency, and a challenge to the attempt to institute clear demarcations of public and private." At this point Mitchell paradoxically backs off from a reading of cruising as undermining capitalism and asserts the opposite: "cruising is...compliant with the dominant ideologies of capitalism," and as a result she begins to link this to Hollinghurst's own political stance, admitting that there is in the criticism on Hollinghurst a "fundamental uneasiness at the author's political ambivalence—particularly his relationship to Thatcherism" (48). Instead of taking her analysis into the working-class subjects that do arise in the novels, she looks at Nick as an outsider in the Fedden's household, who, as the novel makes clear, is keeping his homosexuality under wraps so that he can continue to hang out with Toby in the Conservative atmosphere of the Fedden household. For her, Nick's duplicity is not a failure of political nerve, or a failure to assert his own gay identity, instead she reads it in a favorable light toward Hollinghurst so that he is intentionally constructing a narrative that reveals "a coruscating awareness of the character's complicity in the systems which oppress them" (Ibid). So rather than moving into a critique of Hollinghurst's bourgeois politics, we take the alternative road whereby a queer radical reading of the novel is salvaged:

> This "complicity," however, can be read another way: as indicating the instability of the boundaries separating the homosexual and heterosexual worlds, and thus—to return to my original theme—to the failure of the orthodox narrative of homosexuality to contain and regulate its subject. (Ibid)

So the work of Hollinghurst is praised, in the last instance, for the production of a postmodern kind of gay subjectivity, a fluid unstable subject who is somehow no longer embedded in anything as limiting as a stable self, and even operates within unstable radically decentered novels. Similarly, like the ideal postmodern (classless) subject, the white middle-class gay male takes on a radical quality that "threatens" power and coherence by being nowhere, yet everywhere:

> Hollinghurst's worlds...[show] the gay man as simultaneously insider and outsider, visible and invisible, [and] he introduces ambivalence into homosexual identity which threatens its coherence and intelligibility while also asserting its presence, even its ubiquity. (Ibid)

The stage is set for Mitchell to present us with the postmodern gay subject and the postmodern gay narrative form: "So through the proliferation of representations, homosexuality becomes less, rather than more, intelligible; we find ourselves presented with a series of competing, possibly contradictory, narratives, rather than a unified concept" (50). From this point, as Mitchell begins to close her essay, she brings in Alan Sinfield's analysis that in our own historical moment we have perhaps reached a point where "gay" (and "lesbian") as subject markers and epistemological categories, may be too limiting and need to be abandoned. In a move that is remarkably parallel to other theoretical positions in which we are supposedly in the realm of the "post" (post-feminism, post-Marxism etc.), Sinfield feels that "we may now be entering the period of *the post-gay*—a period when it will not seem so necessary to define, and hence to limit, our sexualities" (Ibid).

Mitchell thus concludes her essay by asserting that Hollinghurst is presenting us with radical narratives that queerly destabilize and "threaten" mainstream culture and its desire to safely contain and pigeonhole him as a gay writer. However, the tricky last element of Mitchell's analysis is that if Hollinghurst is so threatening and destabilizing, how is it that he has managed to achieve "mainstream success" from oppressive heterosexual society? Her answer is that Hollinghurst is providing a chance for "more positive and radical cross-contaminations (both literary and sexual) to occur" because he is "both insider and outsider in the literary establishment..." and is producing "a reflection on the construction of the homosexual identity" through "diverse narratives, with all the ambivalences, contingencies and contradictions which that construction involves" (Ibid).

This reading of Hollinghurst is revealing though for what it fails to discuss. Postmodern critics like Mitchell wish to appear in favor of more fluidity, more contingencies, more undecidability, and they wish to read contemporary authors as being engaged in similar activities.

The result therefore is a smooth fit between author and critic in which the aims of the author are matched seamlessly with the aims of the critic. We saw the same thing in the last chapter, for example, where Julian Wolfreys will praise Ackroyd for echoing Derrida. The embarrassing and difficult alternative is to think differently, and to read the novel not with the grain, but as Terry Eagleton has always reminded us, *against* the grain. In the case of a gay writer like Hollinghurst, it is tricky because the critic runs the risk of simply appearing to be somehow homophobic by refusing to say nice things about his novels. However, this is certainly not the case here, and in going on to critique Hollinghurst's work from a class perspective I hope that we can open up a way of reading his work that enables us to see how class and Mitchell's postmodern gay identity have a more troubled relationship.

Mitchell's reading of *The Line of Beauty* asserts that Hollinghurst is constructing a queer narrative in which we see the emergence of a gay identity that is fluid and multiple as well as less, not more definable, and which radically threatens the coherence of both gay and heterosexual identity. These comments could be taken verbatim out of any textbook definition of the postmodern self, and perhaps it is this comfortable ideological match with our own models of postmodern subjectivity that makes a reading like Mitchell's feel so right and "true." But such a reading is not critical but merely ideological. Surely postmodernism criticism wants us to read the novel in this way and desires to produce such a reading. While we come away holding up the fluid unstable self as our badge of victory, what has to be sacrificed to produce such a reading? What does Mitchell have to leave out to make her conclusions? I would argue that what is really being produced by such a reading is not just a fluid, mobile postmodern gay self, but also a very stable, fixed, and highly immobile working-class subject. In *The Line of Beauty* this working-class subject causes a fascinating problem for the narrative and for criticism (hence Mitchell's silence) because Leo is not only gay and black but thoroughly working class.

As we saw with Carl in Zadie Smith's *On Beauty,* and now in Hollinghurst, in the middle-class novel the black working-class male clearly constitutes a zone of narrative anxiety as they are always conveniently killed off or rapidly removed. Leo is Nick Guest's boyfriend in the novel who will get AIDS and die, and while Mitchell had made it clear that cruising is central to the gay economy and that it is by cruising in Kensington Park that Nick meets Leo, this relationship with Leo is never explored by Mitchell. Mitchell has also made it clear that in her opinion Nick's gay identity is not real until his encounter with Leo, and yet once again, she is silent on his character. It is my contention that in the same way that Mitchell can only produce a reading of a fluid postmodern self by avoiding any analysis of Leo, so too in the novel Hollinghurst needs the fixed working-class world of Leo in relation to which his middle-class and upper-class postmodern selves can be positioned. Once this platform has performed its role then (given that there is no place in this bourgeois novel for the working-class Leo) he is removed and like the African-American Carl in Zadie Smith's *On Beauty* is prevented from participating in any narrative denouement. Looked at in this light we can see that the success of *The Line of Beauty* is quite understandable in that mainstream culture would be happy to absorb a novel that generates a model of a postmodern gay identity as one without foundations, while from a class standpoint the novel keeps the main elements of a class society firmly in place and in fact openly reinforces long held frameworks that work to mitigate against any rethinking of working-class culture or identity. In Hollinghurst's hands, the bourgeois novel here opens up a space for the postmodern neoliberal self (which has plenty of room for a "classless" gay identity, and is quite happy to critique Thatcherism) while denying any kind of parallel space for the black and gay working-class subject.

The position of the novel in mainstream culture should not be gauged by looking at the obvious dislike by the *Sun* and the *Daily Express*, but by looking at the praise that was heaped on the novel from all quarters. Given how close the novel is to her own *On Beauty*, it is telling that Zadie Smith in the *Guardian* called it "the best English novel of the year," Edmund White called it a "deeply informed social satire," and Geoff Dyer named it "Hollinghurst's finest novel." The conservative *Daily Telegraph* called it a "magnificent novel" while the *Sunday Times* felt it was "exquisitely written." The *Sunday Telegraph* felt it was "Jamesian in the best sense" and that he even "surpasses his master." The tabloid *Evening Standard* felt it was "an important novel of twentieth century manners" and finally, Hollinghurst's old employer the *Times Literary Supplement* described it as a "morally exacting satire."[20] All of this praise from very mainstream sources reveals I think that underneath the smoke screen of shock and outrage from some predictable quarters at the gay sex in the novel, this is a novel which is saying something that is far from troubling for bourgeois culture, and is actually saying something that it wants to hear about the placement and identity of working-class culture.

In an interview with Pat Wheeler, Alan Hollinghurst said that in *The Swimming Pool Library* he addressed the idea that "gay men are linked across barriers of class and race by sexuality and puts it up against a system in which the forces of class are still extremely powerful."[21] Yet for all of this awareness of how homosexuality intersects with class, he also admits in the next breath that "the truth is that I don't know a lot about working-class life and so, without its being at all a schematic decision, it hasn't arisen as a subject in my books."[22] Moreover, in an interview in the *San Francisco Chronicle* Hollinghurst describes his own youth: "I was a gay, middle-class only child from the provinces, fairly innocent of real life, with a precocious knowledge of music, literature and architecture…I think I shared something of Nick's snobbery and aestheticism, and these were qualities I sought to explore and expose in this book."[23] We could say that Hollinghurst is being quite honest here in admitting that as an Oxford educated middle-class author he cannot write about working-class characters as it is beyond his sphere of knowledge, and yet talking to Pat Wheeler he states that there is something about working-class subjects that interferes or blocks narrative: "From the novelist's point of view, of course, people who have money and connections give scope for fictional freedoms which working-class characters don't."[24] So in this sense the middle-class author cannot find narratives when looking at the working class and this paucity obviously translates into formal concerns. For example in *The Line of Beauty*, bearing in mind all that Kaye Mitchell has said about Hollinghurst's radically queer narratives and new postgay subjectivities, we find startling different narratives for two of the novels gay men: Wani and Leo. Both men are gay, and not white. Leo is black, and Wani's family is originally from Beirut. Both men also contract AIDS toward the end of the novel. Now if Mitchell was right about Hollinghurst's work, then we would see an equally disruptive narrative that could deal with both men in the same "radical" way, destabilizing the binaries of public/private. Yet this is far from the case. The working-class Leo dies "off stage": the novel avoids confronting his illness directly, and he only returns to the novel once he is dead, and then only for ten pages when his sister Rosemary comes to the Ogee office to tell Nick of his death. In contrast, the illness of the upper-class Wani spans all of part three of the novel, and there are many scenes with Nick helping Wani deal with his struggle against AIDS.

Another reason why the novel would be welcomed by mainstream culture is that the novel, while focusing on the upper and middle classes is also finely attuned to the various shadings of class differences that, far from undermining class, or revealing a classless society, do the opposite: they serve to retrace and to reaffirm demarcations of class. Once again, for all of its desire to generate a "post-gay" sensibility, it does so at the expense of putting class firmly into place along lines that have been unchanged since 1945. On a basic level, the book traces a three part social structure for contemporary Britain: the Feddens and their world is that of the Tory upper classes, Nick and his parents are clearly middle-class representatives and Leo, his lesbian sister Rosemary and people like the black taxi-driver Brentford, function as the working-class characters. For all of its radical questioning or "cross class" sexuality, there is very little serious crossing of classes, other than temporary forays. The relationship between Nick and Leo is cut short after some brief intense sex, as Leo returns to his class roots with his old lover, Peter. Nick never gets to sleep with the (heterosexual) object of his desire, the upper-class Toby, and is finally expelled from the house in which he has always been just a lodger and a guest. The Feddens too are only temporarily drawn into Nick's middle-class/ gay world. The Fedden household is entirely heterosexual (Toby and Catherine are straight) and Gerald's affair that finally pulls him down is with a woman. It is only through coming into contact with Nick that they get into trouble and the upper-class family will suffer no long-term damage from this episode. Nick points out to Penny how "[i]t's rather amazing to resign in disgrace one day and be offered a job at eighty thousand a year the next." To which Penny responds: "That's how this world works, Nick, Gerald can't lose. You've got to understand that."[25] In this sense the novel is doing something that is actually the opposite of what we are told to expect from the contemporary novel. Far from opening up what Mitchell calls narratives of "contingencies and contradictions," it is operating with a limited palette that basically ensures that not only are the three classes of British society clearly mapped out, but that they are also shown to be unable to mix, blend, or unravel in any substantial way.[26]

This restrictive mapping of British society is also elided when we turn to academic criticism that deals with the aesthetic issues in Hollinghurst's work. Writing in *Textual Practice* in 2006, Andrew Eastham takes on the question of Henry James and *The Line of Beauty*. For Eastham, the novel has a "deep involvement in nineteenth century Aestheticism."[27] In this reading Hollinghurst is using the position of the aesthete to signal an ironic detachment from the events around him: "The Aesthete's ironic performance was, to some degree, an aspiration to the ideal independence of the art object itself. . . ."[28] For Eastham, what the novel reveals is that in the world of the Conservative 1980s and the world of postmodernism the detached position of the aesthete is no longer possible. It is not possible, Eastham feels, for two main reasons:

> According to Hollinghurst's representation of the 1980's, then, there are two problems with irony and Aestheticism. The first is in relation to the aristocracy—the Aesthete attempts to reclaim a posture of independence and detachment from the aristocracy but remains bound to the object it mimics: where it aspires to autonomy it remains in a position of patronage—an obliging guest. The second problem is in the arena of post-modernism, where the Aesthete manages an ironically detached appreciation of contemporary culture but fails to assert any independence from capital and commodity consumption. In the first sense Aestheticism is compromised by its specious claim to autonomy, whilst in the second sense it is not autonomous enough.[29]

Although this gives the impression that the novel has to give up the idea of aestheticism altogether in a postmodern moment, Eastham recuperates this loss by claiming that the ending of the novel "invokes a powerful sense of the residual potential of aesthetic experience" and that once Nick has been expelled from the Fedden household and stands alone on the street, we finally see "perhaps the first moment in the novel in which Nick stands in free space, no longer a guest to the culture of Conservatism, and in this sense it is arguably the first moment in the novel where the aesthetic dimension is experienced as a democratic freedom."[30] While this kind of reading makes the novel into a happy ending for the continuation of a bourgeois tradition of the ironic outsider/aesthete, it pushes aside a major issue. From an economic standpoint, this is simply not true as Wani has decided that after his death he will leave Nick the Clerkenwell building so that Nick can finally enter the echelons of the upper classes by not having to work at all and he can simply "live on the rent for the rest of [his] life."[31] Moreover, what this analysis presupposes is that the novel has to deal with only two spaces: that of the upper class (on which the middle-class aesthete is dependent) or the supposedly "independent" middle-class position. The narrative struggle, the search for a "free space" is thus always being played out as either (a) dependent on the upper class or (b) free and independent (i.e., no longer a guest). If the social world of the novel (and British society) were limited to these two classes, then this analysis may have some credibility, but aestheticism takes place precisely in the context of capitalism whereby the working class is structured in opposition to all that is beautiful. The working classes are not included in the aesthete's purview, and in Derridean terms would act as a kind of "dangerous supplement" that can neither be included in the aesthete's equation nor completely eradicated. So while Nick, according to Eastham, finally ends up in a "free space" at the end of the novel, and turns a street corner that is "so beautiful" the working-class world of the novel is never permitted to be beautiful or free.[32]

Hollinghurst makes this quite apparent when Nick visits Leo's house for the first and only time. In the same way that Brentford (the black taxi driver that Catherine buys drugs from) standing in the hall of the Fedden's house is described as being "completely and critically different from everything else in the house," in the same way that Leo's house, or rather, his mother's house, is "critically different" from the world that the aesthete desires.[33] While he may desire Leo as an object that he can collect, Leo's class position insists on surfacing, and it is clear that Leo is unwilling (unlike Nick) to separate and distance himself from his class roots. In a sense this is the aesthetic reason for Leo's removal from the novel: his socioeconomic position is simply ugly and doesn't give the aesthete the "free space" he needs.

Leo, finishing work at his job in the council meets Nick to take him home. The first sign that the working-class world is limiting and restrictive appears in the way that Leo warns Nick that since his mother is religious Nick has to watch what he says: "Don't say, 'Jesus fucking bollocks.' "[34] Leo and his mother and sister don't even have a whole house: they live in a maisonette: "Mrs Charles and her son and daughter lived on the ground floor of a small red-brick terrace house" and therefore there were "two front doors side by side in the shallow recess of the porch" leading into a "tiny flat in unknown Willesden." Once Nick has "disguised [his] shock" what hits him on entering is a "sharp...cooking smell in the hall." We are given a tour of the "tiny kitchen" with its tell tale signifiers of working-class culture: "the sliding frosted-glass doors," the "orange curtains," "scary wiring," and "a bubbling pan."[35] It goes without saying that Leo's house will not be an article in the next issue of Wani and Nick's magazine *Ogee* or *Architectural Digest*.[36] Charles's sister Rosemary returns from work as a "doctor's receptionist" and Nick senses that there are "subdivided rooms at the back" of the flat, and feels that even Leo's bike must feel trapped and is aware of "its own trapped velocity." Nick observes more examples of the sheer ugliness of working-class life: a "shiny ginger leather" sofa, a "gas fire with a beaten copper surround."[37] Working-class food is also part of the anti-aesthetic: "the meal was a bold combination of bland and garishly spicy," while he registers a "shock of class difference" in that they are sitting down to dinner at "five forty five."[38] The dinner is predictably followed by "fruit and ice cream" and Nick cannot wait to leave.[39] Here, then is the working class, and the reason that it cannot be included in Nick's world, nor at any length in Hollinghurst's novel is because it is too stark a reminder of the economic foundations that underpin a world that Nick is unable to eradicate. Remember that Hollinghurst has said that "people who have money and connections give scope for fictional freedoms which working-class characters don't."[40] So here, in this cramped flat, the narrative cannot grow or develop and so it must leave: one cannot be an aesthete in the face of something so "completely and critically different" as Hollinghurst has said of the black taxi driver, Brentford. As Nick and Leo leave and part ways, the geography of the city also reinforces the permanence of class divisions:

> Nick was still in the alien high reach of the road, with the canal and the council estates, and longing for the other end, his own end, the safety and aloofness of white stucco and private gardens. He wondered what Leo thought as he made the transition, which occurred at the dense middle part by the market and the station, under clangorous bridges, where people loitered and shouted.... After that there was a stretch of uneasy gentility, before the Grove climbed, taking palpable advantage of the hill as a social metaphor.[41]

In this way, *The Line of Beauty* operates in a similar fashion in terms of class and narration as we see in Ishiguro's *The Remains of the Day*: the narrative voice pulls us into identification with a bourgeois-subject position while distancing us from both a working-class position as well as an upper-class one. So, as in Ishiguro, we are kept at arm's length from Lord Darlington and from Stevens, while in Hollinghurst we are prevented from identifying with the Feddens or with Leo and his family. The only "free space" that the reader is granted for nearly 500 pages is the individual middle-class consciousness of Nick Guest. In addition, the novel's form also mimics upper-class aesthetic behavior. After Leo's sister visits Nick at the *Ogee* office, to tell him of Leo's death from AIDS, they leave and Nick sees the office as somehow garish and ugly: "It was what you did if you had millions but no particular taste: you made your private space like a swanky hotel; just as such hotels flattered their customers by being vulgar simulacra of lavish private homes."[42] If we rephrase this, we can see how *The Line of Beauty* operates as an aesthetic object of beauty to be contemplated by the bourgeois identifying reader in a class divided British society: "you make your novel like a swanky hotel; just as such novels flattered their readers by being vulgar simulacra of lavish private lives." While such a novel/hotel may delight and be a respite from the working week, it nevertheless remains only a temporary resting place, after which we have to go back to work, and in any case, for the majority of us, the price of staying there is too high.

Graham Swift

As a young boy Graham Swift was educated at Dulwich College that is a private boarding school in London currently charging £8000 per term. From here he went to Queen's College, Cambridge, and then began work on a Ph.D. at York University before becoming a full time writer in 1983. It is clear then that Swift's own class position is certainly not that of his characters in *Last Orders*. None of the characters in the novel have had any education to speak of, let alone a private education, and none of them have been to university or have friends at university. From a sociological perspective, Swift is clearly middle class, while his characters are upper working class at the most. Some commentators have suggested that the characters are "petit bourgeois" perhaps because some of the characters like Jack (a butcher) and Vince (a car salesman) and Vic (a fruit and vegetable stall) have small businesses, but their social-class environment is certainly "working" as opposed to middle class.[43] So, as with many of the novelists we have been looking at, there are interesting tensions here. In the same way that Hollinghurst had admitted that he didn't really know anything about working-class life, so in Swift (a friend of Hollinghurst) we are once again dealing with the view from above: a presentation of a working-class world by someone *outside* of that class. In Hollinghurst we saw how this resulted in a novel in which Nick's middle-class view of the upper class was of a world that was attractive and exciting, while the working-class milieu was seen as cramped and ugly. In this sense Swift's novel (awarded the Booker Prize in 1996) is an extended look into that working-class milieu from a middle-class authorial perspective. The result is a work of fiction that feeds off the identity of a definable working-class group at the very historical moment when, as we are investigating in this entire book, it is supposed to have vanished, or is supposedly no longer important.

Whereas the middle-class characters in Hollinghurst are never limited or defined by what they "do," once we get to Swift the working-class characters are fully defined by their jobs. David Rogers suggests that

> They *are* what they *do* for a living, and, epitomized by Vic Tucker, a mortician, what they do is tantamount to the inability to renew themselves. They need to do their duty ('like there was an order sent down from High Command' as Lenny says 132) which follows from their respective commitments to their jobs, mitigates against change and self-realisation, just as it has historically for the English working-class. Duty in the novel, is, as Gunby realizes, immobilizing.[44]

Rogers claims though that while the majority of the characters are trapped in a form of Englishness that is bounded by class and duty, two of them "resist the immobility associated with doing one's duty." For Rogers, Vince and Ray represent a revision of Englishness, in that they are not known for what they does for a living, but for who they are. Rogers concludes that Ray and the land, "he and England—are one." Vince resists his duty and "overcomes the pressure to become a butcher" while Ray has been "encouraged by his father not to follow in his footsteps as a scrap metal merchant."[45] What do they then choose to do having resisted their outdated Englishness and duty? Vince becomes a used car salesman, and Ray gets a job as an insurance clerk. In this sense they stay firmly rooted into their socioeconomic class, but Rogers, wishing to tease out the ways in which Swift is cleverly drawing out how to recreate a new Englishness, wants to see characters who are not fixed, but who are disembedded from outdated grand narratives and are moving freely into worlds in which they can define themselves: "Ray is not known for his occupation or for what it implies...Instead he's known for his instincts, instincts (feminine in nature) that determine his nature...."[46] Interestingly, the novel quite clearly illustrates that even in the act of "resisting" their duty, the ideological and economic boundaries in these characters lives ensures that there really is nowhere for them to go, and if we read carefully we see that Ray is basically doing what his father told him to, and Jack is not even Vince's real father. However, they remain, even in a supposedly classless contemporary Britain, fully inscribed into a working-class framework. Rogers doesn't feel that this resistance to old ways of being ("blowing the rules") is limited to Ray and Vince though but encompasses the message of the novel. For Rogers, the "deconstruction implicit in Ray's 'blowing the rules' becomes formally complete with the novel's last paragraph... As Gunby observes, Margate signifies the 'shedding of the past,' the groups' 'becoming new people' as if taking, in class terms, their 'last orders.'"[47] The final result then is that the novel offers us, like Kureishi, a new way of being English, and opens up a postmodern world of fluid subjects who are no longer tied to the past, or history, or such outdated things as class: "The rhetoric of the novel posits a nationalism 'beyond an insular Englishness,' a connection with a 'wide world,' fluid and in constant motion, perpetuation transition and renewal."[48] But surely we need to stop and consider that this rewriting of Englishness is emerging from the pen of a middle-class author and if we stop to look at that definition of this new nationalism, it reads like a definition of globalization and international capital. As Eagleton points out, capitalism is always constantly reinventing itself, crossing borders and must be fluid and renewable if it is to maximize its markets: "Capitalism, in short, itself deconstructs the difference between system and transgression."[49] Rogers' reading of Swift thus places it firmly into the postmodern, postnationalist, postclass camp, in which Englishness is now "free" to open itself up to "the local and the global" as part of "spaceship Earth."[50] Although Swift's text may desire to convince us that we live in world in which all are free from "duty" to the outmoded grand narratives of class and nation, I cannot help think that as you read this, thousands of workers across Britain are still engaged in jobs that probably pay as much in a year as Swift's *alma mater* Dulwich College charges for one term.

In *Understanding Graham Swift,* David Malcolm is confident that these characters are speaking "lower class English" and that they are all "drawn from a narrow, drab, South London, lower class world" and that while they are "humble," Swift reveals that working-class people can be "complex figures" and that the novel's "lower class subjects have rich and complex emotional lives."[51] Not only the voices, but the plot also, according to Malcolm, clearly marks it out as a working-class world that we all see in British soap operas: "the novel's story material (adultery, illegitimacy, confused and conflict-ridden family relationships) are the very stuff of *Eastenders.*"[52] However, the novel, thanks to Swift's skill shows that these men and women are "far from stupid" and that the novel is "permeated with references to canonical literary texts."[53] The implication here is that working-class lives are flat and uninspiring (as Hollinghurst has already pointed out) but with the alchemical hand of the middle-class novelist, the leaden flat world of the working class can be transformed into the golden material of a novel that can now deal, not with narrow things like class, but with "centrally human existential concerns." Of course, as Malcolm adds, these literary levels of the novel are not really accessible to a working-class reader but can be "perceived by the informed reader of Swift's novel."[54] These intricate, intertextual levels of the novel are also not available to the working-class characters in the novel because they are "poorly educated."[55] However, for the "informed" (i.e., not working class) reader, one can see that the novel "in a true postmodern, metafictional manner" makes reference to everything from Wordsworth's Preface to the *Lyrical Ballads,* to "Dickens, T. S. Eliot, Chaucer, and Faulkner." These literary references thus serve to "dignify and universalize" what would have otherwise been simply "drab" working-class characters, who, one would assume, without this middle-class canonical stamp of approval, would remain undignified and parochial.[56] In a contemporary British culture that has supposedly done away with class, it is fascinating that not only can we continue to talk of classes in this way, but that also there is an unquestioned assumption that the middle class is clearly there to give credence and meaning to the empty signifiers of the working class, who, not surprisingly are scripted by the middle-class author and critic as being passively unable to construct or possess meaning in and for themselves.

This reading of the novel also gets played out by other literary theorists. Daniel Lea carried out a full-length study of Swift as part of the *Contemporary British Novelists* series. Taking on Swift's oeuvre, Lea neither moves the debate into the realm of history as one would expect given Swift's subject matter over the years, nor does he situate it in the recent debates surrounding Englishness that Rogers is part of. The Linda Hutcheon route of seeing Swift as a master of "historiographic metafiction" has been well mined and is now rather *passé* since *Waterland* (around which most of these debates centered) was published in 1983.[57] The other route that has been taken is to look at Swift's oeuvre as a body of work dealing with "mourning and/or melancholia" as Tamas Benyei calls it, in which the "the melancholic narrative personae" is inscribed in the "broader cultural pathologies of nation, empire or age."[58] It is this latter road that Daniel Lea chooses to take. From the outset of this approach, Lea begins by taking an ostensibly realist novelist who deals with real historical events and recognizably class-based environments since 1945 and jettisons it all, in favor of a Lacanian psychoanalytical model that has the two fold effect of (a) reducing the characters to fragmented psyches impossibly struggling with ontological questions that they cannot fathom or resolve and (b) expanding these subjects into universals who are dealing with issues that are not shaped or troubled by such quotidian factors as class or gender or race. This sweeping micro to macro perspective seems to take in everything yet in its own subtle postmodern way, leaves out the center: the economic and social grounding of Swift's characters. Drawing on Malcolm's basic reading of these novels as texts that "use" limited working-class characters to get at larger, more important issues, so Lea jumps over the class position of Swift's protagonists and moves immediately to the universal. Whereas in Rogers the ending of the novel was an opening out to the future having "shed the past," in Lea the ending is deliberately delayed by the four men as a way of holding on to the past: "Suspending the moment of arrival represents an unwillingness to relinquish a past of shared experience and suggests a hankering for the stabilities of the known that can mitigate the awful moment of loneliness that comes with self-knowledge."[59]

The end of the novel is thus symptomatic of what we witness throughout Swift's oeuvre: not a class based or social sense of cultural meaning but a Beckettian existential isolation in a world devoid of meaning. As Lea says, "[o]n the end of Margate pier, as each dips into the urn and throws Jack Dodds to the winds, there is a creeping acknowledgement that only directly facing the realities of lives half-lived and decisions wrongly made can they accept the commonality of loss and achieve a genuine empathetic understanding of each other" (1–2). What this overlooks, however, is that for working-class people in Britain today of any race, as opposed to middle-class authors and critics of any race, lives are "half-lived" due to class and money, and "decisions wrongly made" are more a matter of decisions that are made for them by economic systems over which they have no control. Lea's reading of Swift thus moves us into psychosocial realms where characters have a "primitive urge" to resist the "uncanny" and where "psychic rupture" is a consequence of the "engagement with the instigating wound" that can only be removed via an "ultimate revelation" in which the unloading of "guilt and sorrow" will bring about a process of "psychological self-immurement" (2). Swift's work is thus seen as questioning the "parameters of contemporary being," and the signal of his genius is that his fiction "has always gone beyond the limits of mechanistic readings." While Lea admits that the work does resemble a form of "self-conscious social realism" the real concerns of his texts "foreground the arbitrariness of semiotic definition and the elusive qualities of any hermeneutic superstructure to life" (4–5). In short, what Lea is saying is that given the death of the grand narratives in the twentieth century and beyond, how is meaning to be constructed and experienced. Lea does suggest that Swift's work is interested in the ways in which "public and private worlds intersect," but the quotidian political issues of what might actually "tie [the characters] to their place in the world" is met with broad ontological concerns in which all subjects experience the world in the same way, and the self that engages with these issues, is, as we have seen all over the pages of the contemporary middle-class novel, a kaleidoscopic self that cannot be reduced to any form of limiting narrative or totality (5–6):

> Swift's principal narrators...all...encounter...the disarticulated shards of former selves which, even when reassembled, fail to proffer a full picture of their lives as continuous, logical and coherent. That sense of lack, of being incomplete, or of glimpsing the potential forever outside the grasp of the self, or the means of expression, is a recurrent theme of Swift's fiction. (7)

History is allowed into this analysis so that it can be removed. For Lea, Swift's novels always "juxtapose the individual's dislocating experience of the historical moment with the form of grand narrative that constitutes History." However, in Lea's Lacanian model, history is reduced to merely "an abstract site" that is of little concern to us, because what really matters is "a more fundamental dislocation" between "subjective and objective realities." Sadly, nothing will come of this dislocation because the protagonists are "isolated in matrices of subjectivity" in which we are "alienated from others" and "another's consciousness" (Ibid). Owing to their inadequate and blinded position, "the experience of selfhood for Swift's protagonists is always characterised by inadequacy, self-alienation and the fear of dissolution into an asymbolic nullity" (9). Now, we could take this Lacanian model back to Althusser and from there we would be close to looking at how it is ideology that causes us to misrecognise ourselves, and that, as Marx pointed out long ago, all of this "alienation" is actually rooted in economics, but in this post-Marxist reading, this "contradictoriness is, for Swift, simply in the way of things and is connected to a primary misrecognition of the world...." Lea moves away from economics and toward Lacan as the prime framework against which to measure our alienation: "the Lacanian Real demands that we see signification as an imprecise approximation of reality that can never wholly describe its totality. Thus a surplus reality always exists outside the ability of language to contain and identify it" (Ibid).

For Jameson, however, this notion of the real as somehow an inaccessible limit is misleading. He has suggested that this Lacanian notion is inaccurate, and that is has been misappropriated by post-structuralist theory to create an "antiteleological formula for history" (neither a subject nor a telos), based as it is on Lacan's notion of the real as that which "resists symbolization absolutely:"

> The sweeping negativity of the Althusserian formula is misleading insofar as it can readily be assimilated to the polemic themes of a host of contemporary post-structuralism and post-Marxisms, for which History, in the bad sense—the reference to a "context" or a "ground", an external real world of some kind—...is simply one more text among others.[60]

As we have seen, this is convenient for critics like Lea as it allows history to be erased, and with it any reliance on class and economic materialism, while simultaneously presenting us with subjects who are now free in a world in which meaning has to be made by themselves alone. Jameson reminds us that while Althusser does speak of history as an absent cause, "what is missing from the formula as it is canonically worded, is that he does not at all draw the fashionable conclusion that because history is a text, the 'referent' does not exist."[61] For Jameson, a revised formulation would be more accurate: "that history is not a text, not a narrative, master or otherwise, but that as an absent cause, it is inaccessible to us *except in textual form,* and that our approach to it and to the Real itself necessarily passes through its prior textualization, its narrativization in the political unconscious."[62]

Without this kind of dialectical criticism what we see is that Lea's work on Swift soon becomes rather two-dimensional. Lea remarks that *The Waste Land* and *Last Orders* "both situate loss and disconnection as fundamental characteristics of modernity's episteme" and both are works of "spiritual crisis in the face of authoritarian absence" and what has been lost is the "instinctive internalisation of belief."[63] As he pointed out in his introduction, what Lea feels we are witnessing in the novel is how the characters "perceptions of the objective realm are naggingly inconclusive."[64] For Lea, Swift is examining how, in the face of Modernity, the self has woken up to find itself without any stable epistemological or spiritual ground on which to live. So they must turn to "the redemptive potential of structure and ritual" even though they are painfully aware of the "mute indifference of an objective realm that fails to offer up persuasive narratives of tradition that would cement a sense of belonging." All of this must take place in the face of the horrifying confrontation, endlessly delayed, with the "Real's asymbolism."[65]

Jameson has stated that Western society is haunted by utopia in that it is an idea that "it can neither access nor dismiss"[66] and that all utopias, whether from the Right or the Left, are thoroughly embedded in their own class ideology:

> The point about ideology is not a particularly complicated one: it sets out from the conviction that we are all ideologically situated, we are all shackled to an ideological subject-position, we are all determined by class and class history, even when we try to resist or escape it... [this] holds for everyone, left or right, progressive or reactionary, worker as well as boss....[67]

All classes or groups then can produce their own utopian narratives and yet, as Jameson points out, these utopias always bring with them the trace of the class or group that constructs it: "No matter how comprehensive and trans-class or post-ideological the inventory [of the Utopian narrative] the imagined resolution necessarily remains wedded to this or that ideological perspective" and that "it cannot but be a class experience and reflect a particular class perspective on society as a whole."[68]

In this way, instead of reading *Last Orders* as simply a novel about "ritual" and "meaning" in the contemporary world, and the inadequacy of the subject to comprehend their own lives (which I feel is how the novel wants to be read) what if we read it as a distinctly middle-class Utopian narrative? In this way the novel, as Jameson would say, is taking hold of the utopian desires for community and connection that are always present in capitalist culture and transforms them. Instead of moving toward any collective consciousness raising, the middle-class utopia that we have here is one in which those desires for coherence are seen to fail, crumble, and are exposed as a futile wish in a world that "naturally" does not provide for such possibilities. Thus, the mechanisms that keep subjects separate and individuated is extrapolated outward and mapped onto the nature of the universe itself so that any desire to try and read history qua history is derailed into a closed hermeneutic in which, as Lea points out, Swift's characters have a "desire for salvation" but this desire must be curtailed so that they all "have to face the traduction of their ideals by the pragmatic relativism of the contemporary episteme."[69] In this sense the text "manages" the working-class desire for radical cultural transformation by placing those desires into a narrative in which they are shown to be futile and pointless. Having shown that the subjects can no longer turn to any grand narratives for comfort (or revolutionary zeal) they are made to fall back on "believing in believing" and "faith" (as Lea says) but it seems to be a faith that not only does not extend to others in society, but can barely be held onto even by the isolated self.[70] While critics may respond that the novel is using Ray and his friends as signifiers of a universal condition, it is surely apposite that they are scripted as *working-class* figures, and thus their sense of being lost is not seen (in the body of the text) to apply to middle-class, or even upper-class characters, but only to these members of the working class. This choice of social setting and class milieu is undoubtedly driven by the class interests (albeit unconscious) of the author, and as Jameson points out, the fact that a text is plotted and shaped in the way that it is raises questions of class, and the question of how texts function as a way of "managing" the cultural tensions that capitalism produces but cannot remove: "the aesthetic act is itself ideological, and the production of aesthetic or narrative form is to be seen as an ideological act in its own right, with the function of inventing imaginary or formal 'solutions' to unresolvable social contradictions."[71]

So in *Last Orders* we are seeing a middle-class utopian narrative impulse in which the traditional white working class (treated as the symbolic core of "the" working class) emerges in a narrative in which they are present on the stage of history but are powerless to act: they are among us, but their power has been curtailed. In this middle-class utopia, the working class suffer in existential silence with the continuation of things as they are, since the revolution will not be coming and is always already out of reach in the real.

Hence in Daniel Lea's reading of Swift, rather than moving toward an examination of the economic framework of the character's class-based malaise, we find ourselves being asked to consider, paradoxically, Swift's "areligious religious novels" in which the working-class characters seem to mean everything and yet nothing:[72] in this novel the actions of the working-class characters are both "intrinsic and irrelevant to the historical process."[73] In addition, the subjects are both "within and without a framework of social reference"[74] and their rituals are both "significant and insignificant."[75] Moreover, the characters' search for a real self among their multiple selves is also therefore put into question as "none and all of these selves are credible," while in true postmodern fashion the analysis soon drifts into how "the self actually consists not in any immanent essentiality, but in the polyphonic multitude of its retelling" in the "subjective void" of a "no man's land of existential indeterminacy."[76] The tentative catharsis that the end of the novel provides, can be read, says Lea, not as an "empty gesture" but as a "poignant moment of rapprochement [which] attests to a trans-substantive action of community," but one which sadly "will not reinvigorate a lost community" although it does provide an opportunity for "individual change and self-realisation."[77]

A parallel reading emerges in Adrian Poole's often cited essay "Graham Swift and the Mourning After" whereby the mourning that the characters engage in will never be enough to recover their "existential" sense of loss:

> There is a residue that can never be recovered because that figure once filled a time and a space from which it cannot be separated. Hence the double sense the reader gets at the end of *Waterland* and *Last Orders*, that we are left both with a knowable pattern, a coherence achieved, and with everything that such knowledge and completion and coherence must omit and can never recover, all the memories, desires and stories. Hence the strange double sense of cheerfulness and desolation.[78]

The result is a disempowered community who are "left to mourn the impossibility of such mourning" and subsequently can only "go on telling stories" but in true Beckettian fashion they are also "waiting for the ideal listener who will never quite arrive."[79] So in *Last Orders* (and in the canonized readings of the novel) we are left with a text that celebrates the individual fractured ego, not the community, the isolated self over the group, and the existentially terrified consciousness, not the raised empowered one. It is a novel that asks us to celebrate the person who cannot change or grow and is in the same place at the end of their life, but who is somehow all the richer for it, and has bravely confronted an essentially empty universe in which they both can and cannot "connect/Nothing with nothing." What the novel also manages, at the level of form, is to assert that social transformation is essentially impossible and unnecessary and that lives must be "half lived" for these working-class characters because nothing else is available to them. As Jameson points out, "some utopians long for the end of the political altogether"[80] and here in *Last Orders* while Swift's conscious desire may have been to construct a text in which Death can be "contained within a network of socially symbolic rituals that desensitize the impact of the unknown" the unconscious utopian desire has formed a middle-class narrative that hopes that working-class history and agency have finally been laid to rest.[81]

Jonathan Coe

Having been educated at Trinity College, Cambridge and then on to Warwick University for his Ph.D., it is clear that Coe is no exception to the rule when it comes to the canonical institution and education of middle-class contemporary British authors. Yet when his work is discussed, Coe's own class position is elided while his work seems to have an almost magical power to take on Thatcherism and be able, single-handedly, to cut it down to size. Dominic Head is unreserved in his praise for what he sees as "the most significant novel about the effects of Thatcherism...an extraordinary literary achievement" "a work of great flair that ranges assuredly between the poles of comedy and tragedy."[82] But as we have seen before, the canonized novel is also one which speaks for the middle class, and here in *What a Carve Up!* the central protagonist is an author, who, as Head admits, "stands for Coe."[83] So, it would seem that the concerns of this novel will be the concerns of the middle class, but simply because the novel is somehow anti-Thatcher does not automatically make it a novel that is in anyway socialist. Yet, Coe is seen by many critics as "the" political writer of the current generation, and in his presentation of strikes, IRA bombings and NHS cuts, comes to be seen as the political realist novelist par excellence. He is seen by Head for example as someone who has realized that "an elaborate fictional form is required to offer a meaningful commentary on fragmented society." More than just creating a kind of postmodern realism that will enable us to see our way clearly in the confusion of postwar culture, Coe, in his privileged position "alludes confidently to both 'highbrow' and popular culture" so much so that Head feels that the narrator/author Michael Owen (i.e., the Coe stand-in) functions "as a kind of Everyman" who offers up his "judgment of Thatcherism."[84] The nasty evil members of the Winshaw family in *What a Carve Up!* thus become symbols of Thatcherism, and as Head points out "[t]hese characters are caricatures of a new unethical elite, and together they represent the full range of social devastation, which the novel lays at the door of the Thatcher era."[85] These evil people are thus representative of Thatcher's "process of abandoning all beliefs, principles, values and policies." Interestingly, it is not the working classes who are shown to suffer from these policies in the novel in any great detail, the main focus is on the author/narrator, the middle-class figure of Michael Owen. As Head points out, the "writing persona becomes the symbolic victim."[86] Given this radical dismantling of the norm by the Thatcher revolution (which is essentially undermining the post war consensus), Coe's textual function is not to politically undermine Thatcherism from a socialist perspective, but to simply restore the culture to a middle class, decent, honorable center.[87] This desire to attack Thatcherism for its greed, callousness, and its inhuman distaste for all things decent, leads Coe directly toward a satire of his social and economic moment, as opposed to any radical desire to overturn capitalism. In many ways this is a very old tradition of epater le bourgeois that can be traced back to Dickens: a tradition in which the middle-class author, stuck between the upper and lower classes turns his anger toward the upper classes and their excesses (as well as those of his own class) while never really having any real economic connection to the working classes. As the novelist Ian Sansom points out, Orwell was clear that "the great disadvantage, and advantage, of the small urban bourgeois is his limited outlook. He sees the world as a middle-class world, and everything outside these limits is either laughable or slightly wicked. Once again, in *The Rotters' Club*, the comparison magnificently holds."[88] At one point in *What a Carve Up!* Michael Owen comments on the Winshaws: "Did they have the same worries that I had, these absurd people? Did they have the sort of feelings I would even understand? It wasn't enough to say that they came from a different walk of life. It was more extreme, more final than that: they belonged to a different genre of existence altogether. One which actually horrified me...."[89] Sadly, these sentiments are also expressed, in less overt ways, toward the working-class figures in the novel as well. So, despite the apparent "postmodernity" of *What a Carve Up!* it is clear that underneath, Coe's text elicits all the trademarks of his own middle-class ideological limits. As Philip Tew points out:

> An emphasis common in British fiction is an authorial notion of a similar conviction of the innocuousness of liberal attitudes; even where there might appear superficially to be a literary transformation—subject matter, inclusion of new cultural values and fashions, generic shifts, self-consciousness—many writers retain a conceptual world-view based on liberal values and the cultural significance of the middle-class. [90]

So, in its extreme attacks on the excesses of the Winshaw family the novel places itself firmly in this tradition whereby the upper class is exposed as perverted, greedy, and callous while the victimized "poor" author who can see all the greed and corruption and seeks to expose it is presented to us as the "innocuous" and unquestioned moral center of the text.

Head points out that the novel "veers dramatically from farce to pathos, realism to metafiction, in a unique satirical statement," while the role of Owen/Coe/Everyman, is thus through the tool of the satirical novel, to bring about a "reinvigoration of social connection" and "an angry repudiation of the Winshaw dynasty." So while Thatcherism and greed tear the culture apart, Coe's text will restore it and reclaim the center ground by generating a novel that will reveal "the social interconnections that remain" and that having been "neglected" are now conduits for "exploitation and suffering."[91] This notion of Coe as a satirist has been repeated by Randall Stevenson who feels that the novel is a "satiric attack on a huge range of targets, including the tabloid press, factory farming, arms manufacture, the aristocracy, and the shortcomings of the National Health Service."[92] I would also suggest therefore that the form of *What a Carve Up!* that Head feels is "unrepeatable"[93] is little more than what Randall Stevenson accurately terms "stylistic pluralism" and that in the same way that Thatcher breaks with the postwar consensus, so Coe breaks with the limits of conventional realism, expanding his palette through an "aesthetic supermarket" but which leaves class formations unaltered.[94] In this sense Coe's text is echoing and manifesting at a textual level what Thatcher's privatization of industry did at the economic level. Coe's work is certainly a critique of Thatcher, and as Eagleton has said it is "one of the few pieces of genuinely political Post-Modern fiction around" but he also goes on to add that "the novel is chiefly political in a pleasantly old-fashioned sense, preoccupied with animal torturers, predatory stockbrokers and the Gulf War...."[95] To this extent, it is the form of the novel that finally brings the novel's politics back to the moral certitude of the center. Eagleton in fact goes further and condemns the novel for its openly ideological denouement:

> [T]he governing elite is not a family, and so cannot be summoned to the drawing room for their just deserts, nor are they hideously evil individuals as the Winshaws most certainly are. In this sense, *What a Carve Up!* is fantastic wish fulfillment, able to establish political justice only by a crafty reshuffling of genres in which fairy tale is projected onto realpolitik.[96]

Pamela Thurschwell has argued that Coe's work, such as *The Rotters' Club* and *The Closed Circle*, explore the "weighty political and moral issues" that have emerged in contemporary Britain as a result of the "collapse of communal structures" that had sustained it since 1945. Coe's novels thus explore "the breakdown of the post-war British consensus that the state ought to look after people 'from cradle to grave.' "[97] This includes the dismantling of the trade unions in the 1970s and the restructuring of the National Health Service in the 1980s. Although it is certainly true that the novel is concerned with these issues, we cannot assume that it has magically escaped from bourgeois ideology. Rather than turning toward socialism, Coe is turning, in her words, to "classical tragedy" to provide him with a narrative structure to represent these events.[98] The result is that the novels then present these political changes in terms of "the roles of contingency, chance and destiny; [alongside] the sense of helplessness that large scale political and economic forces engender in people, and each individual's potentially catastrophic confrontation with a historical situation he or she cannot control and can barely begin to understand."[99] Thurschwell sees Coe, almost like Lea saw Swift, as the contemporary equivalent of "Thomas Hardy" in whose works we see how "History and individual tragic fate seem inescapably intertwined." The epigraph for her essay is Marx's much quoted comment from *The Eighteenth Brumaire of Louis Napoleon*, where, expanding on Hegel, he remarks that all historical personages show up twice, "the first time as tragedy, the second as farce."[100] For Thurschwell, "Marx's words seem appropriate for Coe's oeuvre" with the difference that there is no initial tragic performance that the farce mimes, rather "farce itself becomes the modern form of tragedy." The result is that "Coe's narrative universe is one where parody Gothic and gritty realism coexist, where Groucho and Karl vie for space on the same page, even in the same sentence."[101] For Thurschwell this reading of history as comedy/farce is not so much a sign of weakness in Coe, but becomes his strength, and the sign of a great author. So, while she admits that "farce, as a genre, distances us from everyday life," in Coe "farce is often designed to enrage," and that his "abundant borrowings from popular and high-culture genres actually function to feed anger rather than defuse it." Using Michael Owen's review of a novel in *What a Carve Up!* Thurschwell sees this as a direct expression of Coe's own "strategy" and a "fair description of Coe's project":[102]

> We stand badly in need of novels, after all, which show an understanding of the ideological hijack which has taken place so recently in this country...the appropriate response lies not merely in sorrow and anger but in mad, incredulous laughter.[103]

Thurschwell's aim is to examine the ways that Coe uses Greek tragedy to deal with the "gritty social realities of the 1980s." She draws on Mengham's comment that *What a Carve Up!* mirrors the "cultural psychosis" of Thatcherism and suggests that Coe is clever at showing us how our contemporary lives are governed by "generic rules" and that in the same way that his characters are unable to "escape from a film or a bad novel" this "also functions as a metaphor for the stitching up of narrative possibilities by the ruling classes who control the means of production, textual and otherwise."[104] Strangely though, such a comment seems to assume that Coe is somehow not part of that ruling class, that he is some radically subaltern and subversive author who is outside of such a system, rather than a highly successful Cambridge educated author. For Eagleton, Coe's work shows us the "paranoid world of the Post-Modernist text, where everything is at once arbitrary and obsessively interconnected...aleatory and sinisterly connected,"[105] but Thurschwell insists that Coe's work reveals a "characteristically postmodern nostalgia for better times—when people seemed capable of really relating to each other."[106] Eagleton has made this point too, but added something that Thurschwell seems to be rather quiet about:

> Post-Modernism's compulsive connecting is in part a utopian impulse, a yearning for a non-fragmentary world in which things might once

> more rhyme. But it is quite as much dystopian: the reflection of a society in which the public has so deeply penetrated the private that there seems no room left for chance or free play.[107]

For Thurschwell, Michael Owen in *What a Carve Up!* suffers from "excessive passivity and [a] lack of self-knowledge" but this is not seen as in any way reductive, and in fact, Owen's "autistic withdrawal" is not a problem of his "psychic make-up" but is a symbolic "product of the *zeitgeist*," and his blindness puts him on a par with Oedipus. Coe's novels are thus of value to us, in Thurschwell's view, in that they reveal "the historically traumatized state of the postmodern subject, a state in which the freeze-frame becomes the only way left to experience history."[108] The result is that Michael Owen's "relation to history, and to genre, leaves no room for working through, or human agency," and that in Coe's other novels, such as *The Rotters' Club* and *The Closed Circle* we are repeatedly faced with characters who are "unable to escape defining events of their childhood."[109] As we saw with Graham Swift, Thurschwell feels that Coe's novels provide us with narratives in which "being unable to process history may be the defining condition of what it means to live through it." In addition, as we saw with Graham Swift, Coe always refuses "to let his male fictional alter egos succeed via art; they can't write their way out of their historical predicaments... [and are] trapped by history." Thurschwell basically closes her analysis at this point, but finishes by switching the debate away from history toward gender. Consistently avoiding any consideration of the class of Coe's characters, she feels that Coe's novels are less "tragic" in the field of gender, and that while the men in his texts may be "clueless... Coe's women... react differently."[110] Drawing on the characters Lois and Fiona Trotter, she argues that "these women... want chains of cause and effect which are both simpler and more difficult; historical explanations which allow some room for human agency, farces or tragedies which aren't all determining."[111] Admirable as this may be it is not really clear why these two women, without any consideration of their class position, are somehow able to move beyond the zeitgeist that seems to affect all of the male characters. There is no real answer on this matter but she closes by suggesting that Coe's novels "lead us towards the recognition of modern history as tragedy" while also serving up "incredulous, shared laughter" for the rest of us who are watching "postmodernism's endless historical reruns: our second time farces."[112]

This presentation of Coe is troubling in that Thurschwell is reading Coe's novels in such a way as to leave no room for agency, and despite their overt references to the events of the periods that Coe considers, the sense that class is being examined in any dialectical way is sadly missing. In this sense Coe's work, while seeming on the surface to avoid the route of mourning and melancholia, essentially functions in the same vein as Swift, whereby the real is presented in all its verisimilitude including the sense of powerlessness that ideology engenders in its subjects: it is realism without the real, a historical novel sans history or telos, and which exist only as tragedies in which, contrary to Brecht's advice, all classes of readers should respond by laughing at their own powerlessness.

Although it is clear that the Winshaws are "a family of criminals," the novel's relationship to the working class is clearly problematic.[113] In one scene Michael Owen travels on the underground to go to see his publisher. As in many contemporary novels, the working class is always seen through a very distasteful lens. We read how Owen feels like "Orpheus descending to the underworld" on the Tube, and is "confronted by this throng of pale and sad-looking people" [and] "red-faced passengers." Once inside he takes his "first mouthful of the foul, stagnant air" and has to stand up against the glass next to "a huge slimy patch, exactly at face level, an accumulation of sweat and grease off the back of the earlier passengers heads" (95). He is face to face with "pallid, pimply skin" and "hot breath" and next to him is a "builder's labourer" whose smelly armpit is right in Owen's face: "my nose was right inside his moist gingery armpit" and he hopes that it will "all be over in a couple of minutes" (Ibid). The bodies of the working-class passengers seem to come only in extremes: there was a "wizened old man" and a "plump woman who for some reason had already gone purple in the face" and a "tall asthmatic guy . . . who was taking regular gulps from his inhaler" (96–97). Another passenger is eating a burger and we get a close up of "his gaping jaws" and every "knob of gristle" (98). Like Dante, talking to Paulo and Francesca in the *Inferno*, Owen suddenly faints. While this echoes so many scenes in which working-class people are presented as grotesque or excessive, in this particular case, the scene has no role in the development of the narrative. He is taken to a railway office, given a cup of tea, and then walks to his publisher. Hence this scene is entirely gratuitous, other than to allow us a glimpse into Coe/Owen's unconscious dislike for the working class. In this way we see how the author is caught between a distrust of the upper-class Winshaws and a dislike of the working classes.

The same position emerges in the portrayal of Roddy the art dealer, when he goes to collect Phoebe from her council estate flat. At one point he tells everyone that he doesn't only choose artists to exhibit because he "knew [their] brother at Trinity" but has taken on some "real" artists: "I do go round all the art schools, you know, looking for new work. I've just taken this chap on, and he lives in Brixton. Thoroughly working-class. It's pretty dangerous stuff, too: pretty ground breaking. He takes these enormous canvases and holds them at a sort of angle and then he tips these big cans of paint over them so that it all runs—" (196). In one remark the text has thus opened up two lines of ideological thought. On the one hand it exposes Roddy's superficial attempts to be a "real" art dealer who deals with artists beyond the confines of his own bourgeois world, and thus exposes his callousness but at the same time it also mocks the working-class Brixton artist whose "genuine" talent is certainly put into question. As Phoebe adds, "That sort of stunt was interesting in the sixties for about five minutes" (Ibid). Even Phoebe's position (what Hilary Winshaw refers to facetiously as "a *bona fide*, old-fashioned, dyed-in-the-wool, head-in-the-clouds *socialist*") is undermined in the novel by the fact that she is prepared to sleep with Roddy to become a famous artist (199). The same ideological splitting in the novel is seen when Graham Packard is reading an early draft of Owen's novel. While Thurschwell has quoted the comment made by Owen about "mad incredulous laughter" only one page before, Graham declares his objections to the contemporary novel: "the problem with the English novel is that there's no political engagement. I mean it's all just a lot of pissing about within the limits set down by bourgeois morality, as far as I can see. There's no radicalism" (276). While this comment is unsettling to Owen, it will not be fully undermined until much later in the novel when we see Graham Packard again in 1990 when we are told that "Graham had left college with his ideals intact, but seven years later his student radicalism, was to all appearances, a thing of the past: he now occupied a managerial position with Midland Ironmasters...." (370). Graham Packard will thus be caught up in the arms trade financed by Mark Winshaw. At one point he is sitting in a restaurant in Baghdad and Mark Winshaw is gently teasing him: "You've grown up quite a lot in the last few years it would seem...Politically I mean. Let me see now was it the Socialist Workers, or the Revolutionary Communists who enjoyed your services as treasurer?" Graham can only sheepishly reply "As you say...I've grown up a lot" (Ibid).

Philip Tew suggests that Coe's work, like that of Jenny Diski, represent spaces in which "in portraying a middle-class world, there can exist both a plural and intelligently critical view of middle-class culture and its place in British society."[114] Yet, it would seem that "plural and intelligently critical" really means complacently bourgeois. Tew feels that in *The Rotters' Club* Coe offers us a world in which "All of the classes exist within the city and within the text itself. None is ultimately privileged in a narrative sense, as they all share the pathos of bad judgment...."[115] As in Thurschwell's criticism, nobody escapes, and we are all subject to the same overarching historical forces and we "all share" in the tragedy of our own historical moment. Rather than stopping to think that perhaps not everyone experiences the present under the same economic conditions, Tew asserts that this all inclusiveness makes Coe a great social commentator and "allows [Coe] a plurality of sorts, a cartography of pathos." Coe's value for Tew is that he thus "recuperates the role of the novel, its need to critique and engage, even in a postmodern environment," producing a kind of postmodern political novel:

> It is evident from this kind of contextualization that, very unusually for a post-war British novelist, Coe in his narrative appeals to and integrates a broad public rhetoric, establishing a mixture of ethnic and class positions, and importantly within the voicing of the text he sets out a series of middle-class voices—including his own implied narrative position—where each one exists simply as a contributory viewpoint in the generality that is the order and disorder of social affairs.[116]

Yet this is surely disingenuous because both *The Rotters' Club* and *The Closed Circle* are broadly speaking working in a realist vein, and realism has to engage in a hierarchy of discourses: even the apparent democracy of "all voices being equal" is in itself an artificial textual construct that serves an ideological function.[117] What we see here in Tew's reading of Coe is the logic of multiculturalism in which all voices are accepted and can coexist, which is then being superimposed onto class conflict. Interestingly, such a narrative strategy is not "very unusual" in the post war middle-class novel, as Tew says, rather it is the norm. Ideology cannot expose that different classes in British culture are at odds with each other in insoluble ways, so instead Coe's text fulfills a vital ideological function by creating a coherent stable realist text in which all the classes can be seen to "really" coexist and live alongside each other in an economic space where material conditions no longer matter because everyone is equal in postwar, postmodern British narrative and society: one in which the national narrative privileges no one. In this way the novels are attempting to say that this "is" how we live, this is the "reality" of our relations under capital and the realism of the texts themselves is proof of that reality. In this way, the meaning of "the closed circle" that Coe uses takes on a slightly different meaning. In *The Rotters' Club* the closed circle is the secret elite student group at King Williams School, and in one of Paul Trotter's letters he announces that *The Closed Circle* is powerful because "The Circle is accountable to no one but itself" and does not have to "listen to the voice of the rabble. In essence it is anti-democratic and that is its strength."[118] In this sense, Coe's fiction is also a closed circle which in true postmodern style refers only to itself, while pointing to a simulacrum of history. Lukacs admired realism in that it enabled us to see ourselves and our history in the mirror of the real, but now, like vampires, the working-class subject cannot see themselves reflected in the realist novel. Terry Eagleton has remarked on this process:

> The aesthetics of postmodernism is a dark parody of such anti-representationalism: if art no longer reflects, it is not because it seeks to change the world rather than mimic it, but because there is in truth nothing there to be reflected, no reality which is not itself already image, spectacle, simulacrum, gratuitous fiction. To say that social reality is pervasively commodified is to say that it is always already "aesthetic"—textured, packaged, fetishized, libidinalized; and for art to reflect reality is then for it to do no more than mirror itself, in a cryptic self-referentiality which is indeed one of the inmost structures of the commodity fetish...The commodity is less an image in the sense of a "reflection" than an image of itself, its entire material being devoted to its own self-presentation.[119]

The problem then when considering the arguments of Thurschwell and Tew, is that if all class narratives and class positions are equal, and none are privileged by the form of *The Rotters' Club* and *The Closed Circle* then politically we are truly in a tragic situation in so far as any sense of telos and utopian desire has been effectively unraveled and dissolved. At one point in *The Closed Circle*, Philip Chase is trying to write an essay on contemporary politics but encounters a problem:

> Sometimes he would draft a paragraph or two, and read it back only to discover that he himself had started to sound like a far-right

> sympathizer, and then half an hour later he would look at it again and find that now it seemed to be coming from the radical left. There didn't seem to be a difference between the two perspectives any more, between anybody's perspectives.[120]

Or, in the words of Ian Buchanan: "The only realism left to us is the realism of that experience of being locked inside a hyper-real simulacra."[121] Praising Coe for his powerful "intertwining of actuality with invention," Richard Bradford reminds us that in *The Closed Circle* we see a world in which politicians, by careful management of the media have "insulated themselves from serious scrutiny":[122] it would seem that Coe's fiction, like that of Swift and Hollinghurst, has also moved in step with this trend, by giving us the ultimate commodity: history itself, a history, as Eagleton points out, which comes to us "textured, packaged, fetishized" cleansed of the tensions and contradictions of class struggle.[123]

In conclusion, does the canonical British novel have a history of radicalism? In a recent review of Patrick Parrinder's *Nation and Novel: The English Novel from Its Origins to the Present Day*, Michael Sanders points out that Parrinder clearly outlines how the English novel has adapted itself since the eighteenth century to a host of changed historical circumstances, but while the novel "is a form of national allegory" Sanders asks "what are we to make of its relative distance from existing forms of popular culture throughout much of its history?"[124] Parrinder concludes that while the British novel has an inherently "republican form, it is far from being a democratic one."[125] Sanders' concern is that while the British National Party is currently offering its own version of a racist and xenophobic "toxic Englishness," the canonical British novel cannot turn its back on the popular working class of any race or ethnic origin. If the novel is to be truly democratic in the years to come, it must break with its traditions and find ways of dealing with "the majority of its population" and not just the middle classes. I would concur with Sanders that "throughout its history the national allegory has struggled to represent the majority of its population within its form" and that "[t]he English novel still needs to find a way of representing those experiences... if it is to make good the promise of a radical English identity."[126]

Chapter 5

A Class Act: Representations of Class in British Cinema and Television 1979–2008

The working-class... is a group that is in itself, as a group within the social edifice, a nongroup, in other words, one whose position is in itself contradictory; they are a productive force. Society (and those in power) needs them in order to reproduce themselves and their rule, but nonetheless, they cannot find a proper place for them.

—Slavoj Žižek[1]

This chapter offers an analysis of a variety of texts from British art cinema to mainstream cinema and finally examines television as a way of productively opening up British media to questions of class. To begin with, I examine the work of Mike Leigh, Peter Greenaway, and Derek Jarman. All three have become central to the canon of British art cinema and yet critical work on them has a tendency to erase any troubling class questions in their work. The critical tendency has been to steer clear of treating them as middle-class auteurs, and instead treats their work as offering universal or existential themes, or as echoing "radical" postmodern/poststructuralist concerns that as we have seen, also evade the problem of class. The section on mainstream cinema will briefly examine the class narrative in the Harry Potter movies, as well as Stephen Frears's *Dirty Pretty Things*. In both cases these two highly successful mainstream productions offer ways of seeing how class is managed and positioned for a popular audience. Turning to television I examine the class dynamics of various "makeover" and "lifestyle" programs that have increased in popularity during the period, as well as examining the troubling class and gender aspects of the political drama *The Amazing Mrs. Pritchard*. Some of the concerns that have been raised will then be explored by looking at how the working class has been presented in various television comedies such as *I'm Alan Partridge* and *The Office*. Given that Sam Tyler "wakes up in 1973," I have concluded by looking at *Life on Mars* as a way of examining how the program treats the question of class from the double perspectives of 2007 and 1973. Across the spectrum of all these media, I will be concerned to assess the extent to which, since 1979, collective concerns and the issues of class and society, have been ideologically transformed into poststructuralist abstractions of "identity" and the fulfillment of "personal desire."

Mike Leigh OBE

As the son of a doctor, living above the surgery, Mike Leigh has often reminded us that he was "a middle-class kid growing up in a working-class environment" adding that he was both "an insider and an outsider, all at once"[2] This biographical comment is important because it highlights the central paradox at the heart of his work. Leigh, now Mike Leigh OBE, has become central to the canon of British cinema and has made an international reputation for himself, but his films display some of the central problems that we have been addressing in the fiction of this period. While Leigh is clearly a middle-class auteur, his films have almost exclusively dealt with the working class. This double frame means that as with our middle-class canonical authors of fiction, with Leigh we have a director who is generally accepted as offering a clear window into the truth of working-class experience while it is clear that he is not of this class, but is always already an "outsider." Unlike the films of Ken Loach whose films are often dismissed for pushing an overtly socialist agenda, Leigh's work is always favorably interpreted and received: I would argue that this favorable critical reception is because his work articulates a picture of the working class that is entirely amenable to liberal bourgeois ideology.

One example of how Leigh's work is ideological as opposed to political can be seen if we look at the critics. A recent book length study on Leigh by Ray Carney delineates the ways in which Leigh's films can be dealt with quite comfortably simply by treating them as "profoundly true" studies of the "emotional complexity and tragicomic experiences" of "human beings." Hence, for Carney, Leigh is both "clearly political" and yet "his films carry no political agendas, nor do they offer political alternatives or solutions."[3] In this way, Leigh's work, like many of the textual practices that we have been examining, can give the impression of tackling serious issues (e.g., Carney feels that many of the films "get right to the heart of English class power") while at the same time actually offering no troubling political critique of class at all. Insofar as they can manage to do both is a sign of the films ideological nature.[4]

Carney's work on Leigh thus seeks to draw out, not the political problems with Leigh's work, but instead by moving away from politics, he treats Leigh's oeuvre as one grounded in a kind of existential foundation, whereby politics is merely the window through which to see a much more important human condition that politics can neither help nor hinder. So, for Carney: "What makes Leigh unique is his ability to construct a humorously bleak and desperate world filled with characters whose comic behavior springs from their essence as human beings."[5] Therefore, while the films may have the surface look and feel, to an extent, of traditional social realism the goal is far from that offered by the supposedly rigid and programmatic socialist Ken Loach. In Carney's words: "Leigh's subject is the possibility of personal transformation."[6] However, these transformations seem few and far between in his films, and generally the working-class characters at the center of the films are predominantly unable to change. Carney feels that neither is this an ideological blockage in Leigh, nor is it symptomatic of his own class limits, but in fact is simply the truth of the human condition. To this extent while Loach's films are dismissed as socialist propaganda, Leigh rises above such limits and creates great art:

> Leigh's work dramatizes the individual's capacities for creative performance within inescapable limitations. His characters...cannot transcend the social forms of expression that define them. There is no unconditioned realm of consciousness into which they can withdraw...They must find a way to express themselves, uniquely and creatively, within social and psychological forms and structures that inexorably limit who they are and what they can say and do. (30)

Carney goes on to place Leigh into the British *literary* canon. He is "true to the culture of Jane Austen, Charles Dickens, and George Eliot" (84) and the result is an author who leaves the audience in no doubt that there is no political system or class to blame since Carney is confident that "even the class system" has "eroded" (6) since Thatcher took office. All that is left are isolated figures who have no one to blame but themselves for how their lives are. For Carney, Leigh exposes how his characters often delude themselves and others and that while there is no one to blame the punishment is individualized: "Characters are punished by undergoing a breakdown or simply by suffering due to an inherently contradictory or deluded position" (84) Leigh's plays thus offer for Carney, as in "Greek tragedy... potentially transformative moments of *anagnorisis*" while those who "maintain their routines against all odds clinging to their old understandings with a death grip... are truly lost souls" (85). Carney feels that the point of Leigh's work is "to put the viewer in the most emotionally and intellectually challenging position possible" (88). Since his work is "primarily addressed to an educated middle-class,"[7] what if we take the radical position of proposing that Leigh's work, rather than challenging the middle-class audience, gives them a thoroughly ideological representation that is both emotionally and intellectually satisfying and rewards, reaffirms, and reiterates deeply held ideological beliefs? Carney claims that "The point [of Leigh's work] is to rattle our complacencies, to force us to let go of preconceived notions and actually start thinking freshly, opening ourselves to the actual flow and complexity of experience" so that we can be moved to "a place beyond knowing."[8] In actual fact, I would suggest that Leigh's films take potentially troubling class conflicts and neutralize them by framing them as personal failings and/or family issues. Žižek has commented on this standard Hollywood approach to cinema:

> Numerous treatises have been written about the perception of a historical Real in the terms of a family narrative as a fundamental ideological operation: a story about the conflict of larger social forces (classes and so forth) is framed into the coordinates of a family drama. This ideology, of course, finds its clearest expression in Hollywood as the ultimate ideological machine: in a typical Hollywood product, everything... is transposed into an Oedipal narrative.[9]

For Carney, this reduction to family relationships is what elevates Leigh to the level of high art, but I think we need to see Leigh's work as being complicit with, rather than critical of middle-class ideology.

Leigh's *Abigail's Party* becomes a case in point. Carney reads the film outside of its class context and sees the protagonists, Beverly (an ex-Beautician) and her husband Laurence (an Estate Agent) as existentially empty ciphers who are laboring under "what Sartre here calls 'bad faith'" and that their problem "is less that they are troubled individuals than that they are not individuals at all."[10] Now while this could be read in terms of the material conditions that have shaped their false-consciousness, Carney goes in the opposite direction, so that their problem is not even psychological, but actually, "ontological," so much so that "in a sense, there is no Beverly" since her entire existence is a kind of empty act, in which everything is a sad performance of a self that is painfully empty: she is thus "a ventriloquist's dummy mouthing someone else's words, an impersonation of a person." Every line of dialogue is thus "inauthentic" and "everything is fake."[11] Yet, if Beverly and Laurence are somehow symptomatic of a human condition then surely we would see this in all of the characters in the film, as it would be a universal problem. But if we look closely at other characters in the film a very different picture emerges, one that reveals how Leigh's work is working with class, not ontology.

Carney uses dialogue between Susan and Beverly as an example of how empty Beverly's phrases are, and how they are "all feigned, formulas."[12] Yet Carney cuts off the dialogue right before the all-important punch line: having unwrapped the bottle of Beaujolais that Susan has bought, and thanked her for such a nice gesture, Beverly says "I'll just pop it in the fridge." This one line is crucial in understanding how the film operates at the level of class, because, the in-joke, at Beverly's expense, is that red wine is not to be served chilled and that the suggestion of refrigeration exposes Beverly's ignorance for comic effect. At this point a gulf opens up in the film with the arrival of Susan, who is clearly not working class (her husband is an architect), and who has a definite middle-class sense of detachment during the entire evening and in short operates as the outsider on the inside. Susan, whose phrases are not empty, and who seems untroubled by any existential/ontological hollowness, becomes the surrogate educated middle-class viewer. She enables us to see them, and we see their (embarrassing) actions through her eyes. Susan is manifestly not part of Beverly's world of empty gestures since, I would suggest, her class position removes her from such a vacant existence. The other working-class couple, Angela (a Nurse) and Tony (a Computer Operator, who is embarrassed to admit that he does "shift work" and is not a Computer Programmer like Beverly's brother), both lack the anxieties, insecurities, and aspirations of Beverly and Laurence, and they are not subjected to the same level of satirical criticism. What the film clearly delineates then is that Angela and Tony and Susan are rewarded with our respect by the narrative insofar as they are comfortably accepting of their middle- and working-class positions. Leigh's comic vision is never really applied to Angela and Tony, and Susan is never mocked during the entire film. In fact, she vomits after being forced to consume too many of Beverly's drinks: in symbolic class terms these people literally make her sick. The full force of the film's satire is directed at Beverly and Laurence not simply because they are working class, but because they are trying to cross the boundaries between classes. The film's biting satire is thus reserved for them alone, and as always with satire's conservative impulse, the desire is to see them safely returned to an acceptance of their class position.[13] As Carney tellingly observes, while Laurence may think of himself as a "connoisseur," "we" (the educated middle-class critic/viewer) know that he is "the rankest of Philistines." So, while Susan and Angela and Tony are free to come and go, "Beverly and Laurence are trapped in emotional routines they don't even realize are routines."[14] For Carney, their condition is not produced by anxieties or worries that are rooted in their class, instead, their troubles are all internal, and therefore the only position made available by the film's narrative is one in which "we feel sorry for them" and yet there is nothing we can do for them as "their cries are the screams of the eternally damned."[15]

It is this sense of the working class as somehow alone and cut off from the audience that serves to strengthen the ideological element of Leigh's work. This reading of Leigh continues throughout Carney's text, and every film is viewed through this existential lens, thus ensuring that all political questions are safely bracketed. *High Hopes* is thus simply showing us a world of "private inward turnings and meditative moments of mind that will never be made part of an ideological system of understanding or control. In this sense the film might be said to be Leigh's meditation on the limitations of political understandings of experience."[16] Carney gives the same reading of *Naked* too. While admitting that the film is certainly tinged with a post-Thatcherite despair, the issue of class is not central, and as with *Abigail's Party* we are back in the realm of Sartre, not Marx:

> It is Johnny the individual, not Johnny the homeless social victim or member of a displaced working-class intelligentsia, who is terrified of making personal commitments and incapable of using his powerful intelligence and literate wit in a productive way. The responsibility for his self-destructive behavior is not reductively arrogated to Thatcher, to capitalist greed and exploitation, or even to the inequalities of the English class system. *Naked*'s emphasis is an existential one. It is a film about a variety of isolated, emotionally hobbled characters trying to live with themselves and other people in a meaningless universe. Their pain is determined less by their economic situation than by their psychological and spiritual states of being.[17]

Treating the films in this way means that any troubling questions about class can be sidelined and that instead we should get onto more serious issues like art, truth, and human feeling. I am not arguing that Carney is inaccurate though, in fact I would agree that in many cases the characters are left isolated and cut off from themselves and each other, but he sees their trouble as being rooted in some vague existential void, while I am suggesting that Leigh's own ideology seeps into these narratives so that nothing can be seen as a solution beyond the resources of the self-reliant individual.

John Hill has read Leigh's work in a different light that offers us a far more productive way of seeing how Leigh's narratives function to reinforce conventional ideological frameworks. Looking at *High Hopes*, Hill feels that the emphasis on the individual qua individual (which Carney celebrated as a sign of Leigh's true artistry) means that while offering itself as a critique of Thatcherism, the film cannot "offer an attack on the economic hardship suffered by the losers in Thatcher's Britain" and becomes just "a critique of the cultural 'barbarianism' associated with its economic beneficiaries."[18] Hill quotes Richard Combs who feels that Leigh's films go beyond social realism and produce something which is "riven and contradictory" and that while the camera work may be "quiet" (like Ozu) the acting is often conspicuously "loud" (194–195). For Hill, the acting style, with its emphasis on an "isolation, and exaggeration, of external mannerisms" means that we are left not with deeply complex individuals as Carney would say, but with "social types" (195). The problem with this in class terms is that "the overt 'performativity' of the acting tends not only to inhibit the spectator's emotional identification with characters but also to encourage a degree of critical distance and superiority to them," a "superiority [which] is linked to a sense of 'superior' taste and 'cultural capital' that the spectator is presumed to possess but not the characters themselves" (Ibid). For Hill, this acting style is also adjustable: as it is "the least likeable characters who are associated with the most 'excessive' performances" (196). So in *High Hopes,* the Marxist couple Shirley and Cyril are presented as the moral center of the film and stand for a more caring England that has been swept aside by the likes of the ridiculous middle-class yuppies the Booth-Braines, and by the aspiring working classes, typified by the Burkes, and their acting style is played "without the exaggerated mannerisms" that are attached to the others (Ibid). Although this could possibly lead toward a radical conclusion the narrative in true Hollywood fashion a la Žižek, reinscribes any political excess back into the family. So what Hill feels we see in *High Hopes* is a world in which "families are flawed" but "they seem, none the less to be all the characters have to hold on to, given that other forms of communality, extending beyond the family, are either inadequate or non-existent" (Ibid). The radicalism of their friend Suzi is also dismissed by the film's narrative as we find out that she had an abortion: thus serving to align her socialism with a form of barren inhumanity. For Hill then, the film clearly undermines Cyril and Shirley's political hopes by showing that they "lack any clear sense of connection or involvement with a more broadly based social or political community and tradition" (197), while in relation to their desire to have a baby Hill concludes that:

> As such, a film like *High Hopes* ends up conforming to a conservative ideology of "familialism" that is little different from that associated with Thatcherism, moreover, in celebrating the virtues of the privatized family as a kind of escape route from political impotence and passivity, the film, for all its apparent "socialism," appears to end up reinforcing the very skepticism about more collective (or "socialist") forms of political action that was already such a feature of this era.[19]

The most telling criticism of Leigh has actually come, not from a critic but the highly innovative writer Dennis Potter. On first seeing *Abigail's Party* Potter wrote that Leigh "diminished the characters... to a brilliant puppetry of surface observation. The thin wires of prejudice and superficial mimicry can nearly always be seen, tangled up with words... The force of the yelping derision became a single note of contempt, amplified into a relentless screech. As so often in the minefields of English class-consciousness, more was revealed of the snobbery of the observers rather than of the observed."[20] Interestingly enough, nearly all who write on Mike Leigh's work quote Potter's analysis and go to great lengths to undermine his critique. What would be losing if we accepted that his critique was acceptable? What might we gain?

Peter Greenaway

The other canonical art cinema film director who dominated the 1980s and 90s was Peter Greenaway, and his films have generated a large body of academic criticism that generally takes his films as "postmodern" self-referential expressions in which the subject of the films is film itself. So for example, in her poststructuralist reading of *The Cook, the Thief, His Wife and Her Lover* (1989) (via Barthes *S/Z*) Dayana Stetco states that Greenaway produces "texts" that are "lost in perpetual contemplation of their own abyss, preoccupied with themselves, folded within."[21] Stripped of its historical context the film becomes merely the contemplation of "universal consumption and appropriation" and is "a container of everything and nothing at the same time" and that since Greenaway is prepared to "ask questions and not provide definitive answers, we do not see clearly (through tears of laughter or humiliation) the difference between the cultivated and the base."[22] Such apolitical criticism, while admired by the academy, fails to read Greenaway critically.

Yet Greenaway's cinema is clearly unable to escape into a world of *l'art pour l'art* (Art for art's sake) and finds itself constantly dealing with questions of class and power. Written only five years after Martin Amis's *Money* (1984), *The Cook, the Thief, His Wife and Her Lover* rehearses a parallel framework in which it is the working class (in this case Albert Spica) like Amis's working-class protagonist John Self, are linked to uncultured levels of consumption and greed, and who become the object of scorn and hatred. This emergence of what Tony Parsons calls the "prole nouveau" becomes in the hands of Greenaway, as with Amis's protagonist John Self, "an allegory of Thatcherism [built] around images of grotesque corporeality and consumerism."[23] While Stetco wished to see the film as contemplating its own void, even Greenaway himself has suggested that *The Cook, the Thief, His Wife and Her Lover* be read in political terms:

> The film is a very angry one. The political situation that currently exists at the moment in Great Britain under Mrs. Thatcher is one of incredible sense of self-interest and greed. Society is beginning to worry about the price of everything and the value of nothing, and there is a way in which *The Cook, the Thief* is an exemplum of a consumer society, personified in the Thief, Albert Spica. He is a man who is thoroughly despicable in every part of his character. He has no redeeming features and is consumed by self-interest and greed.[24]

The reference to one of Oscar Wilde's aphorisms in "the price of everything and the value of nothing" keys us into the politics of Greenaway's oeuvre in that his work remains firmly within a desire for a self-referential intertextual postmodern cinema that has its roots in *l'art pour l'art*. Notice too that the film is seen as "angry" and yet the object of this anger is the working-class Spica.

Critics have generally tended to follow Greenaway's lead when commenting on his work and praise it for its postmodern playfulness and its resistance to totalizing grand narratives. So for example, Mary Alemany-Galway looks at *The Draughtsman's Contract* in relation to Robbe-Grillet and the postmodern French novel as well as linking it to Resnais's *Last Year at Marienbad*. Placing Greenaway firmly into the camp of "postmodern/poststructuralist cinema," she proceeds to read the film not against its contemporary political moment but in relation to other (inter)textual contexts. The political ramification is that questions of class are easily bracketed and/or made invisible. For Alemany-Galway, the postmodern novel is characterized by "the presentation of unsolvable enigmas, and the forwarding of multiple meanings and contradictions that are left open for the audience's active interpretation." The result is that Greenaway's cinema also therefore "puts forth a multiplicity of meanings, or 'truths' in order to put into question any fixed or totalizing vision of reality." Alemany-Galway follows Scott Bukatman in asserting that while modernism followed Einstein's relativism, postmodernism goes even further by drawing on quantum physics in which "the universe is cast as a field of possibilities devoid of absolute causation."[25] The problem with such a formulation is that it conflates the structure of the natural universe with our own humanly constructed civil society in which absolute causation (i.e., the realm of economics) is easily located. For such postmodern critics then, postmodern textual practices can "effectively act in a critical manner toward the dominant ideologies even if they do not adopt one universal truth or grand narrative" (118). The question at this point though is quite simple: how? Moreover, by suggesting that postmodern art can confront "dominant ideologies" gives the game away, as it reveals how the space of culture is not some indeterminate equal playing field in which many conflicting narratives circulate in peaceful harmony with no final absolute causation a la quantum physics, but that in fact a system of power is in operation that results in "dominant" ideologies, which aim to silence and exclude ideologies that the dominant state apparatuses find objectionable. Confronting these dominant ideologies with a glittering array of contradictions and "unsolvable enigmas" is rather ineffectual, and may actually be in the interests of the dominant ideology.

Alemany-Galway's analysis of *The Draughtsman's Contract* seems promising at the outset as she aims to discuss how the film uses postmodern techniques "to question accepted values, particularly those of the property-owning bourgeois class" (119). Alemany-Galway feels that the film is effective in drawing out the contradictions inherent in "bourgeois ideology" since it exposes how the property owing bourgeois class sees nature as "an object that can be measured, quantified, and owned," and that "Greenaway's film tries to make us aware of these codes and of their ideological implications" (123–124). Try as he might to control and shape reality, the draughtsman, Mr. Neville finds, in conformity with postmodern theory, "that he cannot control reality." On this note Alemany-Galway makes explicit her preference for postmodernism: "A postmodern perspective recognizes that there are many ways of knowing: postmodern artists, such as Greenaway, allow contradictory ways of knowing to co-exist while 'realist' artists focus the work on a unified, coherent point of view" (125–127). Hence Greenaway, who himself is a middle-class person speaking to a middle-class educated cinema audience, is preferred since his work is somehow open, fluid, and comfortable with paradox, whereas "realist" art, that is, art that may attempt to have a politics, is dismissed as being limited and somehow intellectually immature and naively "coherent."

Having begun her analysis by suggesting that class is somehow at the heart of *The Draughtsman's Contract*, we find that her postmodern form of criticism cannot move into such a territory as it would require the articulation of a definable political position and the articulation of a supposedly defunct "grand narrative" that by definition postmodernism finds anathema. At this juncture Alemany-Galway's analysis turns away from the property owning bourgeoisie and toward Frazer's *The Golden Bough*, much used by Eliot in *The Waste Land*. In a strangely structuralist moment in a predominantly poststructuralist reading of Greenaway, we now find her analysis articulating the belief that

> The narrative structure of this myth has appeared repeatedly over time and is associated with fertility rituals that take place in the autumn and spring of every year, that is, at the times of the death and rebirth of vegetation. In *The Draughtsman's Contract*, this myth is invoked in the murders of Mr. Henderson and Mr. Neville, who can be seen to represent the priestly king figures associated with the golden bough. (129)

This analysis is extended to include Mrs. Herbert and her daughter, in which "Mrs. Herbert's daughter can be taken to represent Persephone, and her sexless, fruitless marriage a descent into the underworld" (Ibid). The analysis then moves into a generalized discussion of gender roles: "Do men use women and nature for their own ends, or do women and nature use men? Which construction of reality is the correct one? As with postmodern works in general, Greenaway's film does not resolve the contradiction" (131). How then is such a film "effectively [acting] in a critical manner toward the dominant ideologies" as she had claimed? (118). We are thus left with an analysis in which Greenaway's cinema draws on the myths of Demeter and Persephone in such a contradictory and complicated way that the differing uses of the myth, "ultimately enrich one another" (131). In this way Greenaway, like Leigh, becomes a "great artist" because his art is polyvalent and invites a multiplicity of readings but can never be reduced to just one. For Alemany-Galway, such "postmodern/postructuralist works follow this turn in scientific epistemology since they, too, do away with the 'supreme determinant' or God-like author, and give us a number of possible conclusions rather than a singular statement" (135). Such a position leads directly into Greenaway's comment (and one that Alemany-Galway's feminism might find rather objectionable) that "we can forget God, Satan, the Communist Party, Freud and our mothers" (305). Notice the liberation of discarding such evil grand narratives in favor of postmodern freedoms: "we are on our own, which I think is fantastically liberating..." (Ibid). But despite Greenaway's own middle-class desires, we cannot forget about class (the communist party) or our mothers for that matter, moreover, why would we *want* to forget those things? In this sense, Greenaway's cinema, aimed at an intellectual art cinema audience serves as a cinema of forgetting, moving away from the troubling contradictions of the real into the fetishized (inter)textual (self-referential) delights of what he calls the "film-film" (307).

A political reading of Greenaway is however not only possible, but desirable. Rather than reading Greenaway through the mise en abyme and self-fulfilling theoretical positions of "postmodernism" in which we always end up with "unsolvable enigmas," reading his work politically reveals how troubling his cinema is, and that far from being a radical destabilization of the norms of grand narratives, the films reproduce a very clear ideological message regarding the "unsolvable enigma" of class. Scott Malcomson points out that Greenaway's early films were aimed at "the British intellectual avant-garde" that is a fairly "limited and homogenous" group.[26] However, *The Draughtsman's Contract* opens by seeming to establish contact with a wider audience, and by developing a narrative based on politics and power the film quickly moves to mold the "sympathies of the audience: the film presupposes audience alienation from a particular version of the ruling class, the rural aristocracy ca. 1695."[27] The non-aristocratic draughtsman of the title, Neville, is shown in the opening scenes as a potent sexual rival to the comically effete aristocratic men. So, the opening of the film, while drawing on the ideological cliché of the potent working class versus the weak and decadent aristocracy, at least appears to engage the audience with the suggestion that in the "psychosexual class struggle [Neville] appears, at this stage, to have cuckolded the ruling class."[28] Our sympathies at this stage are clearly with Neville (in *The Cook, the Thief, His Wife and Her Lover* our sympathies are always with the refined Georgina and her intellectual middle-class lover, Michael), and we are clearly distanced from the aristocratic men, like Mr. Talmann, so much so that Malcomson observes, rightly, I would argue, that Neville becomes (assuming we are not aristocrats) the "surrogate of the audience, acting out our role in the political drama of the film."[29] However, as the film progresses it becomes clear that this initial position of power is soon eroded, and Neville soon finds himself out of his depth and no longer in control. The status of what he is now drawing thus changes as Mrs. Herbert takes charge of his work, so that he is "no longer in control of information" and that now his drawings contain information that "eventually decide his fate and that are decipherable only by his aristocratic employers" (37). He is eventually murdered by a group of aristocratic men who accuse him of the murder of Mr. Herbert. Malcomson suggests therefore that what the film reveals is that Neville cannot control the meaning of his own labor: "it is the aristocrats who control its meaning and importance...the worker/producer has no control over or understanding of 'reality' at all, and that that control is in the hands of the ruling class which employs him" (38). Moreover, the political position of the women in the film is also clear: "the superior position of the two women in the political structure of the film forces us away from them" (Ibid). While Alemany-Galway delights in the "unsolvable enigmas" of the narrative, Malcomson makes it clear that the lack of information in the film is something that Neville and the audience share: "we find ourselves in the same position of inferiority and political impotence as Neville" (Ibid). The same applies to the human "statue" in the film that is always witnessed only by powerless actors in the space of the film, and like the audience, is a powerless and impotent witness to Neville's murder. Alemany-Galway might like to argue that the film cleverly deconstructs and frustrates any traditional murder genre by playfully making the murder unsolvable so that traditional structures of knowing are thrown into doubt by Greenaway's poststructuralist cinema, but as Malcomson perceptively remarks, the solution to the mystery may be unknown to us, the audience, but it is known to the ruling class who control the flow of information/power in the film: "the key information is held collectively by the class that defines his status. Moreover, this information is not discovered or deduced by Neville and the audience, but rather it is given us by the aristocratic class to which we are opposed by the film's structure..." (Ibid). This power imbalance is also not confined to the space within the film: "The departure from the genre is an act of mystification which locates the audience in a position of impotence before the film's ruling class—and ultimately before Greenaway, as he too has positioned himself on the other side of the divide created by the control of meaning" (40). Malcomson's political conclusion follows that "[t]he reality presented in *The Draughtsman's Contract* shows opposition to the political hegemony of the ruling class as a pathetic self-deception...[and although the film] is 'avant-garde' it partakes of the oldest of cinematic traditions: the validation, as phenomenological reality, of a political structure that supports the dominant class" (Ibid).

Derek Jarman

The third and final art cinema director that I would like to briefly consider is Derek Jarman. Jarman's work has come to be central to the cinema canon and his work is consistently praised for its avant-garde technique as well as his radical treatment of sexuality. However, Jarman's position as a *middle-class* auteur, who shifted from art school to art cinema, once again leaves us with an influential British director, much admired and critically established but whose politics circumvent any form of socialist agenda and fall comfortably into line with the identity politics so favored by our current postmodern academic milieu.

Jarman's most obvious foray into political cinema was *The Last of England* (1987). Conservative critics tended to see the film as an attack on England, but Jarman reacted that it was not an attack at all, but a kind of love song for an England that was in the process of being lost. Jarman clearly saw himself during the Thatcher years as being the representative of a tradition of middle-class dissent, and that in essence he was the real conservative, preserving a traditional position that valued history and aesthetics, at a time when Thatcher was taking a hammer to every aspect of an older more paternalistic England.[30] In this respect, for all of his intellectual differences from Greenaway over the nature of cinema, they both articulate a middle-class position in which Thatcherism (like Greenaway's Albert Spica or Martin Amis's John Self) is seen as philistine and destructive. Insofar as Jarman really sees himself as occupying the "center" it would be hoped that his work offered a base on which to build a central collective consciousness, but his films, based in a central position of *middle-class* dissent, fail to offer such a path. Instead, while finding a clear place in the intellectual avant-garde his work offers a meager foundation for a collective response to Thatcherism that would be rooted in class. Significantly, in *The Last of England*, the stereotyped representative of the working class comes in the form of the yobbish young man Spring who (while being erotically positioned by the film) comes to occupy the space of Pan in the narrative and cynically plays his pipes over the ruins of England while the Young Man (Spencer Leigh) is attempting to clear up the debris. The working-class Spring is seen shooting up, smoking, and coughing and defacing and masturbating on Caravaggio's *Profane Love* before disappearing from the film altogether. All the while, as the soundtrack tells us "the swan of Avon dies a syncopated death,"[31] and it will be the death of the Young Man who we will mourn along with Tilda Swinton at the film's end, not Spring. Although it may be fashionable to assume that Jarman's work has something vital to impart in terms of sexual politics and narrative, like Greenaway, his films are much more centripetal and are more about cinema and narrative while only tangentially do they have a political gaze. For example, John Hill is clear that Jarman's cinema, like Greenaway's is "characterized by the cinematic self-consciousness and self-referentiality of modernism...."[32] Jarman's work may be very useful for offering insights into cinema and sexuality and narrative, but we should remember the critics who also suggested that the film was a combination of "inaccessible private images with over-familiar symbols of national identity and urban breakdown...lacking any real social or political insight."[33] John Hill also sees the film as being aesthetically radical but politically impotent: "while the film contains footage of real events (e.g., Jarman's childhood, inner city riots) and real places (e.g., London Docklands), these do not necessarily denote 'actuality' or 'realism' so much as a pattern of symbolism and significance that is anchored in the subjectivity of the director's vision," and therefore for all of Jarman's outspoken criticism of the extremes of Thatcherism, the film is finally a "pessimistic film, but one in which the energy and intensity of the film's vision partly belies the lack of optimism (and sense of political agency) that it has to offer."[34]

More traditional "poststructuralist" critics eager to see the film as a radically unstable "text" thus tend to overlook the film's political weaknesses and instead, as we saw with Greenaway and Leigh, these middle-class art films are read as offering an existential criticism of the human condition rather than any troubling critique of "power." So, for example, in the hands of Rowland Wymer, *The Last of England* articulates a moment of crisis that is somehow beyond quotidian political realities, moving us toward a classless biographical/postcolonial sense of place, in which Jarman's HIV status is raised to a universal existential condition:

> Beyond any specific political or historical context, beyond the 1940s or the 1980s, *The Last of England* also raises other questions. What is "home" and where is love when both your parents are dead and you yourself are under sentence of death. The emotional desperation of the film...is intensified by the fact that it cannot finally articulate what it wants, because whatever government happens to be in power, whatever redistribution of material goods takes place, there is a sense in which we all remain in a permanent state of exile, disturbed by images of a past to which we cannot return....[35]

Mainstream Cinema

Harry Potter has captured the imagination of the Blair years in such a powerful way and among such a range of readers that it must have undoubtedly powerful ideological form/content driving it. The best place to see the ideological aspects of the texts and the films is in their beginnings because it is here that the class aspects of the narratives are most pronounced. In each case the narrative is developed along identical lines: the books invariably open with Harry back "home" during the summer holidays having to deal with his quasi-servitude with his adoptive family and the concomitant horrors of living in the Dursley household. In various openings we see him reduced to a kind of male Cinderella, living under the stairs, cleaning up after visiting relatives, being screamed at by Petunia (Fiona Shaw) to answer the door, or being locked away in his room out of sight. The establishing shots of the films invariably open with the camera flying (as if we the viewer are already magical, like Harry) over an endless array of identical

English suburban homes only to zoom in on one. The Dursley family is thoroughly working class and is offered to us as a figure of contempt due to their snobbery. The household and its occupants are also clearly marked off as being not us, by their extreme consumerism and love of empty consumption. Dudley Dursley (Harry Melling) and Uncle Vernon (Richard Griffiths) physically embody their level of consumption by being overweight (similarly with the visiting Aunt Marge who symbolically gets inflated) and both are regularly seen in relation to excessive eating or drinking. In *The Prisoner of Azkaban,* Dudley is eating and watching television at the same time just to underscore his unbounded desire for consumption (his aunt is floating away but he doesn't care: just to remind us of his selfishness too). The house is a showcase of pretentious horrors of the upwardly mobile and insecure working class: the house is filled with objects that display their (lack of) taste, and their obsession with material goods. We are also distanced from Petunia by her pathetic desire to ingratiate herself with Dudley, and her desire to keep him as a "mummy's boy." They are not marked as middle class, and in fact, for a British audience the home and the people are clearly marked as ordinary working-class people, who see themselves as middle class. Noticeably the family is also seen as philistines: reading and books are not part of their world, they are more comfortable with the television and the newspaper.

The household is entirely claustrophobic and it is also narrative-phobic insofar as the film's real story cannot get underway while the camera (and Harry) remains in the house. This working-class environment cannot be a magical space, and Harry must escape from it if *his* story (the one that we are also asked to desire) is to begin. There are no stories that can be told from within this working-class space, it is an antinarrative location: stories, excitement, magic, friendships, heroism all are to be found outside of this working-class space. In nearly every instance Harry is basically rescued from this carceral environment either by friends from Hogwarts or the Ministry of Magic. As John Kirk says of *Billy Elliot*: Billy, like Harry, is the "exceptional individual" who in a theme "that goes back at least to Lawrence, can fully express himself outside the stifling confines of the enclosed and embattled community... [while] the good, the true life, must lie elsewhere."[36] Moreover, Kirk feels that "[r]ecoding the escaper paradigm to suit postmodern times [thus] conveys the 'New Labour' message of meritocracy and classlessness."[37]

The horrors of the Dursley household are easily contrasted with the family home of the Weasleys: their country house is detached and is full of "character" (unlike the faceless similarity of the Dursley's suburban McHome). The house gives off an air of bohemian insouciance in which family members, mirroring the democratic pluralism of Hogwarts, all exist alongside each other with humor and equanimity. There is not only more physical space, but this middle-class environment (with its plethora of books and its ties to the Ministry of Magic via Ron's father) offers Harry the first chance to be once again back among "his own kind." The narrative could easily disavow this kind of a reading by saying that it is not class that differentiates the families it is just that the Dursley's happen to be Muggles (non-Magic folk) while the Weasleys's are Wizards. While this is true, the way that Magical/Non-Magical is signified to the audience is through markers of status and education and behavior that are clearly based on how we measure class. If the narrative was ideologically innocent, then we could easily switch the families around: but imagine how ideologically odd the film would be if Harry had to escape from a family like the Weasleys to be saved by the fat, selfish, and arrogant and magical Dursleys. The Weasley family is all good looking, with foppish haircuts, and they seem to wear pajamas at all hours, while the warm and loving parents never need to be authoritarian in any way. The family is eccentric and quirky, but this all adds to their magical middle-class "charm." We never see them watching television, or stuffing themselves with cake, and no one is overweight or neurotic like Petunia. This is Harry's "real" family, this is where he "really" belongs, mixing with the powerful families in the ministry and heading back to what can only be described as a private education at Oxford for a small coterie of privileged magical intellectuals. Ironically, as each narrative opens he finds himself thrown back into the horrifying Dursley world each time, and like some economic repetition compulsion must escape it all over again. Although Hogwarts clearly presents itself as a multicultural utopia in which all races and nationalities peacefully coexist (and one in which difference is the order of the day) what this "open" society must exclude is the drab ordinary working-class world that Harry has to constantly keep escaping from. The working-class world is what Hogwarts is not, it is its antithesis: it is everything that the Dursley household wants to be but cannot. Strangely, the narratives suggest, I think, that being "magical" is not something that can be bought, or worked for, like "class" you are born into it, and you either have it or you don't, and no amount of Corinthian pillars on your McHome will give you that elusive "magical" edge. The Weasley's on the other hand don't have to try at all, because they have it: they *are* magic. Harry's class affiliation is clear (and by implication that of the viewers) when he sees the huge inside of the Weasley's small "tent" at the Quidditch World Cup: "I love Magic."

Having clearly distinguished themselves from their inferiors, the audience/protagonist identification also ensures that we are clear that the upper classes also constitute a kind of other that Harry (and the audience) must not identify with or admire. This is the quasi-aristocratic world of the various Lords who Harry encounters: most obviously the evil Lord Voldemort, as well as the Malfoy family. These evil aristocrats (only a baddy would insist on an outdated antibourgeois heraldic system) are marked by their inflexible attitude toward blood, as one would expect, and in addition to having the same vampiric character traits that have gone hand in glove since Stoker's *Dracula*, have a thoroughly evil relationship to power unlike our benign bourgeois hero, Harry.

Dirty Pretty Things (2002)

In a recent interview Stephen Frears tells us: "I was brought up in a completely white, middle-class life. Since I opened up a little, it's got much more interesting."[38] Unlike Frears's earlier "condition of England" films, such as *My Beautiful Laundrette* and *Sammie and Rosie Get Laid, Dirty Pretty Things* moves into the cinematic terrain of the thriller. The writer of the films is also revealing: whereas the earlier films had Hanif Kureishi as their author, this film was written by Steve Knight, one of the co-creators of the hit TV show *Who Wants to Be a Millionaire?*[39] The film has been lauded for its no-holds barred treatment of the horrors of the underclass in contemporary England and was given four prizes by the British Independent Film Awards in London in 2003: Best British film, Best Director, Best Screenplay, and Best Actor for Chiwetel Ejiofor. Worldwide, the film was nominated for an Oscar and garnered sixteen prizes and eighteen nominations. The success of the film comes with a price however, which is that as the film's mainstream audience is opened up so the political engagement of the film diminishes. So while the content of the film aims to expose a side of the economy that is normally invisible, the form of the film and the generic constraints of the thriller mitigate against its political impact, and we actually have a very limited film, one which ironically reinforces the political status quo and undermines any investigation or critique of contemporary class formations.

In his analysis of cinema in the 1980s, John Hill says that films such as *The Ploughman's Lunch, Edge of Darkness, Defence of the Realm*, and *Hidden Agenda* all articulated their political analyses through the format of the political thriller. For John Hill, the problem with this approach is that it severely curtails the depth of the political critique that is made available: such films draw on "both the liberal Hollywood tradition of journalist movies in which a journalist hero exposes wrongdoing in high places...."[40] The film's author Steve Knight has said that "a thriller keeps people guessing and keeps them interested. And at the same time they'll come out of it more aware of some problem or something maybe they didn't think about before...."[41] But as John Hill observes "[t]raditionally, it has been the great strength of political thrillers to reach and maintain the interest of an audience who might normally be turned off by politics, however, the form of the thriller is not neutral and this inevitably has consequences for the way in which political questions are then handled."[42] To begin with, the film lacks the *cinema verite* style of Ken Loach by using "stars" as the main characters who seem to move around on a backdrop of faceless extras in the film.[43] For Hill this leads to a central concern: "mainstream narrative conventions (and the logic of character-based causality) typically encourage explanations of social realities in individual and psychological terms rather than economic and political ones while [emphasizing] interpersonal relations [rather than] economic and political structures."[44] This arises in *Dirty Pretty Things* by quickly establishing the romantic interest between Okwe (Chiwetel Ejiofor) and Senay (Audrey Tatou). Okwe, who we identify with, is thus the "detective" in this narrative, who sets out to uncover the truth that takes place behind the luxurious surface of the Baltic Hotel.[45] However, John Hill felt that in the 1980s the "conspiracy" was always directed upward toward the inner secret workings of the state, in this film from 2002 the conspiracy moves downward and comes to be located in the underclass itself.[46] The illegal transplant operations are being masterminded by Sneaky (Sergi Lopez) who is himself an immigrant who has found a way to survive by exploiting those around him. The thriller moves forward to expose this "crime" and while it takes us on a tour of the sweatshops and hotel/hospital porters and cleaners, all that can be finally exposed is the actions of Sneaky himself. There is obviously a sense in the film that Sneaky is part of a larger conspiracy of medical exploitation, but there is a clear sense that this is beyond the scope of the film. Once Sneaky gets justice served upon him, the narrative can close. Our feelings for him are also clearly shaped by generic constraints: he is a sexual maniac, he drinks, he has no care for his fellow colleagues, in short, he is a stock villain who, like Albert Spica in *The Cook, the Thief, His Wife and Her Lover*, or the Dursleys/Voldemort in *Harry Potter* for that matter, deserve our contempt. Interestingly, the writer of the film, Steve Knight has compared himself to Dickens:

> I see London the same as New York or Birmingham...any big city is lots of different cities; it depends which city you visit. With *Dirty Pretty Things* I spent some time looking at sweatshops, and I'd walk through doors in London and find myself in the Third World. I think if you're a writer and you live in a city, you would be mad not to include all of those other worlds in your territory. If you only want to write about one particular sort of person in London, I think it's a mistake. It's not particularly a crusade for me, it's just that that's where the stories are. If Charles Dickens were around now, he'd be telling their stories, he wouldn't necessarily be telling the stories of middle-class native Londoners.[47]

The parallel is apposite because Dickens's work has the same generic limitations as Knight's work in which an underclass is the focus but the individualization of the issues by the generic constraints finally betray the limits of Dickens/Knights ideological position. Frears says on the film commentary that one of the sweatshops that Senay goes to find work at also looks like "something out of *Oliver Twist*...." As D. A. Miller has pointed out though, the form of Dickens's work always produces an ideological resolution to real contradictions.[48] In Dickens, the melodrama also serves to undermine the political critique, and in this film Sneaky becomes the archetypal villain, preying, at one point, on a seven-year-old Romanian girl. When he first appears, the doorman Ivan (Zlatko Buric) is telling Okwe to watch out for Sneaky at which point he drives into the hotel garage. As we watch him on CCTV, the doorman says "O speak of the fucking Devil himself" and just to underline his position as the Dickensian villain, Sneaky tells Okwe later without remorse, "So, I'm an evil man."[49] As a critique of capital, the role of Sneaky is also ineffective as he is himself nothing more than a working-class immigrant who has a job as a Porter in the hotel and who is trying to find a way to survive. He is also a long way from home and a long way from having access to any kind of bourgeois life, nor is he connected in any way to the (invisible) businessmen and women who own the hotel (or the consortium of which it is part).

The nature of the conspiracy is at the heart of this thriller and is developed by a dialogue between Okwe and Senay as he makes dinner for her and she is trying to have a bath. He is talking in the kitchen asking her if she had seen anything odd going on in Room 510 of the hotel, but at the same time her bath water stops running because he is washing some wine glasses for dinner. She asks him why he is talking about work, and then, talking about the taps asks him "You can fix...?" and then tells him that "everything here is connected to everything else" by which she implies that the plumbing is linked so turning on one tap causes problems for another, but it also becomes a comment on the nature of the conspiracy itself in which everything that goes on in the hotel / British society is linked through some invisible and secretive system of economic "pipes." This all-pervasive system, which never works properly and cannot be fixed, takes us back to Okwe's opening comments to two Middle Eastern men as he tries to pick up passengers at the airport that he is here "to rescue those who have been let down by the system." In this thriller he will be the hero that will expose the dark underbelly of the illegal immigrant worker's world and right all wrongs. However, the nature of the genre means that he can only "rescue" the chosen few, which as it turns out will be himself and Senay.

Paradoxically, Okwe is actually not really part of the underclass but is actually middle class since he was a doctor back home in Nigeria and has studied in America. He is in England not because he is an illegal migrant worker, but because he had to leave Nigeria after standing up against political corruption in Lagos, for which his wife was murdered by government forces. Frears says on the commentary that the actor did a good job of making it clear that Okwe was a man with "a strong moral sense...and that he was articulate and educated and authoritative." So paradoxically, Okwe, who is meant to be part of a powerless underclass, is actually a powerful middle-class individual, who happens to finds himself caught up in these terrible circumstances. Moreover, he doesn't even want to stay in England and desires to leave and return to his seven-year-old daughter. Senay also has no political dimension only what Okwe calls at one point her "stupid dream" of making it to America where her cousin runs a coffee shop. Throughout the film these star actors have only transitory interactions with other "workers," all of who are named actors. The other workers, who are part of the working class in the film, such as the groups of Asian sweatshop women or the long lines of cleaners being bused into the hotel, remain nameless and unexamined.

Frears's own ideological limits can even be seen in his comment on the DVD that the sweatshop in London that they used for Senay's job wasn't really all that bad: "They took me to this sweatshop. I mean this is what they call a sweatshop. It seemed quite nice to me. The windows were open, the radio was playing. You thought, the police must know about this place but it was very nice and the people were making a bit of money on the side, you know it didn't seem, it was very odd...(laughing)." Imagine Dickens saying of one of the original Dotheboys Hall, "well, they say these places are terrible, but it seemed quite nice to me." The comment also opens up a rather wide gap between what the *fiction* of the film wants us to feel: that is, that these places are slave mills with bosses forcing their workers to give them sexual favors, while the personal ideological response from Frears is basically that he is not sure what all the fuss is about, since the working conditions are not all that bad.

John Hill suggests that another problem with the political thriller as a genre is that while the dark forces of the state are seen in personal individualized forms, so "it tends to conceive of opposition to the state as primarily an individual activity as well." This is done through the "investigation of an individual detective (or journalist) and his quest to reveal or make visible, the truth behind a crime or enigma." This figure fits perfectly with Okwe: he is a "loner" with "no apparent family ties."[50] So while the film follows the actions of the "lone individual," the film, true to its generic constraints, downplays "more organized, or collective forms of political protest and opposition," while there is no "link with organized labour."[51] There is always in the thriller a clear sense that the "current social set up [can] triumph over injustice and wrongs" while the problems are transformed into "the responsibility of isolated or 'deviant' individuals, rather than social institutions and regimes" and since it is "those who are in power who are the source of the wrongdoing" it is "much more difficult to identify the means whereby social ills can be remedied." Hill feels that this genre only leaves us "a sense of paranoia (rather than genuine political insight)" and like Okwe, who becomes increasingly caught up in the immoral maze of London, the protagonist in the thriller has "a sense of alienation [that is] less political than existential as he struggles to make sense of the Kafkaesque world in which he has become embroiled."[52]

In this way the thriller genre ensures that the true economic bottom of the society remains hidden and unexplored while the higher economic sources of the illegal organ business are also beyond reach.

The audience is left to hover in the center with the middle-class Okwe. Similarly by the end of the film, nothing will be exposed or changed: Sneaky will have been punished, and Okwe and Senay will leave England. Having left England there is the sense that the problems that the film has addressed have been resolved satisfactorily. The fact that England and its economic system and the situation of the working class (whatever their new ethnic make up) remains need not be our concern: we are happy that Senay and Okwe have escaped to America and Nigeria. As for the economic system that they are leaving behind (or for the English audience a system that "we" live in) the audience no longer care. So whereas the 1980s political thriller directed its critique at the secret workings of the state, so now in *Dirty Pretty Things*, the anger can only be directed toward Sneaky, he and he alone is the source of all of the problems: the state in any form is invisible while beyond critique and analysis is any sense of a collective class of workers (even though we see them in the background of the film all the time). Once Sneaky is dealt with, there is nothing more to say: the system has been cleansed and everything can return to normal, while Okwe and Senay magically leave England and its problems behind. Significantly, Juliette (Sophie Okonedo) the black British prostitute is left standing on the curb as Guo Yi (Benedict Wong) drives Okwe and Senay to the airport.[53] Juliette and Gyo Yi cannot leave England as there is nowhere for them to go, and the elimination of Sneaky from the equation does nothing to change their lives, nor the lives of the workers who, as in the contemporary British economy, are left with a nameless existence on the shadowy margins of the film.

Television

Gareth Palmer has pointed out that while British culture aims to articulate a sense of classlessness in its media, the recent popularity for "lifestyle programming" means that there is a huge demand for TV programs that helps viewers to clearly demarcate their new "classless" position but this turns out to be one based on a rejection of any kind of depth model of the self, and involves an acceptance not only of middle-class values but also an acceptance of a self built purely on image and a rejection of one's individual history.[54] This new classless self, which is carefully reconstructed out of the old self, is thus parallel to the strategies that we have been tracing in the highbrow literature of the period in which the problems of class have constantly been erased or evaded.[55] These lifestyle programs, including such programs as *Changing Rooms, House Invaders, Would Love to Meet*, and *What Not to Wear*, all operate along lines that establish how your original sense of self, taste, décor, or fashion is somehow inadequate and outré and that you must be reconditioned and refashioned to fit in and the contestants can thus become, not only "all that they can be" but if they follow the middle-class experts' advice, they will also become happy.[56] So while the programs present themselves as helping the viewer to shed the past and emerge into a new you, this "empowerment thesis" brings with it very old ideological baggage.[57] As Palmer points out "Lifestyle programming…features the bearers of old middle-classness…bringing apparently effortless 'good taste' to the new and more insecure classes."[58] The clearest example of this is *What Not to Wear* in which two "upper middle-class 'gels' are licensed to abuse in their quest to transform the dowdy."[59] The two middle-class presenters of this show thus become in Palmer's words, the "signifiers of middle-classness" and do not need to go through the process themselves, as they are already "finished." Like Harry Potter's magical birth rights, these presenters are, in the words of John Arlidge, "born posh, have lived posh, worked posh…."[60] In this sense while "real" class is something that you are born with, the working-class TV viewer can acquire it, but only if they submit to humiliation and defeat before being reconstructed. In Orwell's *1984* when Winston Smith is being tortured by O'Brien, the sign that he really does love Big Brother is that he is prepared to reject even his innermost sense of self. Once the makeover is complete, the subjects feel themselves to be happier and free, but paradoxically it is clear that far from having transcended any class limits they have simply engaged in a process of false consciousness conducted in the name of style and have been made to identify with the values and tastes of a class to which economically they may aspire but socially they can never "truly" belong. As Palmer points out, this new self is nothing more than a way of revealing "the power of the norm operated by the middle-class, those whose taste determines an increasing number of areas."[61] Palmer sees all of these programs as part of a larger pattern concerned with a kind of "personal development movement" that covers everything from weight loss shows to décor and fashion as well as dating and self-empowerment "get rich quick" seminars and books. As with Big Brother, this pattern tends to see the self as a "project to be invested in" in which the "brute individualism" of the market economy is morphed into a strategy for "personal" transformation. Hence for Palmer, in this kind of ideological nexus "[l]ife is all about choices for empowered individuals transcending circumstances to self-validate and realize their 'true individuality.' "[62] As the person is moved from being a "citizen to a consumer... [s]ociety, like class and background, are merely the circumstances from which the individual has risen, indeed which she has overcome, on the quest to selfhood."[63] Although this is clearly a legacy of Thatcherism in which society is seen to no longer exist but only individuals, it is also simply part of a much larger ideological framework into which working-class people have long been subjected. As Palmer remarks, for all of their postmodern hipness, these shows are "reincarnations of the etiquette guides that were marketed to the aspirational classes of the Victorian era."[64] As we have been tracing throughout this book, the ways in which class has been erased and evaded and redressed is alive and well on TV and that in these types of popular programs "lifestyle is the home of the view that eradicates, by illustration, the 'end' of class. Class, upbringing, location, education are constructs to be overcome from the vantage point of the self."[65] But as Palmer adds, while the "subjects/victims...are being taught to create a self by learning middle-classness...it is a task that will always feel doomed to failure."[66]

The Amazing Mrs Pritchard (2006) is another useful example of how the myth of classlessness plays itself out in television drama. Drawing in part on Reality TV and the fashion for makeover programs, the six part BBC series follows Ros Pritchard (Jane Horrocks) as she miraculously overcomes all barriers of class and education and goes from an ordinary supermarket manageress to prime minister. In essence the narrative is satisfying a utopian desire on the one hand by showing us how an "ordinary" woman can become the leader of the country, while also affirming the "freedom" inherent in Western democracy in which no one is barred from power and even "ordinary" people can speak up and are allowed to hold the reins of power. In an attempt to prove the "truth" of this unbelievable series of events, the program draws heavily on a Reality TV style as if to confirm that we are watching a documentary and/or the evening news, rather than an ideological fiction. The use of "real" people playing themselves underscores this truth: but, paradoxically the majority of representations of the "real" are from the media itself. So we see journalist/historian/TV presenter Andrew Marr, James Humphreys of the BBC's Today program, as well as familiar figures from TV like Paul Snow, Nick Robinson, Sarah Montague, and Gavin Esler from *Newsnight*, as well as cameo appearances from MP's Roy Hattersley and David Steele. Throughout the series we are kept abreast of what is happening via information from the BBC News. Embedded in this "real" environment is a tale of a quirky ordinary woman who by a sheer "can do" spirit, sets out to give the country a political "makeover."

The series begins with Ros Pritchard at work as a supermarket manageress in the fictional location of Eatanswill in the Midlands.[67] Our first image of her shows her looking in the store mirror before going out to greet the customers and her workers, and next to the mirror is a sign saying "This is how the customer sees You": having shown us her concern for style we then see her moving through the shop chatting personally with her workers. She is shown as a kind, caring manageress who brings a "female" touch to the job by asking her subordinates how they are doing with their personal lives, and in one case a rather overweight black woman thanks Ros for taking her off of the dairy section as it helped her to lose six pounds. The overall image is of someone who understands others because she was (and in essential ways) still is "one of them." There is no suggestion that she has any professional or academic education, and we feel that she is in this managerial position from sheer hard work. On a micro level, this asserts an early example of the meritocratic classless society, in which hard work will lead you to positions of power, mirroring her immanent rise to a position of *national* power. After a fight outside the store between two MPs (one Tory, the other Labour) she decides that she could do better and stands in the local by-election. Thanks to the financial backing of supermarket owner and millionairess Kitty Porter (Frances Tomelty) she wins the election and very quickly a "Purple Alliance" is formed and she is soon whisked into 10 Downing Street as prime minister. While this covers the first two episodes, it quickly emerges that her past will come back and destroy her in the form of some money laundering that her husband, Ian Pritchard (Steven Mackintosh) was involved in fifteen years before. Having been elected as an "ordinary person" who will take back England and give power to the people, it soon becomes clear that class is not going to be part of the agenda, in fact the agenda of the program itself is gender. The policies that are initiated and which take up a large part of the series are concerned not with class as one would expect but with environmental issues. This "female" notion of a mother caring from her planet/children supersedes any overt class politics, while the series is peppered with childish, impotent men.[68] Ros's own husband, Ian, stays behind in Eatanswill in his nondescript accounting job and doesn't even vote for her. He starts drinking from the pressure and is often seen in conventionally female roles such as doing the cooking and shopping. Scenes inside the House of Commons also reproduce a rather gendered political split. New Labour is so fractured by Ros's rise to power that the Tory party is now the opposition, so in the House of Commons the scenes are of Ros surrounded on all sides by women, and one or two men and women of color, while the opposition is a rather homogenous group of old Tory men. This is meant to show that the split in the country is no longer one of class but rather is between "new" selves that emerge from identity politics (and like a post "make-over" program are now "free") versus a white male establishment that is the group that desires to hold onto the past and notions of class and privilege. All the major positions in Ros's government are women but importantly they are neither working-class women nor are there any noticeable women of color in the cabinet. Catherine Walker is an Oxford and Princeton scholar and the Home Secretary Hilary Reese-Benson (Geraldine James) is clearly a middle-class figure (and was Catherine Walker's tutor at Oxford) while the Health Minister Beverly Clarke (Siobhan Finneran) is a partner from a law firm. While this provides ample opportunity to make statements about women and power in an "empowering" yet classless way, the series, as it progresses, uses the issue of gender to unravel her party and its achievements. The actual working-class women in the supermarket that the series began with are never seen again, and none of them are given any position of government responsibility, even though Ros made a point of saying that government was not rocket science and that all that is needed is just "common sense." As Ros and her close supporters move into Whitehall so they are joined by a host of middle-class civil servants, such as Ros's own secretary Meg Bayliss (Sally Phillips) and her advisor Sir Richard Leavis (Jonathan Aris) who she calmly gets to work with, and in fact, has to rely on to figure out how government works. The other very visible example would be Catherine Walker's middle-class secretary Nina Morgan (Sylvestra Le Touzel). Apart from a plan to sell Whitehall (which never happens) and move the center of government to Bradford (which never happens) and a desire to abolish the Monarchy (which never happens) the *only* policy that is seen to be put into effect (which ironically had come from a *man* in the street in the early episodes) is to have "Green Wednesdays" that entails nobody using a car for one day a week. Terrorism makes it into the program when a plane explodes over Walthamstow in London, but it turns out to be a faulty fuel line due to a reduction in safety inspections as a result of some European Union policy changes. As the narrative arc moves to its denouement, so the past, which paradoxically was what Ros claimed to be sweeping away, finally comes back to destroy her. Her husband's weakness in accepting ten thousand pounds (which was due to their own financial troubles in the past) is revealed, not to the country but to Ros, and for the sake of her family (which is clearly seen as falling apart at this point) she resigns and goes back to Eatanswill, while the Oxford educated and unmarried middle-class career politician, Catherine Walker, who was originally a Tory (who only defected to the Purple Alliance as a savvy career move) finally takes over as prime minister.

Although Ros was never really presented as "working class" (she was always a part of an upper working-class managerial sector: intelligent, capable, strong, and articulate), the ending of the narrative clearly returns her to her class position. For all of its liberatory politics, the narrative ensures that she returns home, to her job, to her husband and her children, and to her neighborhood. The implication being that this is where she really belongs, and the time in government is no more than an interregnum (for her and the viewers) and once she has gone the wheels of government can return to their usual middle-class mechanisms. The end credits also tell us that Ros felt that she had "made her point." True, but the country is left unchanged. The series is also ambivalent in that it wishes to engage us in Ros's rise to power, satisfying a popular wish for social transformation, but then punishes her (and by implication "us," the ordinary TV viewers) for having such a wish. Her power in government is shown to be limited and essentially business as usual is fine, and the implication is that we should just leave it to the people who know what they are doing. So, while the program has a desire to show the power of classlessness and to affirm that Britain is a classless meritocracy, in fact the narrative reveals that such a thing is actually unimaginable, and that power must and should remain in the hands of a particular class, a class to which you, the viewer, do not and cannot belong.

A parallel class bias can be seen in recent comedy. Steve Coogan's creation of Alan Partridge and Ricky Gervais and Stephen Merchant's creation of David Brent from *The Office* both display current strategies for simultaneously displaying and evading questions of class. Steve Coogan's character Alan Partridge, like David Brent (and Martin Amis's John Self) is a working-class figure eager to fit into the middle-class milieu to which he aspires. He is essentially a kind of "before" example in the makeover genre. For example, Partridge is hopeless with European languages ("Numero... One", "Aqua, which is French for water"), he has no sense of how to deal with women ("I know a cracking owl sanctuary") or music (his favorite Beatles album: "I'd have to say, The Best of the Beatles...," Joni Mitchell's "blinkered view of the world" or late nights at the Birmingham NEC with *ELO*), or film and TV (his favorite being *James Bond*, especially Roger Moore, and Jet from *Gladiators*). In addition to these egregious displays of his lack of cultural capital, he is also persistently insulting and/or condescending toward those that he considers lower than himself, such as Lynn and Michael and the Linton Travel Tavern employees. This becomes his way of marking out his own class terrain while he also has an ambivalent desire and disdain for those he considers part of the "establishment" above him, such as Tony Hayers at the BBC (with its "gravy train" that he says in episode one that he wishes he was part of) or his disgust with the posh middle-class farmer Peter Baxendale-Thomas. He also sees himself as a good friend with the successful local businessman Dan in the second series and hopes to ingratiate himself with Ms. Colman (daughter of the mustard empire). He also displays his highly politically incorrect view of gender while thinking he is being equal ("I'd love to get my hands on the bastard, or bitch. Might be a lady"). His attempts at being "one of the lads" also fall flat. He cannot hold his drink and tries to chat with some men about getting drunk and being sick or commenting on passing women's breasts, or asking his builders if they saw the "match last night": "Which one?" "Dunno." The failure of his character to fit in, his obvious position outside of the norms that have been carefully shaped by recent class ideology thus becomes the source of the comedy, as we look down upon him (from our standpoint in the norm) and laugh not with, but at him. The implication and relief being that *we* know how to order the right wine, *we* understand what women want, *we* can chat about literature and music and sport and food without making these kinds of social errors that would expose our real roots as part of a philistine working-class culture.

The clearest staging of these class differences occurs when Alan goes to the BBC to see Tony Hayers (David Schneider) in series one, episode one. The meeting with Hayers is important since it might be a chance for Alan to get back on television after the poor ratings and killing a guest from his chat show *Knowing Me, Knowing You*. The trouble begins in the BBC restaurant as Alan, clearly out of place among the tailored suits in his sports casual anorak, gets into a discussion about wine. Hayers admits that he has a weakness for wine and that he has a "cellar." Alan Partridge responds

"So have I, no wine in it though, just a couple of old bikes, a bag of smokeless fuel and an old bag of cement, gone hard." Desperate to impress Hayers in the hopes of future job security, Alan changes his order from a pint of bitter to wine. After looking at the wine list in utter confusion for some moments, he settles on the working-class wine par excellence: a bottle of Blue Nun. He is then upset when the waiter pours out a whole glass, "I want you to pour a little bit, then let me sip it." The waiter has already poured a glass, so Alan quaffs the whole thing, remarking, "That's fine, fill 'er up." Hayers orders fettucine arabiatta, and Alan, eager to impress but clearly unwilling to risk the pronunciation of "fettucine arabiatta" simply orders "the same," although he wants the pasta that is shaped like an "Action Man bow tie." After an embarrassing lunch at which Hayers basically tells Alan that he will not be getting another series for his chat show, Alan is now stuck with the problem of being unable to follow through on the deal he made in the morning on an expensive "five bedroom bastard house."

Living on the edge of fame, Alan Partridge clearly exposes the myth of classlessness while at the same time holding on to markers of what he sees as middle-class status like his driving gloves, and his matching tie and blazer badge set. He is also keen to hold onto his Rover car with its polished wood dashboard, even though Lynn points out that with his own company Peartree Productions having gone bankrupt and with no second TV season in sight, he will have to economize and switch to a Mini Metro. Like David Brent, Alan Partridge has to resort to various jobs to stay afloat, sometimes basking in his former glory as a TV presenter to be a host on the very pathetic "Crash, Bang, Wallop, What a Video!" or giving a corporate motivational speech for Dante Fires (with such brutal economic one-liners to the workers as "hit your targets, or you'll be fired"), or being the star of a Water Breaks advertisement for canal boat holidays. He even manages to transform his temporary living space, the hotel, into a work space as he puts on "An Afternoon with Alan Partridge and Sue Cook" (from which Sue Cook pulls out). This particular offering is also timed to coincide with a visit from two young producers from Irish television who Alan hopes might give him a job. His main job is on the radio, and like Brent, he aspires to something more: "I'm a national TV presenter trapped in the body of a regional disc-jockey" he tells Lynn at one point. His radio slot is a predawn time: "It's 4:35 a.m. and you're Up With The Partridge"—leaving him with the rest of the day to hang out at the Lincoln Travel Tavern and chat with

Michael the Geordie handyman/waiter, who by the second series has lost this job and is now working at a petrol station, which in turn becomes a hang-out for Alan too.

Although it does not have the Reality TV elements of *The Office* and it still retained a laugh track, the series did reveal a parallel contemporary concern with class in that Alan Partridge desires to be free from his working-class limitations, and like Edina and Patsy in *Absolutely Fabulous*, are finally unable to cast off their working-class roots. The attempt and the desire to do so reveals the cultural pressure to move beyond class, as expressed in the appetite for makeover programs, while the failure to achieve any kind of promised freedom, leads not to any (comical) critique of those myths but instead due to the cartoonish nature of the character, and the impersonal camera-work (which prevents us from investing too much into Partridge) allows us to interpret his failure as a *personal* failing. The comedy results in a critique of the individual, not the economic and cultural forces that are driving him to respond as he does to his environment. In this sense the title of the program says it all, "I'm Alan Partridge" but in a world where he has no career to speak off, no wife and nowhere to live, his name is all he has left, and yet it is a name which, since he is not middle class, articulates no economic or cultural capital.

Whereas a certain distance can be maintained with Alan Partridge, the camera work in *The Office* collapses that final barrier and brings us much closer to the character's feelings and their failings.[69] In this way the economic problems that these workers encounter are potentially far more troubling for the audience. Ben Walters is right to point out that *The Office* draws our attention to the paradox of the contemporary working environment for the working class as a mixture of a "mundane, repetitive workload" with a "fundamentally insecure job status."[70] While this creates narrative (as well as workplace) tension, the storyline, while holding onto the prospect of redundancies moves away from questions of class, economics, and unionization and takes the usual soap drama route of resolving conflicts at the level of the personal. So the emptiness of contemporary work is finally resolved at the end of the Christmas Special in the personal relationship between Tim and Dawn, as well as the happy relationship that Brent establishes with Carol from the dating agency. It could be argued that the series, toward the end, offers a critique of current British cultural frameworks in which self development has become a staple of TV programming, in that Brent plays out the clichés of self-empowerment once he is fired, only to find that they come to nothing. As Ben Walters points out

> The business instincts of which he was once so confident have repeatedly let him down: his sideline in motivational speaking came to nothing, his self-released single was a flop...bereft of an institutional framework, his work portfolio now comprises two models of individualist entrepreneurialism, one prototypically old-fashioned and tied to peddling wares, the other quintessentially postmodern and concerned with the promotion of an insubstantial image: travelling salesman by day, jobbing micro-celebrity by night.[71]

However, rather than taking us deeper into the roots of this economic collapse, or taking a route that would expose the myth of classlessness and meritocracy, the show finally retreats into the happy ending of romantic love. As John Corner has pointed out, what we have seen recently in television is a movement in which "the viewing invitation slides from the dynamics of understanding to the...transaction of vicarious witness and empathy."[72] Tim and Dawn, Brent and Carol thus shift the focus away from economics and work, toward, as Walters says "a different, positive narrative."[73] Brent's career prospects are unlikely to change (indeed his narrative is parallel to Ros Pritchard's) in that try as he might to leave behind his class and his anonymous mundane working-class life, he is not permitted to do so and must remain within the limits that his class has established for him: the only flexibility is with the type of personal relationship that he can have. Without this love interest we would be left with our own contemporary "death of a salesman," however, as Walters suggests "Merchant and Gervais achieve a sense of hope for Brent by shifting his and our attention away from professional success—an area in which he seems unlikely to ever meet his own disproportionate expectations—and onto his personal life, specifically the prospect of a relationship."[74] Walters concludes by suggesting that what we are left with is a narrative that asks us to realize that "jobs aren't worth getting too worked up about."[75] But, putting this conservative moral aside, I think that the series also does expose the myth of classlessness in that Brent has taken the culture at its word: that you can be anything, and nothing can stop you, and that you are free to recreate yourself above and beyond anything as limiting as class, and Brent as he crashes and falls, reveals the thoroughly ideological nature of that myth, and what the program does uncover is the harsh economic truths that keep him, and us, in our place.

Life on Mars

For all of the supposed classlessness of contemporary British culture, a program like "The Inspector Lynley Mysteries" (based on the novels of Elizabeth George) flourishes both at home and in the United States. Framed around the traditional hermeneutic code of the police drama, the crimes themselves are less the conduit for the program's ideology as the form of the program. Regardless of the actual episode, we are confronted with a drama in which detectives Tom Lynley (Nathaniel Parker) and Barbara Havers (Sharon Small) stand quite clearly in opposition to each other on class grounds. A "dark moody type" as one character describes him, he is middle class, with a posh voice, he drives an old classic red Daimler, has posh friends, posh acquaintances from "school" and mixes in the higher echelons of British society. Havers on the other hand is working class, is seen carrying groceries, and has a flat London accent. The mysteries are invariably solved by Lynley, with Havers pulling up the rear, or he has to rescue her from some near deadly encounter. There are occasions where this is reversed but this only underscores a notion of class cohesion and mutual support. So while the program allows us to clearly map these two figures as having entirely different class positions, the conservative ideology is that they are still working together to solve crime. Thus the enemy is not the other class: the unifying enemy of both classes is the "criminal." Once this class bonding has been established, the "criminal" can then be located in *any* class since the criminal is identified by their relationship to the norm, not whether they are working, middle or upper class. The narrative's form thus asserts that by working together the bourgeoisie and the working class can make society a better place while the notion that the difficulties of one class may be located in the other is elided at the level of form.

A more sophisticated, but equally troubling police drama series is *Life on Mars* (2007). While containing all of the usual formal limitations of the police serial (in terms of the absence of political concerns in favor of microcriminal problems) and the dominance of the nineteenth-century hermeneutic code of the detective, the series also fails to fully develop any class-based critique while taking on the historical shifts that have taken place from 1973 to the present. One of the largest shifts that has occurred in England is the obvious decline of the manufacturing industry in the North of England. This loss, accompanied by the first hints of globalization and outsourcing is usually taken as a truism that the working class as we know it has vanished. Simply because large numbers of factories are no longer up and running, this argument in itself conflates labor with capital, assuming that if capital has closed up shop and moved abroad, then labor has moved with it. Yet, as we can see from *The Full Monty* (1997) while capital is free to leave, labor has to stay behind. In *Life on Mars*, DCI Sam Tyler (John Simm) working on the Manchester police force has an accident and "wakes up" in 1973, while the mystery is where he is and how he can get back "home." In series one, episode three this presents an interesting problem in the representation of class, as a murder at a textile factory positions the viewer in opposition to the mass of factory workers who all become criminal suspects in the investigation. The episode opens up the narrative to a review of "traditional" and "Northern" working-class attitudes and beliefs as the workers articulate their desire to keep the factory alive and to keep their jobs in the face of closures and cheap immigrant labor. At the beginning of the episode, Sam is spoken to by a medical professional from the present over the police radio telling him that his vital signs are low and that to survive he must "keep fighting." When he arrives at the factory to begin the investigation, he places his hands on a warm brick tower. Ted Bannister (John Henshaw), the protagonist in this episode who serves as the traditional working-class proud father who is trying to keep the factory going, tells him that after "hundreds of years of toil" the heat "just bleeds through the bricks. Makes it a living thing. Living things need to keep working on the inside. Once the inside stops. . . ." In the pause Sam adds: "It's just a shell." Given the medical advice that he was given on the radio there is a blurring here and we can feel that Ted is yet another of Sam's paranoid hallucinations, a doctor speaking through Ted to Sam. But for Ted Bannister this idea of the factory as a living body (like a heart that in turn keeps the community alive) becomes a metaphor for class struggle in which the workers have to keep fighting to stay alive, or else they will die.

The workers in the episode are defined in terms of their class, but Sam, having come from the present is "classless" and thus the class dynamic does not seem to apply to him. We are never asked to consider Sam's own class position in this episode, and having come from a time (2007) where class no longer exists, it is not seen as part of his or our consciousness. In another episode we do see Sam's mother and it is clear that he had an ordinary working-class life in a small terraced house and that his father was a gambler and his mother constantly struggled to make ends meet. However, the drama provides us with clear proof of Britain's meritocracy in that although he came from nothing he is now a "classless" detective. Like looking into a historical mirror, class is something "from the past" like flared trousers or Ford Cortina cars. However, the concept of class struggle is then transformed into a metaphor for Sam's own "personal" situation: since he is in a coma he must also "keep fighting" against the temptation to give up and die. Sam's body thus becomes a factory that is threatened with "closure" and he must adopt the position of the unionized working class and fight the closures/death. While the drama maintains its narrative tension by suspending Sam between life and death, the events of the 1970s (as we saw in Jonathan Coe's *The Rotters' Club*) are seen in comfortable retrospect whereby we know how the period unfolded and we have a privileged knowledge of how history will develop. So in this sense the attempts of the workers to "fight" the closures are always already undermined as we "know" that they failed. The futility of their struggle is underscored in that the factory will be converted into an apartment building and Sam will live there: "Thirty years from now this will all be flats...." This emphasizes the unavoidable and unchangeable course of history, and how powerless the working class are to stop it. As the dead body of the victim lies in front of a loom, so the camera flashes a shot of Sam's very trendy contemporary kitchen: "He's in my flat...He's under my kitchen table!" exclaims Sam. This historical determinism ensures that the viewer can dismiss the antagonistic position adopted by the workers in that we know it to be futile: history proved them wrong, struggle all you like, one day your factory *will* be converted into an expensive apartment building for "classless" professional people like Sam. This is the future, and the drama makes it clear that the working class are not only blind and ignorant to the course of history, but they are inflexible and stuck in the past.[76] The implication being that abandoning the past and their "outdated" socialist views would place them on the side of history, and thus they could become flexible and modernize and move along with the course of history, rather than struggling against it. The ignorance and stupidity of the working class is reinforced in that the murder victim, Saunders, was an anti-unionist, and unlike Ted Bannister and his kind, the boss (the aptly named Mr. Coynes) tells us that "Saunders was the only fella ready to adapt" and like the "little brown army" of immigrants, Saunders was also "happy" to work on three machines at once, which the other workers were reluctant to do so, as it meant job cuts. For his love of modernity, Saunders, who said that the unions were "holding everyone back" is thus murdered by a brutal ignorant working class who are stuck in the past and are blind to the movement of history.[77] The narrative draws out our sympathy for Saunders as the boss tells us that unlike the other workers "he could see the way the future lay."

Paradoxically, while the narrative implies that the workers' struggle is futile, this is a move that the "classless" Sam must *not* take: it is imperative that he fight so that he can get back to the present. In a sense Sam is in Stephen Dedalus's shoes in that "History is a nightmare from which [he] must awake." The only way that the workers can get to the future/present is by giving up, dying, and letting history passively carry them along, while Tyler must do the opposite. When questioning the workers, Sam interviews Ted Bannister's son Derek (Andrew Knott). Unlike his father, Derek feels that there is no point fighting: "Why bother? Textiles is doomed. What's the point in fighting it?" Sam replies that "sometimes the fight's the thing. Without it, you go under." At which point the interview with Derek is over. Sam's immediate "fight" now becomes the fight against the rogue methods of his boss Gene Hunt: Gene wants to frame up Ted Bannister while Sam has to try and use "proper" procedures and is not "giving up" in his search to find the real killer. Sam does feel like giving up at one point and the Jamaican barman, Nelson, gives him some wise advice that perhaps Gene Hunt is not the real enemy that he should be fighting. This parallels with the working-class narrative in which Derek Bannister had told Sam that his father always said there was two enemies: "management and government," and a worse enemy, the "enemy within." In political terms Saunders was the enemy within, the class traitor that must be killed. For Sam, the focus thus also shifts from fighting the boss/enemy Gene Hunt, as he shifts his attention to fighting the "enemy within" his own body: the desire to give up.

When it emerges that Saunders appears to have been killed by accident and that Ted Bannister covered up the "accident" to keep the factory open, WPC Anne Cartwright (Liz White) tells Sam that it is good because this way "nobody goes down for life." Sam responds that a "whole community goes down for life," to which she replies, "You don't know that for sure." But of course his historical position means that he does, and so do we. A subplot about some stolen guns and some bad policing by DCI Litton (Lee Ross) ends up moving into the main story as the guns are being used by Derek Bannister to pull a wages robbery on the factory. Derek thus becomes the desperate working-class young man who, having rejected his father's old style union desire to protect the factory and the workers, has turned to armed violence and robbery to look after his family: as Derek says "it's war." In essence what we have here is the two generations of post-war working-class response to living under capitalism: the former is the old style labor fighter who just wants to do an honest day's work for a decent wage, while the latter becomes the violent thug who will kill and rob to get what he wants. The nostalgia of the series clearly sees Ted Bannister as a preferable role model for the younger working class. In the ambulance and under arrest, Derek confesses to his father that he was "scared" because he "didn't see a future for us" to which his father replies "You could have come to me." It is clear that while both father and son agree on the need to fight, the approach is what is being critiqued. The program quite clearly pulls us away from the contemporary notion of the working class as fragmented, violent, and self-motivated and wants to draw us back to a notion of a more benign form of the working class as happy to struggle *within capitalism*. Ted Bannister turns to Sam and says "it is a war. But at least I know what I'm fighting for." Sam says nothing, but the reading we can make is that Sam in his classless postmillennium world has nothing to fight for and does not really know who he is fighting.

The episode ends with Sam arresting the corrupt DCI Litton as he and Gene Hunt knock him out with a combined punch. The final scene in the pub extends this bonding between Sam and Gene as they are again united, hitting a can of Party Seven beer with two screwdrivers and two hammers at the same time, because as Gene Hunt says "it takes two." The notion that he must "fight" Hunt to stay alive is abandoned as Sam has learnt that fighting against his boss is not the answer, and that like Derek and Ted Bannister, any kind of struggle against "the boss" whether of the traditional union kind, or the selfish greed of armed robbery, is doomed to failure. The ideological message that remains is that only by cooperating with the boss can one get results.

In terms of class politics and the medium of television, let us conclude by going back to the night in the pub where Sam gets advice from Nelson about "picking your fights." That same night while Sam is "asleep" the TV test card girl (Rafaella Hutchinson) "visits" him in his dreamlike hallucination and asks him if he feels "helpless" and "unappreciated" and "scared." Like a worker thrown on the scrap heap of history, Sam agrees with her, and like the Bannister family who are "scared" of the future/unemployment (i.e., social and economic "death") so Sam says that "if I stop fighting then I'm scared I'll die" while in the background we can hear the slow steady beep of his heart monitor. The test card girl tells him to trust her and says that she is his "only friend" and she encourages him to "lie down and sleep...No more nastiness. Just sleep...forever." Surely it is important that "television" is here the instrument, not of struggle and fight, but is a soporific tool encouraging the subject to give up fighting and to sleep. This moment in *Life on Mars* is a sort of postmodern confession of television's class bias and a powerful admission and self-referential critique of the role that television has played since its inception in erasing and evading class conflicts.

Notes

Introduction: Questions of Class in the Contemporary British Novel

1. Martin Amis, *London Fields* (New York: Harmony Books, 1989), 24.
2. The full text of Tony Blair's 1999 speech can be found at http://news.bbc.co.uk/2/hi/uk_news/politics/460009.stm (accessed on December 9, 2008).
3. Terry Eagleton, *After Theory* (New York: Perseus Books, 2003), 16.
4. Ibid.
5. Peter Hitchcock, "'They Must Be Represented': Problems in Theories of Working-Class Representation," *PMLA Special Topic: Rereading Class* 115 no. 1 January (2000): 20. Savage, Bagnall, and Longhurst have also pointed out that "Over the past twenty-five years, this sense that the working class 'matters' has ebbed. It is now difficult to detect sustained research interest in the nature of working class culture" (97).
6. Gary Day, *Class* (London and New York: Routledge, 2001), 202. This point is also echoed by Ebert and Zavarzadeh: "By advancing singularity, heterogeneity, anti-totality, and supplementarity, for instance, deconstruction has, among other things, demolished 'history' itself as an articulation of class relations. In doing so, it has constructed a cognitive environment in which the economic interests of capital are seen as natural and not the effect of a particular historical situation. Deconstruction continues to produce some of the most effective discourses to normalize capitalism and contribute to the construction of a capitalist-friendly cultural common sense..." (8).
7. Slavoj Žižek, *In Defence of Lost Causes* (London and New York: Verso, 2008), 404–405 (Hereafter, *Lost Causes*).
8. Andrew Milner, *Class* (London: Sage, 1999), 9.
9. Gavin Keulks, ed., *Martin Amis: Postmodernism and Beyond* (New York: Palgrave Macmillan, 2006), 73.
10. Žižek, *Lost Causes,* 295. For more on the relationship between class and gender in contemporary theory see Skeggs.
11. Following Andrew Milner, by "postmodern" I am referring to "the combination of Derridean deconstruction, Foucauldian genealogy and Lacanian psychoanalysis... which in many respects still continues to 'frame' theoretical debate across the humanities" (9).

12. Eagleton, *After Theory*, 7.
13. Milner, *Class*, 9. While this book will focus on the British experience, I would suggest that the trends are also occurring throughout the Northern Hemisphere. For example, an interesting analysis of these trends in the United States can also be found in Timothy Brennan's *Wars of Position: The Cultural Politics of Left and Right* (New York: Columbia University Press, 2006). As Bernard points out "Brennan advances a broad thesis on the state of contemporary theory…Brennan argues that mainstream cultural criticism, a category that for him includes both 'middlebrow' journalism and scholarship in the humanities (xi), has been a 'secret sharer with American liberalism' following the 'turn' to the right that took place in American cultural life between 1975 and 1980." See Anna Bernard, review of *Wars of Position: The Cultural Politics of Left and Right* by Timothy Brennan, *Textual Practice* 20, no. 4 (2006): 777–816.
14. As Linda Zerilli points out there is "a growing consensus that poststructuralist political theories are incapable of generating a viable alternative to the collective fragmentation that characterizes late modernity" (3).
15. Milner, *Class*, 163. Milner directs us to Altick's 1962 study of 1,100 British authors from 1800 to 1935 in which the great majority were university educated. While there will always be working-class exceptions, the vast majority of canonized authors come from within the middle classes, as I go on to demonstrate in the introduction. Milner reminds us that studies in America and Australia have produced similar findings.
16. Philip Tew, *The Contemporary British Novel* (London and New York: Continuum, 2004), 67, 84–85, 183.
17. Ibid., 86.
18. Ibid., 87. Clearly, writers and academics don't consciously "refuse" to deal with it, but I think it is a sign of ideology's power that class bias passes by undetected, slipping through the critical border by passing itself off as an unquestionable "truth" or "nature."
19. John Kirk, *Twentieth-Century Writing and the British Working Class* (Cardiff: University of Wales Press, 2003), 190.
20. Malcolm Bradbury, *The Modern British Novel: 1878–2001* (London: Penguin, 2001), 519.
21. Ibid., 28.
22. Milner, *Class*, 9–10.
23. Ibid., 10. The same theoretical evasion of class is present also in the American humanities. As Rita Felski has recently pointed out: "There is a noticeable silence about class in much contemporary theory" (34).
24. Ian Parker, *Slavoj Zizek: A Critical Introduction* (London: Pluto Press, 2004), 89.
25. Milner, *Class*, 53.
26. Ibid.
27. Ibid., 10.
28. Ibid., 10–11.
29. Will Atkinson, "Not All That Was Solid Has Melted into Air (Or Liquid): A Critique of Bauman on Individualization and Class in Liquid Modernity,"

Sociological Review 56, no. 1 (2008): 1. For more on the paradox of a "classless" society, see Chapter Seven of Edgell.

30. John H. Goldthorpe and Michelle Jackson, "Intergenerational Class Mobility in Contemporary Britain: Political Concerns and Empirical Findings," *British Journal of Sociology* 58, no. 4 (2007): 526.
31. Atkinson, "Not All That Was Solid," 2.
32. For the full report see http://www.jrf.org.uk/knowledge/findings/housing/2077.asp
33. Another section of the report also concluded that "Over the last 20 years, a large and enduring majority of people (73 per cent in 2004) have considered the gap between high and low incomes too large." http://www.jrf.org.uk/knowledge/findings/socialpolicy/2097.asp (accessed on December 9, 2008).
34. Nicholas Abercrombie and Alan Warde, eds., *The Contemporary British Society Reader* (Cambridge, MA: Polity, 2001), 67. I would concur with Westergaard's definition of class as "a set of social divisions that arise from society's economic organization" (67), and that people "may be said to be in different classes in so far as they occupy... distinct and unequal places in that economic organization" (67). For more on inequality in British society see Westergaard's *Who Gets What?: The Hardening of Class Inequality in the Late Twentieth Century* (Cambridge, MA: Polity, 1995).
35. Ibid., 67. For similar conclusions see also Mike Hout, Clem Brooks, and Jeff Manza. "The Persistence of Classes in Post-Industrial Societies" reprinted in Terry Nichols Clark and Seymour Martin Lipset, *The Breakdown of Class Politics: A Debate on Post-Industrial Stratification* (Baltimore, MD: Johns Hopkins University Press, 2001), 55–75.
36. Ibid., 70.
37. Ibid., 72.
38. Kirk, *Twentieth-Century Writing*, 3.
39. Ned Temko, review of *Thatcher and Sons* by Simon Jenkins in *Observer* (November 5, 2006). www.guardian.co.uk/theobserver/2006/nov/05/politics
40. Susan Watkins, "A Weightless Hegemony: New Labour's Role in the Neoliberal Order," *New Left Review* 25 (January–February 2004): 10–13.
41. Žižek, *Lost Causes*, 189.
42. Arthur Marwick, *British Society since 1945* (London: Penguin, 2003), 382.
43. Ibid., 460.
44. David Cannadine, *Class in Britain* (London: Penguin, 2000), 1.
45. Abercrombie and Warde, *Contemporary British Society Reader*, 72.
46. Ibid., 73.
47. Ibid., 74.
48. Fredric Jameson, *Postmodernism, or, The Cultural Logic of Late Capitalism* (Durham, NC: Duke University Press, 2005), 3.
49. Ibid., 74.
50. Ibid., 75.
51. Milner, *Class*, 99.
52. Abercrombie and Warde, *Contemporary British Society Reader*, 75.
53. Ibid., 76.
54. Ibid., 76–77.

55. Ibid., 77.
56. Ibid. For more on the recent geographical class differences in Britain see Bethan Thomas in "Identity in Britain: A Cradle to Grave Analysis" (published by the Social and Spatial Inequalities Research Group). See http://www.sasi.group.shef.ac.uk/ (accessed on December 9, 2008).
57. Andrew Adonis and Stephen Pollard. *A Class Act: The Myth of Britain's Classless Society* (London: Hamish Hamilton, 1997), 19–21. Subsequent references to this text are made parenthetically by page number.
58. For more on the relationship between class and education see Ball, Stephen J. *Class Strategies and the Education Market: The Middle Classes and Social Advantage* (London: Routledge, 2003).
59. John Kirk, "Recovered Perspectives: Gender, Class, and Memory in Pat Barker's Writing," *Contemporary Literature* 40, no. 4 (1999): 607.
60. Ibid.
61. Ibid.
62. Pierre Macherey frames this question as "What is Literature thinking about?" in *The Object of Literature,* trans. David Macey (Cambridge: Cambridge University Press, 1995).
63. Aijaz Ahmad, *In Theory: Class, Nations, Literatures* (London: Verso, 2008), 6.
64. Ibid., 7.
65. Terry Eagleton, *Literary Theory: An Introduction* (Minneapolis: University of Minnesota Press, 2008), 19–20.
66. As John Kirk points out, this "constant reference to the proliferation of new identities [is] predicated on the postmodern condition…and this purported fluidity of ontological boundaries seemed to seal the fate of the working-class subject" (*Twentieth-Century Writing*, 14). Kirk concludes that identity politics thereby "disenfranchises class through its embeddedness in the discourse of individualism" (16).
67. It is worth noting also that out of this list many of these authors have been knighted, or given various different levels of the Order of the British Empire, such as a CBE, an OBE, or an MBE. Recipients include Sir Salman Rushdie, Iris Murdoch (DBE), Hanif Kureishi (CBE), Jeanette Winterson (OBE), Peter Ackroyd (CBE), A. S. Byatt (CBE), Margaret Drabble (DBE), Sebastian Faulks (CBE), Pat Barker (CBE), and Ian McEwan (CBE).
68. Tew, *Contemporary British Novel*, 84.
69. Raymond Williams, *Marxism and Literature* (Oxford: Oxford University Press, 1977), 52.
70. Ibid., 49.
71. Žižek, *Lost Causes*, 404.
72. Ibid.
73. Eagleton, *After Theory*, 2.
74. Ibid., 13.
75. Ibid., 18.
76. Ibid., 190.
77. Brian Finney, *British Fiction since 1984: Narrating a Nation* (New York: Palgrave Macmillan, 2006), 2–3. Subsequent references to this text are made parenthetically by page number.

78. As John Kirk (2003) reminds us, "classlessness means becoming middle-class" (7), and thus becoming the "norm"—"the authorative and authorized place to be" (7).
79. Tew, *Contemporary British Novel*, 85–87.
80. Slavoj Žižek, *The Ticklish Subject: The Absent Centre of Political Ontology* (London and New York: Verso, 1999), 187.
81. Tew, *Contemporary British Novel*, 87.
82. Ibid., 89.
83. Fredric Jameson, *The Political Unconscious: Narrative as a Socially Symbolic Act* (New York: Cornell University Press, 1981), 85.
84. Ibid., 86.
85. Kirk, *Twentieth-Century Writing*, 191.
86. Ian Buchanan, *Fredric Jameson: Live Theory* (London: Continuum, 2006), 63.
87. Ibid.
88. Jameson, *Political Unconscious*, 81.
89. Ibid., 79.
90. Philip Tew and Rod Mengham, eds., *British Fiction Today* (London: Continuum, 2006), 56.
91. Jameson, *Postmodernism*, 368.
92. See Andrzej Gasiorek, *Post-War British Fiction: Realism and After* (London: Edward Arnold, 1995).
93. Dominic Head, *The Cambridge Introduction to Modern British Fiction 1950–2000* (Cambridge: Cambridge University Press, 2002), 225.

1 "Unworkable Subjects": Middle-Class Narratives in Pat Barker, Ian McEwan, and Kazuo Ishiguro

1. Jameson, *Political Unconscious*, 102.
2. Cannadine, *Class in Britain*, 2.
3. Richard J. Lane, Rod Mengham, and Philip Tew, eds., *Contemporary British Fiction* (Cambridge, MA: Polity, 2003), 15.
4. Rob Nixon, "An Interview with Pat Barker," *Contemporary Literature* 45, no. 1 (Spring 2004): 4, my emphasis.
5. Peter Kemp, "Pat Barker's Last Battle?" *Times Online* July 1, 2007. http://entertainment.timesonline.co.uk/tol/arts_and_entertainment/books/article1995669.ece
6. Nixon, "Interview," 6.
7. Nick Bentley, ed. *British Fiction of the 1990s* (London and New York: Routledge, 2005), 168.
8. Sharon Monteith, *Pat Barker* (Tavistock: Northcote House, 2002), 168.
9. Nixon, "Interview," 4.
10. James Acheson and Sarah C. E. Ross, eds., *The Contemporary British Novel since 1980* (New York: Palgrave Macmillan, 2006), 135. Subsequent references to this text are made parenthetically by page number.

11. John Kirk, "Recovered Perspectives: Gender, Class and Memory in Pat Barker's Writing," *Contemporary Literature* 40, no. 4 (Winter 1999): 612.
12. See Brannigan's essay in Lane, Mengham, and Tew, *Contemporary British Fiction*.
13. See Hubble's essay in Tew and Mengham, *British Fiction Today*.
14. Lane, Mengham, and Tew, *Contemporary British Fiction*, 15.
15. Ibid., 17–18.
16. Ibid., 23.
17. Ibid., 20.
18. Ibid., 24.
19. For an interesting reading of Woolf's *Mrs. Dalloway* and class, see Alex Zwerdling.
20. Lane, Mengham, and Tew, *Contemporary British Fiction*, 24.
21. Ibid.
22. Tew and Mengham, *British Fiction Today*, 153.
23. Ibid., 163
24. Bentley, *British Fiction of the 1990s*, 177, 170.
25. The desire to transcend binaries is surely mirroring a deep seated desire to also transcend *class* binaries: to this extent postmodern theory finds a comfortable echo in Major, Thatcher, and Blair's desire for a classless, nonbinary society.
26. Tew and Mengham, *British Fiction Today*, 164.
27. Pat Barker, *The Ghost Road* (New York: Plume Books, 1995), 257. Prescott sees this as revealing that Barker is interested in "the power of language" (Bentley, *British Fiction of the 1990s*, 177). However, such a reading surely overlooks that Prior intends his words "us, them, we, they" to be connected to something: that is, class.
28. Barker, *Ghost Road*, 276.
29. Philip Tew has noted that the middle classes are prone to universalizing their predicament. The crisis that the bourgeoisie have undergone in the postwar world has thus been rewritten so that their "crisis of definition and exposition became that of the world as a whole" (71).
30. Brian Finney, "Briony's Stand against Oblivion: The Making of Fiction in Ian McEwan's *Atonement*," *Journal of Modern Literature* 27, no. 3 (Winter 2004): 76. Subsequent references to this text are made parenthetically by page number.
31. Finney, *British Fiction since 1984*, 91.
32. Pierre Macherey, *A Theory of Literary Production* (London and New York: Routledge, 2006), 146.
33. Finney, *British Fiction since 1984*, 78.
34. Finney, "Briony's Stand," 82.
35. Ibid., 79–81.
36. Daphne Merkin, *Los Angeles Times*, *Atonement* book jacket.
37. Terry Eagleton, "A Beautiful and Elusive Tale," *Lancet* 358, no. 9299 (December 22, 2001) www.thelancet.com/journals/lancet/article. Eagleton also points to how the "novel form teaches us a politics of liberal tolerance, engaging in a plurality of perspectives, but…it is after all, the all-privileged novelist who decides to whom to hand the microphone to next."

38. Ian McEwan, *Atonement* (New York: Anchor, 2003), 38.
39. Ibid.
40. Finney, "Briony's Stand," 80.
41. McEwan, *Atonement,* 38.
42. Finney, "Briony's Stand," 80.
43. McEwan, *Atonement,* 6.
44. Finney, "Briony's Stand," 76.
45. McEwan, *Atonement,* 47.
46. Ibid., 46.
47. Ibid., 47.
48. McEwan, *Atonement*, 142.
49. Ibid., 21.
50. Ibid., 36. These aspects of the novel always leave me with the feeling that perhaps Jack Tallis is Robbie's biological father. This means that Robbie and Cecilia are incestuous lovers, like Jack and Julie in McEwan's first novel *The Cement Garden*. This would also explain the narrative desire to have these "class-crossed lovers" killed off. Žižek's argument about Cameron's *Titanic* is that the iceberg is there to prevent a cross-class relationship.
51. Finney, "Briony's Stand," 76.
52. McEwan, *Atonement,* 7.
53. Ibid., 8.
54. Aida Edemariam, "'Enduring Fame': An Interview with Ian McEwan," *Guardian Online* August 18, 2007. http://books.guardian.co.uk/interviews/story/0,,2151430,00.html
55. Zadie Smith, "Interview with Ian McEwan," *Believer,* August 2005. www.believermag.com
56. In the novel, clear links are made between writing and surgery, which is important considering that Perowne will operate on Baxter, not someone of his own class.
57. Interview with Ian McEwan, *Der Spiegel*, July 19, 2005.
58. All comments are from the book jacket for *Saturday*.
59. Tew and Mengham, *British Fiction Today*, xv.
60. McEwan, *Saturday*, 8. In Britain "comprehensive schools" are schools designed with the working class in mind, as opposed to "public schools" like Marlborough, Eton, and Charterhouse that, paradoxically, are not public, but *private*, fee-paying schools. Subsequent references to this text are made parenthetically by page number.
61. Will Self's aggressive cab driver Dave, in *The Book of Dave* is also "meaningless." In his own words he is simply "ex-fucking everything."
62. McEwan, *Saturday*, 276. Subsequent references to this text are made parenthetically by page number.
63. Ibid., 218. If the novel attached the same equation of violence to Andrea's racial/genetic make-up, I assume we would laugh at such a stereotyped notion that black violence is "genetic": but attached to the working-class Baxter, this thoroughly ideological notion passes by almost unnoticed.
64. Andrew Sanders, ed., *The Short Oxford History of English Literature* (3rd edition) (Oxford: Oxford University Press, 2004), 451.

65. Ibid.
66. Ibid., 453. *Saturday*, with its cast of Andrea Chapman as the Barbarian turned aristocrat (the "African queen"), Perowne the Philistine bourgeois and of course, Baxter the Unlettered Populace is strikingly close to Arnold's three classes in *Culture and Anarchy*.
67. Ibid.
68. McEwan, *Saturday*, 109.
69. Paradoxically, in Pat Barker, the "science" of psychoanalysis was supposedly deconstructed by River's encounters in Melanesia. Here science is used as proof of Perowne's unassailable position, as well as Baxter's genetic class fate.
70. McEwan, *Saturday*, 100.
71. Ramona Koval, Interview with Ian McEwan. April 2004, no. 4, www.eruditiononline.com/04.04/ian_mcewan.htm
72. McEwan, *Saturday*, 265.
73. Ibid., 266, 282. Fredric Jameson reads *Wuthering Heights* with Heathcliff being the "embodiment of history" threatening the agricultural preindustrial world of the Earnshaws and the Lintons: he is there in the text to "rejuvenate" (Buchanan, *Fredric Jameson*, 76) the two families. So, I would argue, Baxter functions in a parallel way: he is drawn into the text and then removed from it so as to reassert the validity of the bourgeoisie and the nuclear family: it has faced the ultimate terror of facing the working class head on, and survives.
74. Ibid., 121.
75. Ibid., 109.
76. Ibid., 279.
77. McEwan, *Atonement*, 6. It would be easy for a critic to say that such immunity is "cleverly deconstructed by other elements in the novel" that serve to ensure that "no final closure is possible," and that "all immunities are always already infected from the outside" and so on. But such postmodern readings only serve to put McEwan back in the driving seat, and the critic would be once again working "for" literature, showing how McEwan's genius enables him to deconstruct such "simple" notions as middle class/working class, inside/outside and so on.
78. If we think back to McEwan's *The Cement Garden* (1978), it is worth noting that the strange, bizarre incestuous family is thoroughly working class. The novel ends with the excessive desires of this "family" being contained as the police lights signal that they are to be safely taken into care by the government.
79. Jameson, *Postmodernism*, 188.
80. Ibid.
81. Ibid.
82. Finney, *British Fiction since 1984*, 140.
83. "Memory Is the Terribly Treacherous Terrain," Ishiguro: Interview with Graham Swift. *BOMB* 29 (1989): 22–23.
84. Richard Bradford, *The Novel Now: Contemporary British Fiction* (Oxford: Blackwell, 2007), 216.

85. Head, *Modern British Fiction*, 156.
86. Finney, *British Fiction since 1984*, 139.
87. Head, *Modern British Fiction*, 157.
88. Ibid., 158.
89. Acheson and Ross, *Contemporary British Novel since 1980*, 14.
90. Ibid., 12.
91. Ibid., 14.
92. Cynthia Wong, *Kazuo Ishiguro* (Devon: British Council/Northcote House, 2005), 54.
93. Ibid., 55.
94. Wong, *Kazuo Ishiguro*, 55, 65.
95. See John P. McCombe. "The End of (Anthony) Eden: Ishiguro's *The Remains of the Day* and Midcentury Anglo-American Tensions," *Twentieth Century Literature* 48, no. 1 (Spring 2002): 77–99.
96. McCombe, "The End of (Anthony) Eden," 77. Subsequent references to this text are made parenthetically by page number.
97. Jameson, *Political Unconscious*, 76.

2 "Our Economic Position": Middle-Class Consciousness in Zadie Smith and Will Self

1. See "Only Connect: From *White Teeth* to the Ivory Tower": An interview with *On Beauty* novelist Zadie Smith by Joy Press. September 16, 2005, The Village Voice. http://www.villagevoice.com/2005-09-13/books/only-connect/
2. E. M. Forster, *Two Cheers for Democracy* (New York: Harcourt Brace and World, 1951), 56–57.
3. Parallel to the usual readings of Zadie Smith, Alistair McCormack reads Monica Ali's *Brick Lane* as a similar novel of postcolonial hybridity in which we have a fully democratic "multitude of voices" (697). But again, his argument proceeds with no mention of Ali's own middle-class background and education, nor does it take into consideration the extremely complex class positions of the characters in the novel.
4. Tew and Mengham, *British Fiction Today*, 129. Tolan argues that in *On Beauty* "aesthetic concerns predominate and inform an ongoing ethical inquiry" (128). Tolan concludes that "Smith connects this affirmation of beauty with the capacity to relinquish the self and care about the other... " (137). Tolan's analysis makes no attempt to consider that this aesthetic is being articulated on behalf of any particular class.
5. Mary Pinkerton, "Ambiguous Connections: Leonard Bast's Role in *Howards End*," *Twentieth Century Literature* 31, no. 2/3, E. M. Forster Issue (Summer–Autumn, 1985): 243.
6. Henry Turner, "Empire of Objects: Accumulation and Entropy in E. M. Forster's *Howards End*," *Twentieth Century Literature* 46, no. 3 (Autumn 2000): 339.
7. Kathleen O'Grady "White Teeth: A Conversation with Author Zadie Smith," *Atlantis: A Women's Studies Journal* 27, no. 1 (Fall 2002): 107.

8. David James has suggested that Smith draws on Forster not as simple imitation but to "enunciate her own parable of ethical consequence" (694). As with Widdowson (2006), I feel that James also desires to read Zadie Smith as an author who is radically "rewriting" her origins. However, a reading of the novel that takes the question of class into consideration reveals that her text has a rather more troubling relationship to ideology.
9. It is almost as if the publishers are trying to convince us that we have in our hand a thoroughly *working-class* author of mixed race, however, as the epigraph to this chapter makes clear, this is evidently not the case.
10. Turner, "Empire of Objects," 329.
11. Ibid.
12. Pinkerton, "Ambiguous Connections," 236.
13. Kathleen O'Grady, "White Teeth," 109.
14. Zadie Smith, "Love, actually," *Guardian Unlimited*, Saturday November 1, 2003. http://www.guardian.co.uk/books/2003/nov/01/classics.zadiesmith (All subsequent comments are from the transcript of this lecture, unless indicated otherwise).
15. This same division occurs throughout the contemporary British novel. An example would be how Perowne in McEwan's *Saturday* is meant to feel adrift in his post-9/11 world, but it is an anxiety that is not shared by the working-class character, Baxter.
16. E. M. Forster, *A Room with a View, Howards End* and *Maurice* (New York: Quality Paperbacks Book Club, 1971), 365.
17. Forster, *Howards End*, 365.
18. How can we accept this slippage between ourselves and the bourgeois Lucy Honeychurch? Would Smith accept that "we" can be used to include a white man and her own self? Obviously not, but here ideology allows us to assume that "we" includes any reader regardless of class.
19. Zadie Smith, *On Beauty* (New York: Penguin, 2006), 418.
20. Peter Widdowson, *E. M. Forster's Howards End: Fiction as History* (London: Sussex University Press, 1977), 33.
21. Widdowson, *Fiction as History*, 13. Peter Widdowson has recently argued that a large section of contemporary British fiction is engaged in a radical revision of its origins. He suggests that these novels, including such authors as Smith, Barker, Faulks, Boyd, and others, "invariably 'write back' to canonic texts of the English tradition" and that they take novels that have a high profile in our literary heritage "and re-write them 'against the grain'" (2006, 501). As can be seen from my reading of Zadie Smith, such "re-visionary" fiction sometimes falls rather short of offering "a very different reality" (501). Contrary to Widdowson's thesis, Zadie Smith's own warm comments regarding Forster also make it clear that she has no desire to read him "against the grain." After all, as she has pointed out, she is "one of them."
22. Widdowson, *Fiction as History*, 113.
23. These reviewers' comments are all taken from the inside pages of the novel.
24. Terry Eagleton, *The Illusions of Postmodernism* (Oxford: Blackwell, 1996), 87.

25. Ibid.
26. Ibid., 95–96.
27. Smith, *On Beauty*, 44.
28. Forster, *Howards End*, 29–30.
29. In the same way that Tibby and Margaret are worried about their Ricketts painting being stolen by Bast in Forster, so Zora worries that Carl chatting her up will only lead him closer to "the safe in the basement" (139). While Smith has different plans for Carl, it will turn out to be Choo, the African street vendor who ends up being the real art thief of this novel.
30. Smith, *On Beauty*, 44 (Hereafter *OB*).
31. Eagleton, *Illusions of Postmodernism*, 105.
32. Smith, *OB*, 180. Subsequent references to this text are made parenthetically by page number.
33. Ibid. The novel contains another line "borrowed" from Philip Larkin (i.e., "and brings to bloom the million-petalled flower of being here" (211) from Larkin's poem "The Old Fools"). This treatment of the working-class home is also redolent of Larkin's middle-class perspective. See, for example, Larkin's distaste with working-class domestic spaces in "Mr. Bleaney" and "Afternoons."
34. Forster, *Howards End*, 357.
35. Smith, *OB*, 418–419. Subsequent references to this text are made parenthetically by page number.
36. Nick Rennison, *Contemporary British Novelists* (London: Routledge, 2005), 150.
37. Lane, Mengham, and Tew, *Contemporary British Fiction*, 84.
38. Bradford, *The Novel Now*, 51.
39. Tew, *Contemporary British Novel*, 106.
40. Ibid.
41. Bradford, *The Novel Now*, 52–53.
42. Ibid., 53.
43. Tew, *Contemporary British Novel*, 105.
44. Ibid.
45. Lane, Mengham, and Tew, *Contemporary British Fiction*, 81.
46. Will Self, *Junk Mail* (London: Penguin, 1996), 151.
47. Ibid.
48. Here is a sample from one about a new statue that was erected in Aldeburgh, Suffolk in memory of the homosexual composer Benjamin Britten: An Aldeburgh Taxi Driver Writes: "I say, guvnor, that sculpture really is a bit of a shocker. Completely ruins the shoreline…I've got nothing against Ben Britten personally…he played for the other side…running off to America…dreary operas about paedophiles and so on, no it's the council I blame…If you ask me they should all be strung up, it's the only language they understand…" (*Private Eye Annual* 2004, 44).
49. Will Self, *The Book of Dave* (New York: Bloomsbury, 2006), 51.
50. Ibid., 81.
51. Paradoxically, the novel replicates the very social strategy it is designed to avoid in the real: Dave's murder means that Davinity will emerge in the

future where Dave's rants will be taken as gospel and society will be reduced to following the dictates of a working-class man.
52. Will Self "In the Beginning: Will Self on the genesis of *The Book of Dave*," *Guardian*, June 16, 2007. http://books.guardian.co.uk/bookclub/story/0,,2104020,00.html
53. Self, *Book of Dave*, 284.
54. Helen Brown, "A Writer's Life: Will Self," 1.
55. Forster, *Howards End*, 164.
56. Self, *Book of Dave*, 403.
57. Ibid., 403, original italics.
58. Ibid., 392, my emphasis.
59. Ibid., 404.
60. Ibid., 405.
61. Ibid., 400, original italics.
62. John Harrison, "The Gospel According to Dave," *Guardian*, Saturday May 27, 2006, 1.
63. Self, *Book of Dave*, 92, 202, 203, 205, 227, 264, 267, 315, 335, 345, 350, 390.
64. Ibid., 455. Notice that the normal, biological *middle-class* union of father and son in the form of Carl and Cal and the future reunion of Carl Devenush and his real father, the Beestlyman, are not mocked by the authorial voice. Subsequent references to this text are made parenthetically by page number.
68. Ibid., 362–363. There is a line of middle-class satire that can be seen to run from Will Self right back to William Hogarth. John Leonard on the cover of the novel also suggests that Self is the rightful successor to Jonathan Swift.
66. Once again, by seeing how Cal Devenish is the textual mask for Will Self, we have another novel in which the middle-class author (as in McEwan's *Atonement* and *Saturday*) is folded back into the middle-class hero of the text.
67. Mary McGlynn, "Middle-Class Wankers and Working-Class Texts: The Critics and James Kelman," *Contemporary Literature* 43, no. 1 (Spring 2002): 61.
68. McGlynn, "Middle-Class Wankers," 60.
69. Ibid.

3 Classless Fictions?: Middle-Class History/Working-Class Subjects in Martin Amis, Peter Ackroyd, and Hanif Kureishi

1. Martin Amis, *Success* (New York: Vintage International, 1978), 58–59.
2. Terry Eagleton, *Ideology* (London and New York: Verso, 2007), x.
3. Ibid.
4. See Terry Eagleton, "Rebuking Obnoxious Views Is Not Just a Personality Kink," *Guardian Online Comment* October 10, 2007.

5. Eagleton, *Ideology*, xi.
6. See Terry Eagleton, "Only Pinter remains," *Guardian Online* July 7, 2007.
7. All quotes are from "Only Pinter remains" unless otherwise noted.
8. Bradford, *The Novel Now*, 28.
9. Ibid., 184.
10. Ibid., my emphasis.
11. Lane, Mengham, and Tew, *Contemporary British Fiction*, 247.
12. Ibid., 247. Self's promiscuity is really only the promiscuity of capitalism itself. As Eagelton points out "the only norm now is money, but since money has no ideas or principles of its own, it is no kind of norm at all. It is utterly promiscuous..." (Eagleton, *After Theory*, 16–17).
13. Laura L. Doan offers a valuable comparison of *Money* with Caryl Churchill's *Serious Money*. See Laura L. Doan "Sexy Greedy Is the Late Eighties: Power Systems in Amis's *Money* and Churchill's *Serious Money*," *The Minnesota Review: A Journal of Committed Writing* 34, no. 5 (Spring 1990): 69–80.
14. Jon Begley, "Satirizing the Carnival of Postmodern Capitalism: The Transatlantic and Dialogic Structure of Martin Amis's *Money*," *Contemporary Literature* 45, no. 1 (Spring 2004): 80.
15. Ibid., 81.
16. Ibid., 83.
17. Amis, *Money*, 238.
18. Begley, "Satirizing the Carnival," 73.
19. Ibid., 87–88.
20. Ibid., 91.
21. John Haffenden, *Novelists in Interview* (London: Methuen, 1985), 14.
22. Begley, "Satirizing the Carnival," 94.
23. Gavin Keulks, ed. *Martin Amis: Postmodernism and Beyond* (New York: Palgrave Macmillan, 2006), 55. Subsequent references to this text are made parenthetically by page number.
24. Tew, *The Novel Now*, 85.
25. Ibid., 81.
26. Keulks, *Martin Amis: Postmodernism and Beyond*, 71.
27. Ibid., 72.
28. Ibid., 73. Tew's conclusion seems rather muted. He tells us that "Finally, it is left me for to wonder whether, for all its grotesqueries, the quotidian in Amis can sufficiently rise above the bitter class perspectives, the ranting opinions of occluded world-views and the parodic. I am not sure I can answer that question..." (85).
29. Ibid., 81.
30. Ibid., 78–79.
31. Ibid., 79.
32. Ibid., 82.
33. Ibid.
34. Haffenden, *Novelists in Interview*, 7–8.
35. Keulks, *Martin Amis*, 82.
36. Ibid., 85.

37. Ibid.
38. Haffenden, *Novelists in Interview*, 14–24.
39. Keulks, *Martin Amis*, 81.
40. Amis, *Money*, 354.
41. Martin Amis, *Heavy Water and Other Stories* (New York: Vintage, 2000), 38–41.
42. Ibid.
43. Ibid., 41.
44. Ibid., 53–60.
45. Ibid., 68.
46. Ibid., 71.
47. See Cannadine, *Class in Britain*, 11.
48. Del Ivan Janik, "No End of History: Evidence from the Contemporary English Novel," *Twentieth Century Literature* 41, no. 2 (Summer 1995): 160.
49. Janik, "No End of History," 160.
50. Ibid., 162.
51. Acheson and Ross, *Contemporary British Novel since 1980*, 217.
52. Ibid., 217.
53. Ibid.
54. Ibid.
55. Ibid., 221.
56. Finney, *English Fiction since 1984*, 29.
57. Laura Colombino, "Negotiations with the system: J. G. Ballard and Geoff Ryman writing London's architecture," *Textual Practice* 20, no. 4 (2006): 615. Significantly, Colombino traces this to the ideas of the Dutch painter and sculptor Nieuwenhuis Constant. As she points, his idea "had always been to apply Marxist thought to art, *not in the form of real socialism*, but rather in the form of total spontaneism, in the unleashing of public and private creativity, bringing the 'social revolution' into line with an 'artistic revolution' " (616, my emphasis).
58. Ibid.
59. Ibid. Colombino wants to draw a distinction in her reading between the traditional Neo-Gothic and a far more radical alternative offered by J. G. Ballard and Geoff Ryman. For Colombino, Ballard and Ryman's texts "[f]ar from trying to counteract the predetermination of our commodity culture by means of 'secret knowledges' [are] 'anti-democratic in' their 'love of the arcane', they are engaged with the integration of the subject…into the degraded, commonplace world of capitalist economy…Neo-Gothic novels visualise London as a text perpetually enriched whose meanings are enlarged by recollection and positively expanded by creativeness. Contrariwise, Ryman and Ballard's works conceive the capital as a claustrophobic site of entrapment" (615–617). To me this alternative is simply the flip side of the same bourgeois coin, where the city is not the playground of the flaneur, but the oppressive ugly home of the poor and the wretched that bourgeois subject must flee from. Indeed Colombino implies as much when she shows that this alternative tradition comes not from a socialist tradition but from "Dada's capitalist nihilism" (616).

60. Finney, *English Fiction since 1984*, 32, my emphasis.
61. See Susan Onega, "Interview with Peter Ackroyd," *Twentieth Century Literature* 42, no. 2 (Summer 1996): 208–220.
62. Susan Onega, "Interview with Peter Ackroyd," 216.
63. Ibid., 209. Being brought up in a working-class "area" does not automatically make one working class. This bifurcation is also clear in the case of Mike Leigh who admits that he was a middle-class boy who grew up in a working-class area. See my comments on Leigh in chapter five.
64. Tew and Mengham, *British Fiction Today*, 56.
65. Ibid., 62–63.
66. Ibid., 64.
67. Ibid., 64–65.
68. Ibid., 65.
69. Jameson, *Postmodernism*, 365.
70. Alex Link, " 'The Capitol of Darknesse': Gothic Spatialities in the London of Peter Ackroyd's *Hawksmoor*," *Contemporary Literature* 45, no. 3 (Autumn 2004): 518.
71. Ibid., 519.
72. Ibid.
73. Ibid., 520, my emphasis.
74. Ibid.
75. Bradford, *The Novel Now*, 83.
76. Jameson, *Postmodernism*, 362.
77. Link, *The Capitol of Darknesse*, 520.
78. Ibid.
79. Ibid., 520, my emphasis.
80. Ibid., 521.
81. Onega, "Interview with Peter Ackroyd," 209.
82. Ibid., 210.
83. Ibid., 214.
84. Ibid., 215.
85. Ibid.
86. Ibid.
87. Ackroyd, *Hawskmoor*, 78.
88. Head, *Modern British Fiction*, 203.
89. Tew and Mengham, *British Fiction Today*, 65.
90. Jameson, *Postmodernism*, 367.
91. Ibid., 368.
92. Ibid.
93. Ibid.
94. Finney, *English Fiction since 1984*, 24.
95. Jameson, *Postmodernism*, 369.
96. Ibid.
97. Onega, "Interview with Peter Ackroyd," 220.
98. Terry Eagleton, *Figures of Dissent: Critical Essays on Fish, Spivak, Zizek and others* (London: Verso, 2003), 220.
99. Kirk, *Twentieth-Century Writing*, 170.

100. Head, *Modern British Fiction*, 220–223.
101. Ibid., 222.
102. Ibid.
103. Kirk, *Twentieth-Century Writing*, 173.
104. Hanif Kureishi, *The Buddha of Suburbia* (London: Penguin, 1990), 160 (Hereafter *B of S*).
105. Lane, Mengham, and Tew, *Contemporary British Fiction*, 101.
106. Kureishi, *B of S*, 217.
107. Ibid.
108. Ibid., 216.
109. See Anthony Ilona's chapter on Kureishi in Lane, Mengham, and Tew, *Contemporary British Fiction*, 88–105.
110. Lane, Mengham, and Tew, *Contemporary British Fiction*, 87.
111. Ibid., 88.
112. Ibid.
113. Ibid., 88–89.
114. Ibid., 89–90.
115. Hanif Kureishi, *My Beautiful Laundrette and Other Writings* (London: Faber and Faber), 99–100.
116. Lane, Mengham, and Tew, *Contemporary British Fiction*, 93. Subsequent references to this text are made parenthetically by page number.
117. Eagleton, *Illusions of Postmodernism*, 134.
118. Hanif Kureishi, *The Black Album* (London: Faber, 1995), 236 (Hereafter *TBA*). Subsequent references to this text are made parenthetically by page number.
119. Ibid., 287. This same retreat into the personal occurs in Kureishi's *Sammie and Rosie Get Laid*. As bell hooks has pointed out: Sammie and Rosie are "fucked up and fucked over by political systems that they do not effectively challenge or change. They hide in desire, in that narcissistic space of longing where difference... becomes the setting for high spectacle, the alternative playground" (Sen, 76).
120. Terry Eagleton, *The Idea of Culture* (Oxford: Blackwell, 2000), 74–75.
121. Ibid., 42.
122. Ibid., 86.
123. Ibid., 122.
124. *The Body* is strikingly absent from critical work on Kureishi, as is work on *Intimacy*, *Gabriel's Gift*, and *The Mother*. It would seem that once Kureishi stopped writing about race he ceased to be of much interest to the critical community. In part, as his fiction returned to the private world of self and family, it exposed aspects of Kureishi's middle-class ideology that do not fit comfortably with postcolonial criticism. Even though reviewers seem to agree that Kureishi has matured as a writer, his later work has been overlooked in favor of writers like Monica Ali and Zadie Smith. As Linklater points out: "Having stepped out with *Intimacy*, Kureishi has made another pit-stop on his journey to literary maturity with *The Body*. The cinematic and novelistic multiculturalism that he largely pioneered in Britain with *My Beautiful Laundrette* and *The Buddha of Suburbia* has given way to

compressed tales of family and the self. These may be less ambitious in scope than his earlier fiction; but the writing has become more concentrated, more certain of what is being said, and more durable." See "Death of the Ego" by Alexander Linklater, *Guardian Online* November 16, 2002. His work may be more "durable," but it is of much less interest to the postmodern scholarly community since Hanif Kureishi (ironically awarded the Honor of Commander of the British Empire) no longer seems to be "on message" with these later works.

125. Kureishi, *The Body*, 2. Subsequent references to this text are made parenthetically by page number.

4 We're All Bourgeois Now: Realism and Class in Alan Hollinghurst, Graham Swift, and Jonathan Coe

1. Ellen Meiksins Wood, "Issues of Class and Culture: An Interview with Aijaz Ahmad," *Monthly Review* October 1996: 1–9.
2. Head, *Modern British Fiction*, 49. For recent data on the widening class divisions since the 1950s see my remarks on Cannadine, Westergaard, and Adonis and Pollard in the Introduction.
3. Head, *Modern British Fiction*, 49–50, my emphasis.
4. Ibid., 50.
5. Ibid., 69, 72.
6. Ibid., 80.
7. Ibid.
8. Ibid., 81.
9. Williams, *Marxism and Literature*, 53.
10. Ibid., 193.
11. Tew and Mengham, *British Fiction Today*, 40.
12. Ibid., 42.
13. Ibid.
14. Ibid., 44.
15. Jameson, *Political Unconscious*, 200.
16. Ibid.
17. Tew and Mengham, *British Fiction Today*, 44.
18. See John Freeman, "London Calling."
19. Tew and Mengham, *British Fiction Today*, 45. Subsequent references to this text are made parenthetically by page number.
20. All of these comments are from the jacket of *The Line of Beauty* (New York: Bloomsbury, 2004).
21. Sharon Monteith, Jenny Newman, and Pat Wheeler, *Contemporary British and Irish Fiction: An Introduction through Interviews* (London: Arnold/Hodder Headline, 2004), 82 (Hereafter *CBIF*).
22. Ibid., 83.

23. Edward Guthmann, "From Literary Underdog to Prestigious Prize Winner: A Soft-Spoken Hollinghurst Takes It in Stride," Interview with Alan Hollinghurst *San Francisco Chronicle,* October 22, 2004.
24. Monteith, *CBIF*, 83.
25. Hollinghurst, *The Line of Beauty*, 435.
26. Tew and Mengham, *British Fiction Today*, 50.
27. Andrew Eastham, "Inoperative Ironies: Jamesian Aestheticism and Postmodern Culture in Alan Hollinghurst's *The Line of Beauty*," *Textual Practice* 20, no. 3 (2006): 509.
28. Ibid.
29. Ibid., 526.
30. Ibid.
31. Hollinghurst, *The Line of Beauty*, 383.
32. Ibid., 438.
33. Ibid., 130.
34. Ibid., 133.
35. Ibid., 134–135.
36. It is worth comparing this description with an almost parallel sense of claustrophobia and ugliness when Howard visits his working-class father in Zadie Smith's *On Beauty*.
37. Ibid., 135.
38. Ibid., 138.
39. Ibid., 141.
40. Monteith, *CBIF*, 83.
41. Hollinghurst, *The Line of Beauty*, 145.
42. Ibid., 357.
43. Daniel Lea, *Contemporary British Novelists: Graham Swift* (Manchester: Manchester University Press, 2005), 166.
44. David Rogers and John McLeod. *The Revision of Englishness* (Manchester: Manchester University Press, 2004), 182.
45. Rogers and McLeod, *Revision of Englishness*, 183.
46. Ibid.
47. Ibid.
48. Ibid., 184.
49. Eagleton, *Illusions of Postmodernism*, 62.
50. Rogers and McLeod, *Revision of Englishness*, 184.
51. David Malcolm, *Understanding Graham Swift* (Columbia: University of Southern Carolina Press, 2003), 165, 169, 170.
52. Ibid., 172.
53. Ibid., 172, 180.
54. Ibid., 174.
55. Ibid., 181.
56. Ibid., 185.
57. Tew and Mengham, *British Fiction Today*, 40. A recent return to the argument of Swift's *Waterland* and the idea history as a fiction without end can be seen in Damon Marcel Decoste's "Question and Apocalypse: The Endlessness of *Historia* in Graham Swift's *Waterland*," *Contemporary Literature* 43, no. 2 (Summer 2002): 377–399.

58. Tew and Mengham, *British Fiction Today*, 40.
59. Lea, *Graham Swift*, 1. Subsequent references to this text are made parenthetically by page number.
60. Jameson, *Political Unconscious*, 34–35.
61. Ibid., 35.
62. Ibid., 35, my emphasis.
63. Lea, *Graham Swift*, 161.
64. Ibid., 163.
65. Ibid., 164–165.
66. Buchanan, *Fredric Jameson*, 59.
67. Fredric Jameson, "The Politics of Utopia," *New Left Review* 25 (January–February 2004), 46–47.
68. Ibid., 47–50.
69. Lea, *Graham Swift*, 13.
70. Ibid.
71. Jameson, *Political Unconscious*, 79.
72. Lea, *Graham Swift*, 166.
73. Ibid., 9.
74. Ibid., 13.
75. Ibid., 169.
76. Ibid., 175–180.
77. Ibid., 184–185.
78. Rod Mengham, *An Introduction to Contemporary Fiction: International Writing in English since 1970* (Cambridge, MA: Polity, 1999), 164.
79. Ibid., 165, 153.
80. Jameson, "The Politics of Utopia," 47.
81. Lea, *Graham Swift*, 187.
82. Head, *Modern British Fiction*, 35.
83. Ibid., 36.
84. Ibid., 35–36.
85. Ibid., 36.
86. Ibid.
87. We have seen this in Amis's attack on John Self, and we will examine it in more detail in the next chapter with the work of Greenaway and Jarman both of whom engage in a form of middle-class dissent, and distance themselves from the brute ugliness of Thatcherism while simultaneously being unable to create any meaningful political link to working-class culture.
88. Ian Sansom, "Through Plate Glass," *London Review of Books*, May 10, 2001.
89. Jonathan Coe, *The Winshaw Legacy or What a Carve Up!* (New York: Vintage International, 1994), 235.
90. Tew, *Contemporary British Novel*, 61.
91. Head, *Modern British Fiction*, 36–37.
92. Stevenson, *The Last of England?* 459.
93. Head, *Modern British Fiction*, 37.
94. Ibid., 459.
95. Terry Eagleton, "Theydunnit," Review of *What a Carve Up! London Review of Books*, April 28, 1994, 12.

96. Ibid., 12.
97. Tew and Mengham, *British Fiction Today*, 28.
98. Ibid.
99. Ibid.
100. Ibid.
101. Ibid., 28–29.
102. Ibid., 28–29.
103. Ibid., 30.
104. Ibid.
105. Eagleton, "Theydunnit," 12.
106. Tew and Mengham, *British Fiction Today*, 32.
107. Eagleton, "Theydunnit," 12.
108. Tew and Mengham, *British Fiction Today*, 34.
109. Ibid., 36.
110. Ibid., 37.
111. Ibid., 38.
112. Ibid.
113. Coe, *What a Carve Up!* 88. Subsequent references to this text are made parenthetically by page number.
114. Tew, *Contemporary British Novel*, 80.
115. Ibid.
116. Ibid., 80–81.
117. Interestingly enough Tew says that if there is "any priority in Coe, it is to the instinct of the working-classes and those of the lower middle-class when uninfluenced by its love affair with aesthetic intellectualism" (81).
118. Jonathan Coe, *The Closed Circle* (New York: Vintage Contemporaries, 2004), 301.
119. Terry Eagleton, *Against the Grain: Essays 1975–1985* (London: Verso, 1986), 133.
120. Coe, *The Closed Circle*, 233.
121. Buchanan, *Fredric Jameson*, 97.
122. Bradford, *The Novel Now*, 45.
123. Eagleton, *Against the Grain*, 133.
124. Michael Sanders, review of *Nation and Novel: The English Novel from Its Origins to the Present Day*, by Patrick Parrinder, *Textual Practice* 21, no. 3 (2007): 807.
125. Ibid.
126. Ibid., 808.

5 A Class Act: Representations of Class in British Cinema and Television 1979–2008

1. Slavoj Žižek, "Against the Populist Temptation," *Critical Inquiry* 32, no. 3 (Spring 2006): 551.
2. Mike Leigh, *Naked and Other Screenplays* (London: Faber, 1995), xi.

3. Ray Carney, *The Films of Mike Leigh* (Cambridge: Cambridge University Press, 2000), 4–6.
4. Ibid., 4.
5. Ibid., 12.
6. Ibid., 17. The conclusion of Garry Watson's *The Cinema of Mike Leigh: A Sense of the Real* (2004) repeats this assertion that Leigh's films are about moving us "towards self-transformation" via the "transforming power of love" (190). Subsequent references to this text are made parenthetically by page number.
7. John Hill, *British Cinema in the 1980s* (Oxford: Clarendon Press, 1999), 195.
8. Carney, *Films of Mike Leigh*, 95.
9. Žižek, *Lost Causes*, 52.
10. Carney, *Films of Mike Leigh*, 99, 109.
11. Ibid., 99, 101.
12. Ibid., 102.
13. John Hill suggests that the same brutal humor is also directed at Valerie in *High Hopes*, who is a kind of Beverly for the 1980s. She is saturated by consumerism and aspires way above her class: "such is the degree of Valerie's grotesquerie in *High Hopes* that the film extends her virtually no sympathy at all, and as in earlier working-class realism, effectively 'punishes' her by making her suffer in a way that none of the other characters have to and by reducing her to a state of hysterical collapse" (194). Hill remarks that in this way both her husband, Martin and the film itself, join hands in abusing Valerie.
14. Carney, *Films of Mike Leigh*, 108–110.
15. Ibid., 115.
16. Ibid., 202.
17. Ibid., 237–238.
18. Hill, *British Cinema in the 1980s*, 193. Subsequent references to this text are made parenthetically by page number.
19. Ibid., 198. Edward Trostle Jones also asserts that *High Hopes* is a film in which an indictment of Thatcherism is presented "through individual lives and personal relationships." See *All or Nothing: The Cinema of Mike Leigh* (Peter Lang Press: New York, 2004), 44.
20. Carney, *Films of Mike Leigh*, 96.
21. Paula Willoquet-Maricondi and Mary Alemany-Galway, *Peter Greenaway's Postmodern/Postructuralist Cinema* (London: Scarecrow Press, 2001), 207.
22. Ibid.
23. Paul Dave, *Visions of England: Class and Culture and Contemporary Cinema* (Oxford and New York: Berg, 2006), 89.
24. Hill, *British Cinema in the 1980s*, 162.
25. Willoquet-Maricondi and Alemany-Galway, *Peter Greenaway's Postmodern/Poststructuralist Cinema*, 116–117. Subsequent references to this text are made parenthetically by page number.
26. Scott Malcomson, review of *The Draughtsman's Contract* by Peter Greenaway, British Film Institute; BBC Channel 4 Source: *Film Quarterly* 37, no. 2 (Winter, 1983–1984): 34.

27. Malcomson, *Draughtsman's Contract*, 35.
28. Ibid.
29. Ibid., 37. My concern with Malcomson's reading is that it seems to push Neville into a working-class category, whereas the film makes it clear that he is "a tenant farmer's son" and as such would clearly have a bourgeois and middle-class position in the film. However, Neville's position as a "surrogate" for a *middle-class* audience certainly holds true. The working-class in the film, the servants, the gardeners, and the shepherds occupy no space in the narrative other than to silently work, and they are removed from the landscape at Neville's instructions. Subsequent references to this text are made parenthetically by page number.
30. For more on Jarman's position of middle-class dissent see my chapter on Jarman and the British tradition in *By Angels Driven: The Cinema of Derek Jarman* ed. Chris Lippard.
31. This middle-class position is almost identical to the nostalgia of T. S. Eliot who also laments the emergence of that "Shakespeherian rag" that reduces the Swan of Avon to a popular song in *The Waste Land.*
32. Hill, *British Cinema in the 1980s*, 164.
33. Rowland Wymer, *Derek Jarman* (Manchester: Manchester University Press, 2005), 113.
34. Hill, *British Cinema in the 1980s*, 156, 161.
35. Wymer, *Derek Jarman*, 120. This comment is parallel to Salman Rushdie's similarly class evaporating comment that "we are all exiles from the past." Clearly, in economic terms "we" do not all share the same relationship to the past or the present for that matter.
36. Kirk, *Twentieth-Century Writing*, 27.
37. Ibid., 28.
38. Stephen Frears, BBC Interview November 27, 2002. http://www.bbc.co.uk/films/2002/11/27/stephen_frears_dirty_pretty_things_interview.shtml
39. I feel that it would be valuable to examine Steve Knight's *Amazing Grace*, and *Eastern Promises* alongside *Dirty Pretty Things* so as to see how similar ideological patterns would emerge. The question of "wage slavery" is central to all three films.
40. Hill, *British Cinema in the 1980s*, 147.
41. Adrian Hennigan, "Tales of the City": Interview with Steve Knight. http://www.bbc.co.uk/dna/filmnetwork/A28343711 (accessed on December 9, 2008).
42. Hill, *British Cinema in the 1980s*, 148.
43. The lack of realism in the film is remarked on by Frears who says that given the increased restrictions for filming in England, such as in airports, "film has been forced to become more genre based, more artificial" (DVD commentary).
44. Hill, *British Cinema in the 1980s*, 149.
45. In the commentary Frears says that Okwe is like "Clint Eastwood." In this way Okwe becomes the loner who rides into town to clean up, shoots the drunken evil Sheriff and having got the girl to fall in love with him, rides off into the sunset alone.

46. For more on British cinema in the 1990s, see Robert Murphy.
47. Hennigan, "Tales of the City."
48. See D. A. Miller, *The Novel and The Police* (California: University of California Press, 1992).
49. If Sneaky is a devil, then at one point the prostitute with a heart of gold, Juliette, says that Okwe is "an angel." The Manichean nature of the film is clear.
50. Hill, *British Cinema in the 1980s*, 150–151.
51. Ibid., 151.
52. Ibid., 151, 153.
53. The same ideology of the "make-over" narrative that we see in the television programs of this period also arises at this moment in the film when Senay tells Okwe as they head to Heathrow Airport that thanks to their new passports they have escaped from history and their old lives have been erased: "Now we are someone new."
54. Su Holmes and Deborah Jermyn, *Understanding Reality Television* (London and New York: Routledge, 2004), 173. For a history of British television drama, see Lez Cooke. Cooke's survey reveals that since 1979 the number of dramas that have dealt seriously with politics and class has almost vanished, a trend which deregulation since the 1990s seems to have only encouraged. Cooke's conclusion is that the strength of British television, as it goes into the future (like postmodern theory), will be found in its "diversity and its pluralism" (196). Symptomatically, even though Cooke's history covers television drama from 1936 to the present, "class," and "working-class" do not appear in the index.
55. Although I don't have the space to follow it up here, Palmer points out, that "the subject of class has increasingly been marginalized on the agenda of television and cultural studies since the 1980s" (Holmes and Jermyn, *Understanding Reality Television*, 173).
56. The power of this slogan is surely evidenced in its use by the American military's recruitment advertisements in which they also encourage potential applicants to "be all they can be."
57. Holmes and Jermyn, *Understanding Reality Television*, 174.
58. Ibid., 178.
59. Ibid., 182.
60. Ibid., 183.
61. Ibid., 184. In America this can be seen in *Take Home Chef*, in which an Australian chef collars an unsuspecting female shopper and offers to cook her and her family a delicious meal. Once again "random" participants are always people with rather affluent homes and seem to be already very middle-class (even by American standards), it seems that having acquired the property of the middle classes they once again lack the middle-class values of good taste to go with it.
62. Holmes and Jermyn, *Understanding Reality Television*, 185–186.
63. Ibid., 186.
64. Ibid., 188.
65. Ibid., 187–188.

66. Ibid., 188.
67. Eatanswill ("Eat and Swill") is taken from Dicken's *Pickwick Papers*. Jane Horrocks role in *Little Voice* is a valuable point of comparison in that *Little Voice* is also a narrative in which the "exceptional individual" (as John Kirk says of *Billy Elliot*) escapes from the vulgar imprisonment of the past and her vulgar working-class mother. Jane Horrocks's role as Bubble in *Absolutely Fabulous* also brings us to another working-class mother like Ros, who in trying to reach beyond her class becomes absolutely ridiculous. In contrast the calm, respectable Saffi (Julia Sawalha) becomes the point of viewer identification. She accepts and knows her place, and doesn't try to be part of a class she doesn't belong to, and is thus treated sympathetically by the narrative.
68. The subplot also universalizes this perspective in that Ros's Chancellor of the Exchequer, Catherine Walker (Janet McTeer), is dating her speechwriter, Ben Sixsmith (Tom Mison) who is twenty-five but is jokingly referred to at one point as being "15 year old Ben" and Catherine also complains that she is "old enough to be his mother."
69. Walters has commented that Partridge "probably remained too large to be considered naturalistic, even if those around him could be." Ben Walters, *The Office: A Critical Reading of the Series* (London: BFI, 2005), 103.
70. Walters, *The Office*, 136.
71. Ibid., 156.
72. Ibid., 64.
73. Ibid., 157.
74. Ibid., 158.
75. Ibid.
76. Another layer of paradox is that while watching sixteen episodes of *Life on Mars* the television audience is placed in the position of being stuck in the past, in fact the program hopes that we delight in being there. Sam's suicide/return to 1973 at the end of the series affirms that he too would rather live in the past. The sequel *Ashes to Ashes* is set in the 1980s and its southern location means that it can avoid the issues of class and unemployment that plagued the North after 1979. In the sequel, DCI Alex Drake (Keeley Hawes) wakes up in 1981. Her "problem" is to figure out how to get back to her daughter, which is rooted in the death of her parents in a car bomb when she was eight years old: once again, as Žižek has pointed out, problems of class are folded back into an Oedipal narrative.
77. Sam's boss, Gene Hunt (Philip Glenister) is convinced that Ted Bannister is guilty of murder simply because he is a "Commie bastard" and when questioning the workers decides that he wants to "make mincemeat of these Bolsheviks."

Bibliography

Abercrombie, Nicholas, and Alan Warde, eds. *The Contemporary British Society Reader.* Cambridge, MA: Polity, 2001.

Acheson, James, and Sarah C. E. Ross, eds. *The Contemporary British Novel since 1980.* New York: Palgrave Macmillan, 2006.

Ackroyd, Peter. *Hawksmoor.* New York: Harper and Row, 1985.

Adonis, Andrew, and Stephen Pollard. *A Class Act: The Myth of Britain's Classless Society.* London: Hamish Hamilton, 1997.

Ahmad, Aijaz. *In Theory: Class, Nations, Literatures.* London: Verso, 2008.

Amis, Martin. *Heavy Water and Other Stories.* New York: Vintage, 2000.

———. *London Fields.* New York: Harmony Books, 1989.

———. *Money: A Suicide Note.* London: Penguin, 1986.

———. *Success.* New York, Vintage International, 1978.

Atkinson, Will. "Not All That Was Solid Has Melted Into Air (or Liquid): A Critique of Bauman on Individualization and Class in Liquid Modernity." *Sociological Review* 56, no. 1 (2008): 1–17.

Ball, Stephen J. *Class Strategies and the Education Market: The Middle Classes and Social Advantage.* London: Routledge, 2003.

Barker, Pat. *The Eye in the Door.* London: Penguin, 1994.

———. *The Ghost Road.* New York: Plume Books, 1995.

———. *Regeneration.* New York: Plume Books, 1993.

Begley, Jon. "Satirizing the Carnival of Postmodern Capitalism: The Transatlantic and Dialogic Structure of Martin Amis's *Money.*" *Contemporary Literature* 45, no. 1 (Spring 2004): 79–105.

Bentley, Nick, ed. *British Fiction of the 1990s.* London and New York: Routledge, 2005.

Bernard, Anna. Review of *Wars of Position: The Cultural Politics of Left and Right* by Timothy Brennan. *Textual Practice* 20, no. 4 (2006): 777–816.

Blair, Tony. Speech to the Labour Party Conference, 1999. BBC News Network, September 28, 1999, http://news.bbc.co.uk/2/hi/uk_news/politics/460009.stm

Born, Daniel. "Private Gardens, Public Swamps: *Howards End* and the Revaluation of Liberal Guilt." *Novel: A Forum on Fiction* 25, no. 2. (Winter 1992): 141–159.

Bradbury, Malcolm. *The Modern British Novel: 1878–2001.* London: Penguin, 2001.

Bradford, Richard. *The Novel Now: Contemporary British Fiction*. Oxford: Blackwell, 2007.

Brennan, Timothy. *Wars of Position: The Cultural Politics of Left and Right*. New York: Columbia University Press, 2006.

Brown, Helen. "A Writer's Life: Will Self." www.telegraph.co.uk May 28, 2006. http://www.telegraph.co.uk/arts/main.jhtml?xml=/arts/2006/05/28/boself.xml

Buchanan, Ian. *Fredric Jameson: Live Theory*. London: Continuum Press, 2006.

Buford, Bill, ed. *Granta: Best of Young British Novelists: 1*. Middlesex: Granta, 1983.

———. *Granta: Best of Young British Novelists: 2*. Middlesex: Granta, 1993.

Cannandine, David. *Class in Britain*. London: Penguin, 2000.

Carney, Ray. *The Films of Mike Leigh*. Cambridge: Cambridge University Press, 2000.

Ciecko, Anne. "Representing the Spaces of Diaspora in Contemporary British Films by Women Directors." *Cinema Journal* 38, no. 3 (Spring 1999): 67–90.

Clark, Terry Nichols, and Seymour Martin Lipset. *The Breakdown of Class Politics: A Debate on Post-Industrial Stratification*. Baltimore, MD: Johns Hopkins University Press, 2001.

Coe, Jonathan. *The Closed Circle*. New York: Vintage Contemporaries, 2004.

———. *The Rotters' Club*. New York: Vintage Contemporaries, 2003.

———. *The Winshaw Legacy or What a Carve Up!* New York: Vintage International, 1994.

Colombino, Laura. "Negotiations with the System: J. G. Ballard and Geoff Ryman Writing London's Architecture." *Textual Practice* 20, no. 4 (2006): 615–635.

Conradi, Peter. "Art, and the Cruelty That Goes with It." Review of *The Line of Beauty* by Alan Hollinghurst. *Independent*, April 11, 2004.

Cooke, Lez. *British Television Drama: A History*. London: BFI, 2003.

Cowley, Jason. Review of *the Body* by Hanif Kureishi. *Observer*, November 3, 2002.

Dave, Paul. *Visions of England: Class and Culture and Contemporary Cinema*. Oxford and New York: Berg, 2006.

Day, Gary. *Class*. London and New York: Routledge, 2001.

Decoste, Damon Marcel. "Question and Apocalypse: The Endlessness of *Historia* in Graham Swift's *Waterland*." *Contemporary Literature* 43, no. 2 (Summer 2002): 377–399.

Devine, Fiona, Mike Savage, John Scott, and Rosemary Crompton. *Rethinking Class: Culture, Identities and Lifestyle*. New York: Palgrave Macmillan, 2005.

Doan, Laura L. "Sexy Greedy Is the Late Eighties: Power Systems in Amis's *Money* and Churchill's *Serious Money*." *The Minnesota Review: A Journal of Committed Writing* 34, no. 5 (Spring 1990): 69–80.

Eagleton, Terry. *After Theory*. New York: Perseus Books, 2003.

———. *Against the Grain: Essays 1975–1985*. London: Verso, 1986.

———. "A Beautiful and Elusive Tale." *Lancet* 358, no. 9299, December 22, 2001.

———. *Figures of Dissent: Critical Essays on Fish, Spivak, Zizek and Others.* London: Verso, 2003.

———. *The Idea of Culture.* Oxford: Blackwell, 2000.

———. *Ideology: An Introduction.* London and New York: Verso, 2007.

———. *The Illusions of Postmodernism.* Oxford: Blackwell, 1996.

———. *Literary Theory: An Introduction.* Minneapolis: University of Minnesota Press, 2008.

———. *Marxism and Literary Criticism.* Berkeley: University of California Press, 1976.

———. "Only Pinter remains." *Guardian Online* July 7, 2007, http://www.guardian.co.uk/commentisfree/2007/jul/07/comment.politics

———. "Rebuking Obnoxious Views Is Not Just a Personality Kink." *Guardian OnlineComment* October 10, 2007, http://www.guardian.co.uk/commentisfree/2007/oct/10/comment.religion

———. "Theydunnit." Review of *What a Carve Up! London Review of Books,* April 28, 1994: 12.

Eastham, Andrew. "Inoperative Ironies: Jamesian Aestheticism and Post-modern Culture in Alan Hollinghurst's *The Line of Beauty.*" *Textual Practice* 20, no. 3 (2006): 509–527.

Ebert, Teresa L., and Masud Zavarzadeh. *Class in Culture.* London: Paradigm, 2008.

Edemariam, Aida. "Enduring Fame." Interview with Ian McEwan in *Guardian Unlimited,* August 18, 2007, http://books.guardian.co.uk/interviews/story/0,,2151430,00.html

Edgell, Stephen. *Class.* London and New York: Routledge, 1993.

Felski, Rita. "Nothing to Declare: Identity, Shame and the Lower Middle Class." *PMLA,* 115 (January 2000): 33–45.

Finney, Brian. "Briony's Stand against Oblivion: The Making of Fiction in Ian McEwan's *Atonement.*" *Journal of Modern Literature* 27, no. 3 (Winter 2004): 68–82.

———. *British Fiction since 1984: Narrating a Nation.* New York: Palgrave Macmillan, 2006.

Forster, E. M. *A Room with a View, Howards End* and *Maurice.* New York: Quality Paperbacks Book Club, 1971.

———. "Two Cheers for Democracy." New York: Harcourt Brace and World, 1951.

Frears, Stephen. BBC Interview, November 27, 2002, http://www.bbc.co.uk/films/2002/11/27/stephen_frears_dirty_pretty_things_interview.shtml

Freeman, John. "London Calling: Interview with Alan Hollinghurst." www.nerve.com/screeningroom/books/interview_alanhollinghurst/

Gasiorek, Andrzej. *Post-War British Fiction: Realism and After.* London: Edward Arnold, 1995.

Goldthorpe, John H., and Michelle Jackson. "Intergenerational Class Mobility in Contemporary Britain: Political Concerns and Empirical Findings." *British Journal of Sociology* 58, no. 4 (2007): 525–546.

Guthmann, Edward. "From Literary Underdog to Prestigious Prize Winner, a Soft-Spoken Hollinghurst Takes It in Stride." Interview with Alan Hollinghurst. *San Francisco Chronicle,* http://www.sfgate.com/cgibin/article.cgi?file=/c/a/2004/10/22/DDGU69DK7J1.DTL&type=printable Friday October 22, 2004.

Haffenden, John. *Novelists in Interview*. London: Methuen, 1985.

Harrison, M. John. "The Gospel According to Dave." *Guardian,* Saturday May 27, 2006, http://www.guardian.co.uk/books/2006/may/27/fiction.hayfestival2006

Head, Dominic. *The Cambridge Introduction to Modern British Fiction 1950–2000*. Cambridge: Cambridge University Press, 2002.

Hennigan, Adrian. "Tales of the City: Interview with Steve Knight." http://www.bbc.co.uk/dna/filmnetwork/A28343711

Hill, John. *British Cinema in the 1980s*. Oxford: Clarendon Press, 1999.

Hitchcock, Peter. "'They Must Be Represented': Problems in Theories of Working-Class Representation." *PMLA Special Topic: Rereading Class* 115, no. 1 (January 2000): 20–32.

Hollinghurst, Alan. *The Line of Beauty*. New York: Bloomsbury, 2004.

Holmes, Su, and Deborah Jermyn. *Understanding Reality Television*. London and New York: Routledge, 2004.

Ishiguro, Kazuo. "Memory Is the Terribly Treacherous Terrain." Interview with Graham Swift. *BOMB* 29 (1989): 22–23.

———. *The Remains of the Day*. New York: Vintage International, 1990.

Jack, Ian, ed. *Granta: Best of Young British Novelists: 3*. London: Granta, 2003.

James, David. "The New Purism." *Textual Practice* 21, no. 4 (December 2007): 687–714.

Jameson, Fredric. "Fear and Loathing in Globalisation." *New Left Review* 23 (September–October 2003): 105–114.

———. *The Political Unconscious: Narrative as a Socially Symbolic Act*. New York: Cornell University Press, 1981.

———. "The Politics of Utopia." *New Left Review* 25 (January–February 2004): 35–54.

———. *Postmodernism, or, the Cultural Logic of Late Capitalism*. Durham, NC: Duke University Press, 2005.

Janik, Del Ivan. "No End of History: Evidence from the Contemporary English Novel." *Twentieth Century Literature* 41, no. 2 (Summer 1995): 160–189.

Jenkins, Simon. *Thatcher and Sons: A Revolution in Three Acts*. London: Penguin, 2006.

Jones, Edward Trostle. *All or Nothing: The Cinema of Mike Leigh*. New York: Peter Lang, 2004.

Kay, Sarah. *Zizek: A Critical Introduction*. Cambridge, MA: Polity, 2003.

Kemp, Peter. "Pat Barker's Last Battle?" *Times Online* July 1, 2007, http://entertainment.timesonline.co.uk/tol/arts_and_entertainment/books/article1995669.ece

Keulks, Gavin, ed. *Martin Amis: Postmodernism and Beyond*. New York: Palgrave Macmillan, 2006.

Kirk, John. "Recovered Perspectives: Gender, Class, and Memory in Pat Barker's Writing." *Contemporary Literature* 40, no. 4 (1999): 603–626.

———. *Twentieth-Century Writing and the British Working Class*. Cardiff: University of Wales Press, 2003.

Koval, Ramona. Interview with Ian McEwan. April 2004, no. 4 www.eruditiononline.com/04.04/ian_mcewan.htm

Kureishi, Hanif. *The Black Album*. London: Faber, 1995.

———. *The Body*. New York: Scribner, 2002.

———. *The Buddha of Suburbia*. London: Penguin, 1990.

Lane, Richard J., Rod Mengham, and Philip Tew, eds. *Contemporary British Fiction*. Cambridge, MA: Polity, 2003.

Lea, Daniel. *Contemporary British Novelists: Graham Swift*. Manchester: Manchester University Press, 2005.

Leigh, Mike. *Naked and Other Screenplays*. London: Faber, 1995.

Link, Alex. "'The Capitol of Darknesse': Gothic Spatialities in the London of Peter Ackroyd's *Hawksmoor*." *Contemporary Literature* 45, no. 3 (Autumn, 2004): 516–537.

Linklater, Alexander. "Death of the Ego." Review of *The Body* by Hanif Kureishi. *Guardian*, November 16, 2002.

Lippard, Chris, ed. *By Angels Driven: The Cinema of Derek Jarman*. Trowbridge: Flicks Books, 1996.

Lodge, David. "The Novel Now: Theories and Practices." *Novel: A Forum on Fiction* 21, no. 2/3, "Why the Novel Matters: A Postmodern Perplex Conference Issue." (Winter–Spring 1988): 125–138.

Macherey, Pierre, trans. David Macey. *The Object of Literature*. Cambridge: Cambridge University Press, 1995.

———. *A Theory of Literary Production*. London and New York: Routledge, 2006.

Malcolm, David. *Understanding Graham Swift*. Columbia: University of Southern Carolina Press, 2003.

Malcomson, Scott. Review of *The Draughtsman's Contract* by Peter Greenaway. British Film Institute; BBC Channel 4 Source: *Film Quarterly* 37, no. 2 (Winter 1983–1984): 34–40.

Marr, Andrew. *A History of Modern Britain*. London: Macmillan, 2007.

Marwick, Arthur. *British Society since 1945*. London: Penguin, 2003.

Mengham, Rod, ed. *An Introduction to Contemporary Fiction: International Writing in English since 1970*. Cambridge, MA: Polity, 1999.

McCombe, John P. "The End of (Anthony) Eden: Ishiguro's *The Remains of the Day* and Midcentury Anglo-American Tensions." *Twentieth Century Literature* 48, no. 1 (Spring 2002): 77–99.

McCormack, Alistair. "Migration and the Politics of Narrative Form: Realism and the Postcolonial Subject in *Brick Lane*." *Contemporary Literature* 47, no. 4 (2006): 695–721.

McEwan, Ian. *Atonement*. New York: Anchor, 2003.

———. *The Cement Garden*. London: Jonathan Cape, 1978.

———. Interview with *Der Spiegel*, July 19, 2005.

———. *Saturday*. New York: Anchor, 2006.

McGlynn, Mary. "Middle-Class Wankers and Working-Class Texts: The Critics and James Kelman." *Contemporary Literature* 43, no. 1 (Spring 2002): 50–84.

Miller, D. A. *The Novel and the Police*. California: University of California Press, 1992.

Milner, Andrew. *Class*. London: Sage, 1999.

Monteith, Sharon. *Pat Barker*. Tavistock: Northcote House, 2002.

Monteith, Sharon, Jenny Newman, and Pat Wheeler. *Contemporary British and Irish Fiction: An Introduction through Interviews*. London: Arnold/Hodder Headline, 2004.

Morrison, Jago. *Contemporary Fiction*. London: Routledge, 2003.

Murphy, Robert, ed. *British Cinema of the 90s*. London: BFI, 2000.

Nixon, Rob. "An Interview with Pat Barker." *Contemporary Literature* 45, no. 1. (Spring 2004): 1–21.

O'Grady, Kathleen. "White Teeth: A Conversation with Author Zadie Smith." *Atlantis: A Women's Studies Journal* 27, no. 1 (Fall 2002): 105–111.

Onega, Susan. "Interview with Peter Ackroyd." *Twentieth Century Literature* 42, no. 2 (Summer 1996): 208–220.

Parker, Ian. *Slavoj Zizek: A Critical Introduction*. London: Pluto Press, 2004.

Pinkerton, Mary. "Ambiguous Connections: Leonard Bast's Role in *Howards End*." *Twentieth Century Literature* 31 no. 2/3, E. M. Forster Issue. (Summer/Autumn, 1985): 236–246.

Press, Joy. "Only Connect: From *White Teeth* to the Ivory Tower: An Interview with *On Beauty* Novelist Zadie Smith." *Village Voice*. September 16, 2005, http://www.villagevoice.com/2005-09-13/books/only-connect/

Rennison, Nick. *Contemporary British Novelists*. London: Routledge, 2005.

Rogers, David, and John McLeod. *The Revision of Englishness*. Manchester: Manchester University Press, 2004.

Rowntree Foundation. "Poverty and Wealth across Britain from 1968 to 2005." July 2007, http://www.jrf.org.uk/knowledge/findings/housing/2077.asp

Sanders, Andrew, ed. *The Short Oxford History of English Literature* (3rd edition). Oxford: Oxford University Press, 2004.

Sanders, Michael. Review of *Nation and Novel: The English Novel from Its Origins to the Present Day* by Patrick Parrinder. *Textual Practice* 21, no. 3 (2007): 801–808.

Sansom, Ian. "Through Plate Glass." *London Review of Books* May 10, 2001, http://www.lrb.co.uk/v23/n09/sans01_.html

Self, Will. *The Book of Dave*. New York: Bloomsbury, 2006.

———. "In the Beginning: Will Self on the Genesis of *The Book of Dave*." *Guardian* June 16, 2007, http://books.guardian.co.uk/bookclub/story/0,,2104020,00.html

———. *Junk Mail*. London: Penguin, 1996.

Sen, Asha. "Re-writing History: Hanif Kureishi and the Politics of Black Britain." *Passages* 2, no. 1 (2000): 61–80.

Skeggs, Beverley. *Class, Self, Culture*. London and New York: Routledge, 2004.

Smith, Zadie. Interview with Ian McEwan. *Believer*, August 2005, www.believermag.com/issues/200508/?read=interview_mcewan

———. "Love, Actually." *Guardian Unlimited*, Saturday November 1, 2003, http://www.guardian.co.uk/books/2003/nov/01/classics.zadiesmith

———. *On Beauty*. New York: Penguin, 2006.

Stevenson, Randall. *The Last of England?: The Oxford English Literary History: Volume 12. 1960–2000*. Oxford: Oxford University Press, 2004.

Swift, Graham. *Last Orders*. New York: Vintage International, 1997.

Temko, Ned. Review of *Thatcher and Sons* by Simon Jenkins. *Observer*, November 5, 2006. www.guardian.co.uk/theobserver/2006/nov/05/politics

Tew, Philip. *The Contemporary British Novel*. London and New York: Continuum, 2004.

Tew, Philip, and Rod Mengham, eds. *British Fiction Today*. London: Continuum, 2006.

Thomas, Bethan. "Identity in Britain: A Cradle to Grave Analysis" (published by the Social and Spatial Inequalities Research Group). http://www.sasi.group.shef.ac.uk/

Turner, Henry. "Empire of Objects: Accumulation and Entropy in E. M. Forster's *Howards End*." *Twentieth Century Literature* 46, no. 3 (Autumn 2000): 328–345.

Walters, Ben. *The Office: A Critical Reading of the Series*. London: BFI, 2005.

Watkins, Susan. "A Weightless Hegemony: New Labour's Role in the Neoliberal Order." *New Left Review* 25 (January–February 2004): 5–33.

Watson, Garry. *The Cinema of Mike Leigh: A Sense of the Real*. London: Wallflower Press, 2004.

Westergaard, John. *Who Gets What?: The Hardening of Class Inequality in the Late Twentieth Century*. Cambridge, MA: Polity, 1995.

Widdowson, Peter. *E. M. Forster's Howards End: Fiction as History*. London: Sussex University Press, 1977.

———. "Writing Back: Contemporary Revisionary Fiction." *Textual Practice* 20, no. 3 (2006): 491–507.

Williams, Raymond. *Marxism and Literature*. Oxford: Oxford University Press, 1977.

Willoquet-Maricondi, Paula, and Mary Alemany-Galway. *Peter Greenaway's Postmodern/Poststructuralist Cinema*. London: Scarecrow Press, 2001.

Wong, Cynthia. *Kazuo Ishiguro*. Devon: British Council/Northcote House, 2005.

Wood, Ellen Meiksins. "Issues of Class and Culture: An Interview with Aijaz Ahmad." *Monthly Review* (October 1996): 1–9.

Wymer, Rowland. *Derek Jarman*. Manchester: Manchester University Press, 2005.

Zerilli, Linda M. "This Universalism Which Is Not One." Review of *Emancipation(s)* by Ernesto Laclau. *Diacritics* 28, no. 2 (Summer 1998): 2–20.

Žižek, Slavoj. "Against the Populist Temptation." *Critical Inquiry* 32, no. 3 (Spring 2006): 551–574.

———. *In Defence of Lost Causes*. London and New York: Verso, 2008.

———. *The Ticklish Subject: The Absent Centre of Political Ontology*. London and New York: Verso, 1999.

Zwerdling, Alex. *Virginia Woolf and the Real World*. California: University of California Press, 1987.

Index

Printed by Printforce, the Netherlands